Lessons From International/Comparative Criminology/Criminal Justice

Lessons From

International/Comparative

Criminology/Criminal Justice

Edited by

John A. Winterdyk

Mount Royal College

and Liqun Cao

Eastern Michigan University

de Sitter Publications

CANADIAN CATALOGUING IN PUBLICATION DATA

Lessons From International/Comparative Criminology/Criminal Justice
Edited by John A. Winterdyk and Liqun Cao

ISBN 0-9733978-6-1 (hbk)

Cover design: de Sitter Publications
Front cover: Photos donated by the authors.
Back cover: Clipart from Hemera

de Sitter Publications
374 Woodsworth Rd., Willowdale, ON, M2L 2T6, Canada

http://www.desitterpublications.com
sales@desitterpublications.com

PRINTED IN CANADA

Acknowledgments

To all the contributors who took the time to provide their "story," we are very grateful. Without their contribution this project would have remained little more than an idea. In addition to their participation in this anthology, the authors share of themselves in ways we seldom learn about in textbooks.

Without the patience, support, and encouragement of the publisher Shivu Ishwaran at de Sitter Publications, the book might never have made it to print. Due to circumstances beyond everyone's control, the process was confronted with a number of "snags." Ishwaran stood by us and offered insightful guidance and at times assistance to ensure that the anthology could be completed. It has been a pleasure to work with de Sitter Publications.

John would like to acknowledge the passive and active support of his partner Rosemary and their two sons. Much of the work on this project had to take place during awkward hours when deadlines required certain compromises. These exercises provide invaluable life lessons unto themselves! Liqun is grateful to his wife Meiling for taking on considerable chores and her devotion to their daughter's education. Because of her support, Liqun is able to concentrate on writing.

Contents

Introduction   1

Chapter 1

Peter Grabosky, Where To, Next?   8
    Beginnings   8
    Undergraduate Years   9
    Lost Innocence   10
    Graduate Studies   11
    Early Career Successes   14
    Drastic Change   18
    A Return to Research   19
    A Close Call   20
    An Offer Too Good to Refuse   21
    Lessons Learned   22
    Acknowledgements   23
    Notes   23
    Selected Bibliography   23

Chapter 2

Philip Reichel, From Air Force "Brat" to Comparativist   25
    Developing an Interest in Comparative Studies   25
    The Role of Events and Colleagues   28
    A Teaching Philosophy and a Research Orientation   30
    Things Learned   32
    What's Next?   34
    If You Are Intrigued   35
    Parting Words   37
    Selected Bibliography   37

Chapter 3

Irvin Waller, Harnessing Criminology and   39
Victimology Internationally
    The Origins of My Interest in Criminology 40
    Criminology at the University of Toronto   41
    Criminology Inside Government   43
    Criminology and International Advocacy   44
    Moral Entrepreneurship for Victims of Crime 45

Moral Entrepreneurship for Crime Prevention–   47
    Gilbert Bonnemaison
Criminology Inside International Agencies   49
Criminology and Advocacy–Next Steps   50
Conclusions for Young Criminologists   52
Selected Bibliography   52

Chapter 4

Pat Mayhew, Comparative Research in a   55
Government Environment
    Entering Criminology   56
    The British Crime Survey   57
    NIJ Fellowship   57
    The International Crime Victimization Survey (ICVS)   59
    Life after the ICVS   61
    Australian Institute of Criminology   61
    Theoretical Orientation   64
    Advice to Comparative Researchers   65
    Note   66
    References   67
    Selected Bibliography   70

Chapter 5

Jan J.M. Van Dijk, On the Victims' Side   71
    The First Years   71
    My First Job at Nijmegen University   72
    Working for the Dutch Government   73
    Society and Crime   74
    Promoting Victim Support   75
    Leiden University and the International   76
        Crime Victimization Survey (ICVS)
    More International Networking   77
    Working for the UN   78
    The Human Security Dimension   81
    Dealing with the Media   82
    Theoretical Underpinnings   83
    With Hindsight   85
    Lessons Learned   86
    Selected Bibliography   87

Chapter 6

David P. Farrington, Reflections On A Cross-National   89
    Criminological Career
        School   89
        University   90
        Over to Criminology   91
        Ottawa and Washington   93
        Longitudinal and Criminal Career Research   95
            in the 1980s
        Diversifying in the 1990s   97
        Intervention Research   100
        Conclusions   101
        Selected Bibliography   102

Chapter 7

Matti Joutsen From Criminology to Applied Comparative   106
    Criminology: Life as a Peripatetic Comparativist
        Prologue: Cultural Blinkers and Criminology   106
        Growing up on Two Continents   108
        Getting my Feet Wet: Applied Comparative Studies   109
            within the United Nations Framework
        Diving in Head First: Working at an Institute for   111
            Comparative Criminal Justice
        Victimology and Victim Policy   114
        Comparing What Shouldn't be Compared: 116
            Working on International Statistics on
            Crime and Justice
        Changes in the Rules of the Game–Going From   119
            National to Intergovernmental Policy
        Applying Comparative Criminology and Criminal   122
            Justice in Europe Today
        Selected Bibliography   123

Chapter 8

Lode Walgrave, Restorative Justice in Comparison   125
    An Autobiographic Introduction   125
    Developments in Restorative Justice   128
    Analyzing the Differences   129
        Common Law vs. Civil law   130
        Community vs. "Citoyenneté"   131
        First Nations and Other Indigenous People   132
    Conclusion   133
    Selected Bibliography   134

Chapter 9

David Nelken, Being There   138
The Personal Informs the Professional   138
Comparative Criminology: What's the Point?   140
Phenomenology and the Comparativist   143
The "Insider-Outsider" Problematic   146
Notes to Budding Scholars   151
Notes   152
Selected Bibliography   152

Chapter 10

Frances Heidensohn, Finding New Frontiers   154
  to Cross in Criminology
Setting Out   154
Framing Feminist Perspectives   155
  Naming   156
  Discovering   156
  Spreading   156
  Debating   156
Coming to Comparisons   157
The Theory Gap   165
Selected Bibliography   166

Chapter 11

Roy King, On Being a Comparative Criminologist   170
What is Comparative Criminology?   170
On Becoming a Comparative Criminologist   172
The Potentialities and Problems of
    Comparative International Work   177
References   183

Chapter 12

Hans-Joerg Albrecht, From Legal Doctrine
  to Criminology   185
The First Steps   185
Why Criminology?   186
The Max Planck Institute for Foreign and   187
    International Criminal Law
Drifting into Criminology   188

Going Further   189
Studying Crime and Criminal Justice   190
   Immigration and Ethnicity   192
   Organized Crime and Informal Economies 194
      Organized Crime   194
      Informal Economies   195
      Safety and Safety Legislation 196
Summary   197
Selected Bibliography   198

Chapter 13

Shlomo G. Shoham, Searching for Answers   200
An Auspicious Start   200
Capitalizing on One's Situation–Opportunity   201
The Value of Theory   202
Linking Theory to Practice   203
Searching for Answers   205
Responding to the Evolution of Theory   205
Juvenile Sentencing   206
Purposes of Punishment   207
International Interests   207
Fruits of a Labor of Love   207
Lessons Learned and Shared   207
Selected Bibliography   208

Chapter 14

Charles Hou, Adaptations   210
Culture Shock: An Awakening   210
Back to My "Roots"   212
Finding My Way   213
First "Wave" of Criminology in Taiwan   213
The Growth of Criminology in Taiwan   214
My View on Crime and Deviance   215
Summary and Perspective   221
The Future of Criminology   221
Notes   222
Selected Bibliography   223

Introduction and Overview

Lessons

John Winterdyk

and

Liqun Cao

In this collection of "stories," the authors share of themselves in ways we seldom learn about in textbooks.

While the particulars of the stories may fade, the passion will always remain strong.

This anthology got its roots from a modest Appendix that appeared in the first edition of Winterdyk's *Canadian Criminology: An Introduction* in 2000. In Appendix 4, John profiled six pioneers in Canadian criminology. The objective was to provide students with a social, historical, and academic insight into some of the leading Canadian criminologists/criminal justice academics. Each profile was relatively brief in length but based on feedback from students and colleagues, a noteworthy element of the text. Subsequently, Gilbert Geis and Mary Dodge prepared a wonderful anthology entitled *Lessons of Criminology* in 2002, in which they invited thirteen eminent American criminologists and criminal justice scholars to prepare a chapter on their "life and times."

As Geis and Dodge note, their names are well known among most academics and students are regularly required to read various works by these scholars. To obtain insight into how they came into the discipline, how they developed their perspective, where they see comparative criminology going, and some helpful insights for those who are interested in engaging in such research. Their contributions provide both a human context to who these people are as well as offer an honest look into what it takes to become respected in one's field of interest. Aside from hard work and a degree of academic potential, it also requires at times a degree of good fortune, inspirational mentors, and a passion for learning.

So when we met at the ASC meetings in Chicago in 2002, we discussed the opportunity of taking the theme that John had used and combined with the inspiration from the work of Geis and Dodge, and apply it to a somewhat modified approach to our joint interest in comparative/international criminology/criminal justice.

Comparative criminology as an area of study has been around for some 40-odd years but it has only been in recent years that we've seen a growing interest in this approach. Although Bayley (1996) argued that comparative criminology was a misnomer and Friday (1996) proposed that the term comparative could carry a pejorative connotation and value judgment, it is difficult to discuss the study of two or more societies by completely avoiding the word. Both Bayley and Friday preferred to use the word international which implies that if one finds a difference it is a difference, not that one element is somehow either better or worse than the other. Furthermore, it is said that when the Division of International Criminology, American Society of Criminology was created in 1989, the choice of the name was more than mere semantics.

The word international reflects different values and a different orientation than is captured in the concept of comparative. Indeed, one cannot make sense of any phenomenon or event without placing it into some kind of comparative context. What distinguishes comparative criminology is not comparison as a method, but political geography—that is, whether the cases of interest to be analyzed occur within a single country or in several nations.

The use of comparative criminology to indicate international criminology, however, has a long history, beginning with Hermann Mannheim's *Comparative Criminology* (1965). In general, it refers to the systematic study of crime and its related activities in more than one society. Because of its long history and its wide use, it has become difficult to avoid the word comparative in studies of two or more cultures/nations. As a result, in this book, we will use comparative and international interchangeably.

Criminology in a global context is not merely a cross-cultural look at rates, the description of a different system, or a test of theory in another milieu. It is a perspective that relies on both macro- and micro-analysis to place crime in a broader social context. It seeks to identify both commonalities and differences between cultural, legal, political, social, and historical contexts, subdue the variations within a larger context, and search for an extensive explanation.

With the advance of communication, transportation, and commerce, the world has been increasingly shrinking into a global village. The speed and profundity of changes in the world are echoed in the rapidly changing character of criminology's subject matter— crime is no longer contained by traditional nation-state boundaries. Since 1965, the field of comparative/international criminology has gradually become more and more burgeoning. Within the largest criminologist association in the world—American Society of Criminology, the Division had the largest number of registered members of all the Divisions in 2003.

The most recent addition to this enterprise is the *International Journal of Comparative Criminology*. Furthermore, one can find numerous books ranging from a general approach to being topic specific (see Reichel 2003—see the contribution in this text; Fairchild and Dammer 2001; Terrill 1999) to comparative research on such topics as policing (see Deflem 2002; Marenin 1996), victimology (van Dijk et al. 1999—see Van Dijk's contribution in this text), corrections (see Winterdyk 2004), international law (see Smit 2002), penal populism (see Roberts et al. 2003), among others. In addition, there are a host of additional books relating to the same topic areas but which appear in the native language of the author(s) or editor(s). A wonderful resource centre for such material is the Max Plank Institute in Freiburg, Germany (see the contribution from H-J Albrecht).

Although there are today many scholars who are involved to some degree in international and comparative research, there are arguably a limited number who have become highly recognized and respected (regardless of geographical, language, or cultural barriers) for the work that they have done in their respective fields. To compile such a list is somewhat risky since it can be argued that others might be equally deserving of such recognition. It is not our intention to slight anyone. We based our selection on a review of various sources and used a variety of simple indicators (e.g., frequency of publications and perceived quality of contribution to their field within a comparative context) to help compile the list presented in this reader. And since not all international/comparative scholars publish regularly in English, it is likely that several key experts have been overlooked. For example, Denise Sabo, at the University of Montreal, not only helped to establish criminology in Canada, but he has produced some key international and comparative works—the majority of which were written in

French. Rather this anthology is simply intended to offer the reader with a diverse and yet comprehensive overview of some of the key players who have made significant contributions to the field.

We are extremely grateful to those who have contributed to this project. While it is unfortunate that some were not able to contribute for justifiable reasons and that we had to limit the number of individuals profiled, we feel that we have still been able to provide a rich cross-section of experts bridging a broad range of subject areas (from victimology to organized crime, corrections, and restorative justice) and geographical areas of America, Europe, and Asia—a reasonably global representation. Nevertheless, neither the topics nor the authors fully cover the potential range of approaches in comparative/international criminology. They, however, reflect the contingencies of putting together such an anthology.

The resulting selections serve well for our original intention. The diversified paths to criminology by authors in this collection testify the rapid spread and development of international criminology. They also demonstrate the challenges posed for criminology by the changes brought by economic, cultural, and political transformations. The insight from different societies broadens our understanding of criminology and it is just too tempting to ignore. Ever since its emergence in the industrialized, urbanized world, criminology has been, or has sought to be, a contemporary, timely, worldly subject (Cao 2004). Criminologists have always attempt to broaden their views on the nature of human behavior.

This reader anthology should not be viewed as an exercise in narcissism or egotism. Rather, it provides an enriched opportunity for some of the leading experts to share their autobiographical stories in their own preferred way that will hopefully provide existing scholars and, perhaps more importantly, aspiring scholars of comparative and/or international criminology and/or criminal justice the motivation to engage in similar work. Unfortunately, we are not all able to access the wisdom of some, let alone all, of those who have helped to move this area of research forward.

Before you move on to the diverse collection, we felt it appropriate, without detracting from the content, to present a few general observations that might prove helpful in guiding the reader through each contribution. But first, we should mention that the chapters are not organized in any systematic way. We thought alphabetically, regionally, theoretically, but in the end we agreed that the order is irrelevant. In the spirit of *Lessons,* the order of the contents is based on a random draw. Finally, we included boxes in each chapter to highlight key lessons, stories, sayings, and insights.

Overview

First, the community of international/comparative scholars is relatively small. It is interesting to note how many of those covered in this anthology have worked with one or more of the others found in these pages—regardless of country of current residence.

Second, the role of a mentor is significant for most of the contributors. Not only does this speak to the quality of education one should endeavor to pursue but also the joy of working with individuals who while having their own schedules make the time to nurture the growth of aspiring scholars.

Third, the willingness to be mobile. Although today many of us have traveled outside our country of residence, most of those presented in this text have either taught, engaged in research, or been otherwise involved in projects outside their country. This obviously helps to promote collaboration and networking.

Fourth, it is inspiring to read that the field of criminology and criminal justice is immensely diverse and that no matter where one is in their academic career, it is never too late to embrace or expand ones' provincial interests into a broader global context.

Fifth, we were also struck by the frankness and conviction with which most of the contributors expressed their perspectives. Being committed and dedicated to a vision appears to be a benchmark that they all share. For example, **Van Dijk** has virtually dedicated the bulk of his work to issues related to victimology while **Waller** has worked on many high-powered levels promoting the benefit of crime prevention over more traditional means of addressing the social ills around the world. Yet, inspite of all his successes he has returned to his roots in education and is an inspiration to his students. **Joutsen** shares with us the benefits (and at times frustrations) of engaging in international research and policy making with such organizations as the UN and HEUNI, and **Heidenson's** story speaks to the importance of attending a "good" school. Yet her involvement into comparative work (as is the case with several others) did not begin until her career was already well established. Among her areas of interest is the study of women and crime from a feminist perspective. Her concluding comments will likely prove helpful to those aspiring to engage in comparative work. **Hou's** story serves to illustrate that a passion and commitment to a subject matter can be overcome regardless of ones roots and heritage. Coming from virtual poverty, Hou talks about the value of theory and comparative research but also the value of returning to ones' roots to apply international and comparative work in ones' "own backyard." **Walgrave**, like several others, came into criminology from another discipline. Yet, his passion for human good and seeking alternatives to conventional social control has prompted him to dedicate the bulk of his work since the early 1990s to restorative justice initiatives. His insights and observations are compelling and inspire us to remain open to evolving one's ideas and views. **Nelken's** account of not only engaging in comparative work but living in a "foreign" land (i.e., "being there") is both entertaining and insightful as he touches on some of the social and cultural factors that one must sometimes contend with. **Mayhew** acknowledges that sometimes "things just happen" and that by being receptive and willing to embrace new challenges (e.g., the British Crime Survey and the International Crime Victimization Survey) other opportunities are likely to unfold. Yet, she is frank in admitting that international and/or comparative research is not without its challenges. While there are a number of high pro-

file Americans' whom we could have approached to participate in this project, we choose **Reichel** because he embodies the lesson that as someone who works at a university that emphasizes teaching, he has managed to pursue a strong interest in comparative work. We also learn how ones' personal life tends to play a significant role in developing an interest in comparative work. **Grabosky**'s career represents a continual renewing himself and moving into new areas of research. As is epitomized by most of the contributors, a passion for what one does is instrumental to success and to "open doors" of opportunity. Yet, he is also generous to point out that a good sense of humor, or in some cases thick skin can be an asset when engaging in comparative/international work. Of all the contributions, **Albrecht's** account is reflective of someone who from his early years of schooling was destined to become involved in comparative/international work. However, given the social and educational environment in which he was largely educated in, his story speaks to the passion for learning and continually challenging and searching for solutions. **King** offers an equally fascinating account of the importance of mentors and the willingness to venture down new paths and challenge existing ideologies. His story also serves to reinforce the importance of combining theory with practice and he is unbashful in acknowledging the importance of working with inspiring individuals. The account of **Shoham** is equally inspiring. He, like most of the other contributors speaks to the importance of mentorship, following ones passion, and the importance of applying theory to practice within a national and international context. He provides an overview of the three theories he has developed/adapted in his career. His story also speaks to the importance of capitalizing on the environment in which one lives and ultimately in recognizing that criminal policy must be guided by the study of "human behavior on both the individual and groups levels." Finally, but not least of all, **Farrington's** contribution is a wonderful account of how important it is to feel a sense of commitment to one's field of study and the value of having good mentors early in one's career can serve to lay down a rewarding (if not hectic) career. Farrington reminds us of the value in collaboration and blending theory with sound research and methodology regardless of what kind of research one engages in.

Finally, this anthology is a collection of "stories" which we hope will provide some entertainment but more importantly inspiration to join (or continue working in) the community of international/comparative criminology/criminal justice. While the particulars of the stories may fade; if you have learnt something in relation to the lessons offered and feel inspired and motivated to pursue your passion in the field then the stories have served a very useful purpose in a manner which we alone could not have conveyed. As one of the contributors noted: "choose your collaborators carefully."

References

Bayley, D. H. 1996. "Policing: The World Stage." *Journal of Criminal Justice Education* 7:241-251.

Cao, Liqun. 2004. *Major Criminological Theories: Concepts and Measurement*. Belmont CA: Wadsworth.

Deflem, M. 2002. *Policing World Society*. Oxford, NY: Oxford University Press.

Fairchild, E., and H.R. Dammer. 2001. *Comparative Criminal Justice Systems*. 2d ed. Belmont, CA: Wadsworth.

Friday, P. 1996. "The Need to Integrate Comparative and International Criminology into a Traditional Curriculum." *Journal of Criminal Justice Education* 7: 227-239.

Geis, G., and M. Dodge. 2002. *Lessons of Criminology*. Cincinnati, OH: Anderson.

Mannheim, H. 1965, *Comparative Criminology*. New York: Houghton Mifflin.

Marenin, O. ed.
1996. *Policing Change, Changing Police: International Perspectives*. NY: Garland.

Reichel, P.L.
2002. *Comparative Criminal Justice Systems: A Topical Approach*. 3d ed. Upper Saddle River, NJ: Prentice Hall.

Roberts, J.V., L.J. Stalans, D. Indemaur, and M. Hough. 2003. *Penal Populism and Public Opinion: Lessons from Five Countries*. Oxford, NY: Oxford University Press.

Smit, D. van. 2002. *Taking Life Imprisonment Seriously in National and International Law*. The Hague, NL: Kluwer Law International.

Terrill, R.J. 1999. *World Criminal Justice Systems: A Survey*. 4th ed. Cincinnati, OH: Anderson.

Van Dijk, Jan .J.M, Ron G.H. van Kaam, and JoAnne Wemmers, eds. 1999. "Caring for Crime Victims— Selected Proceedings of the 9th International Symposium on Victimology. New York: Criminal Justice Press.

Winterdyk, J. ed. 2004. *Adult Corrections: International Perspectives*. Monsley, NJ.: Willow Press.

Winterdyk, J. 2004. *Canadian Criminology: An Introduction*. Toronto: Pearson Education.

About the Editors

John Winterdyk is an Instructor of criminology/ criminal justice at Mount Royal College where he has been teaching since 1988. John teaches a wide range of courses with a special emphasis on combining interdisciplinary and comparative approaches to the study of crime and criminal justice policy. Professor Winterdyk is currently the Editor of the *International Journal of Comparative Criminlogy*.

Liqun Cao is a Professor of Sociology and Crim-inology at Eastern Michigan University. Liqun has a special interest in the areas of social control, criminological theory, community policing, and comparative criminology. He has recently published a book on the measurement of criminological theories. Professor Cao is currently a Book Review Editor for the *International Journal of Comparative Criminlogy*.

Chapter 1

Where to, Next?

Peter Grabosky

Research School of Social Sciences,
The Australian National University,
Australia

While I would encourage students to explore and to follow their interests, they should do so with open eyes.

Beginnings

In 1962, the year I graduated from high school, a piece of music entitled "Cast Your Fate to the Wind"[1] won a Grammy Award for best original jazz composition. This turned out to be personally prophetic (it is just as well that the prophetic theme wasn't "Purple Haze," of which I became immensely fond of some six years later). My path from a New Jersey high school student with a vague interest in business administration to a Professor at the Australian National University specializing in policing and computer crime has been marked by some strange turns indeed. It has, however, been exciting.

The community in which I was raised was middle-class, and racially homogeneous. Situated about 15 miles due west of New York City, it could hardly be described as insular. Perhaps because of the proximity of cosmopolitan New York, and the fact that both of my maternal grandparents were born in Europe and my paternal grandmother was a great traveler, I was intrigued with the wider world, and wanted to experience more of it.

One tends to pursue what one does well. My best subject in high school was French (I was more than a little inspired by Brigitte Bardot). By the time I arrived at university, I had given some thought to a career in the diplomatic service. Eventually, I settled on a major in political science (or government as it was sometimes called in those days). Awakened by the Kennedy Administration, and by Theodore White's book *The Making of the President 1960* (White 1961), I also developed an interest in elections. A career as what one today would refer to as a "political consultant" began to intrigue me.

I came of age during one of the great social transformations of American history—the civil rights movement. Space constraints will not allow me to do justice to its significance (see Garrow's 1986 Pulitzer Prize winning biography of Martin Luther King, Jr.). Beyond the obvious considerations of justice, it struck me as hypocritical in the extreme for a nation that purported to be the leader of the free world to tolerate discrimination on the basis of race. While I became increasingly sympathetic to the cause of civil rights, I observed events with total passivity. One of my regrets in life is not having contributed to the movement.

Undergraduate Years

I did my undergraduate degree at Colby College, in Waterville, Maine. Ironically, it was about as far from the front lines of the civil rights struggle as you could get, without actually being in Canada. A major in Government, at least at Colby College in the mid-1960s, entailed the study of political philosophy, American constitutional law, and foreign and domestic political institutions. I took a course in comparative government, which was limited to the description of the major institutions of government in England, France, and Germany, but I found it uninspiring.

Somewhat more interesting was a course in totalitarian government, which looked at Nazi Germany, the Soviet Union, and gave a glimpse of Mao's China. Also interesting, because it was so exotic, was a course in African Politics—basically the history of East African constitutional development.

Although the student body at Colby was overwhelmingly white and middle class, there were two students from Kenya there, and I remember celebrating Kenya's independence day with them on December 12, 1963. I had another classmate from the Ivory Coast, and one from Somalia. The Ivoirian stimulated my interest in Francophone Africa, and I thought that I might like to devote my career to the study of West African politics. I remember writing, with great enthusiasm and fulfillment, a paper during my senior year in which I compared the regimes of Ghana's Kwame Nkrumah and Senegal's Leopold Senghor. I predicted that Senghor's regime would soon founder because of resistance from conservative Muslim elements, but that Nkrumah's rock-solid support would see him remain in power for years to come. I received a solid A grade for the paper, and just in time. A couple of days later, Nkrumah was deposed in a coup. Fourteen years after that, Senghor became one of the few African heads of government to retire voluntarily from office. He died in 2001 at the age of 95.

Despite this inauspicious start, I continued to harbour career aspirations in the study of West African politics. These were to remain on hold for three years, while I paid the price for my youthful naiveté.

Lost Innocence

Although by most objective standards I was relatively intelligent, I was, even by the standards of the time, somewhat gullible. John Kennedy was elected President during my third year of high school, and as an impressionable 15 year old, I was seduced by his rhetoric of "ask not what your country can do for you, ask what you can do for your country." I decided to do my bit by volunteering for military service after university. I sealed that commitment three years before graduation by joining the Naval Reserve just short of my eighteenth birthday, while Kennedy was still President. My timing proved to be most unfortunate. I was commissioned as a naval officer in August 1966 and spent the following three years on active duty, eighteen months of which saw me serving on a light cruiser in the Far East.

This, of course, was at the height of the Vietnam War. At university, I had faith that Lyndon B. Johnson, in his wisdom, was doing the right thing. As I sailed towards Vietnam, I became increasingly uncomfortable about the war—in terms of both ends and means.

I never really felt at risk. Actuarially, I was much safer where I was than I would have been back home, speeding along the New Jersey Turnpike. I spent countless hours directing gunnery radar during bombardment of the Vietnam coast. On one occasion in May 1967, a very skilled Vietnamese gunner eight miles distant succeeded in hitting one of my ship's radar antennas; my job was to shoot back while the ship sailed out of range of the shore batteries. I recall the subse-

<table><tr><td>*Lessons*</td></tr><tr><td>*The Vietnam War, and my naval experience more generally, had a great effect on me. I shall always regret my involvement.*</td></tr></table>

quent revulsion at having had to aim a gun and direct fire at another person. On the second such occasion, my response was more efficient, my revulsion somewhat less. Fortunately, that was the last time I was called upon to shoot at anyone. It was my good luck to have been below decks some weeks later when another officer on watch was ordered to fire on a small group of fishing boats that were in an area that was deemed to be a "free fire zone." I don't know how many people were killed. The survivors, some of whom were seriously injured, were described to me as women, children, and old men.

From then on, my opposition to the war increased, although never to the point at which I contemplated deserting, or even requesting a transfer.

The Vietnam War, and my naval experience more generally, had a great effect on me. I shall always regret my involvement. I came out of it disgusted with myself and with my country, with a strong dislike of hierarchy, a growing distrust of government, and contempt for authority. Despite his monumental contributions to civil rights I had developed a deep loathing of Lyndon Johnson, and was euphoric when he chose not to contest the 1968 election. My allegiance was to Eugene McCarthy. As history would have it, my loathing of LBJ was soon to be replaced by an even deeper loathing of Richard Nixon.

My navy days did, however, allow me to see Asia. I spent a fair bit of time in Japan, Hong Kong, the Philippines, Korea, Singapore, and Taiwan. I never did set foot on Vietnamese soil, although my shipboard activities contributed to the despoliation of Vietnam's magnificent coastline.

Not long after returning to the United States to serve my last year of service on board an aircraft carrier undergoing an overhaul, the Democratic National Convention was held in Chicago. The massive anti-war protests that were held in Grant Park were met with a degree of repression that was described as a "police riot." This and less heinous (but nonetheless repressive) police behavior directed at anti-war protestors and other members of the "counterculture" engendered a contempt for police on my part that took many years to abate.

Graduate Studies

The approaching end of my military obligation was accompanied by the rekindled ambition of one day returning to graduate school in political science, and of becoming a more astute analyst of West African politics than I had been in January 1966. My applications for admission to graduate school produced three acceptances: Boston University, UCLA, and Northwestern. Each had strong African studies programs, but I was advised to choose Northwestern because its political science department was considered the more prestigious.

Lessons
We were all required to read a new book on comparative research by Przeworski and Teune (1970). Their lasting message is that the essence of comparative study is generalization.

The NU graduate program in political science was very unusual for the time. In the forefront of what was then referred to as the "behavioral revolution," Northwestern's Ph.D. program had a rigid core curriculum that included philosophy of science, research design, and three courses of statistics.

None of this seemed relevant to the study of West African politics. The statistics requirement was particularly daunting. My experience with high school algebra had been traumatic (I had recurring nightmares about math well into my forties). Concerned about whether I could cope with the rigid Northwestern curriculum, I wrote to the Director of Graduate Studies, Professor Kenneth Janda. I mentioned that I had an unpleasant high school math career, had avoided math altogether at University, and was concerned about my ability to handle the statistics requirement. He sent me back a charming letter, saying that he too had not excelled in high school math, nor had he done any math at University. He disclosed that it was he who taught introductory statistics in political science. "I'll keep your secret if you keep mine," he said. That clinched it for me, and I headed for Chicago in September 1969.

No sooner did I arrive in Chicago

than I eagerly availed myself of the numerous and frequent opportunities to protest the Vietnam War. I was keen to see whether the Chicago Police had changed their methods since August 1968. They had indeed, at least as far as peaceful protests were concerned. But they showed no such restraint during a midnight raid in December 1969 when they shot and killed two Black Panther Party members, Fred Hampton and Mark Clark. I marched peacefully and attended numerous non-violent rallies, activity that paled in comparison to the Weathermen's Days of Rage. From time to time, I flaunted the fact that I was a returned veteran, assuming that this would enhance my credibility.

Having just been liberated from three years in the Navy, and bolstered by Ken Janda's reassurances, the idea of a rigid graduate curriculum did not bother me in the least. I often admitted to my colleagues that I would stand on my head and read Greek if that were required; anything was better than the Navy. Many of my colleagues were less captivated with graduate study than was I. Most were beginning their seventeenth consecutive year of formal education; some were facing conscription for an increasingly horrible war. And the president of the day was Richard Nixon.

Among the few elective courses I took was a course on Political Socialization taught by the late Lee Anderson. With his encouragement, I set about studying children's orientations to domestic and international violence. This was based on classroom observation and on short interviews, during which I showed children dummy

newspaper headlines and asked which ones they would read first. I hypothesized that they would be more interested in local news, regardless of whether or not it entailed violence; my findings were ambiguous.

My course in the philosophy of science exposed me to the logic of inquiry. Although I did not find it captivating at the time, I recognize in retrospect that like spinach, it was good for me. We were all required to read a new book on comparative research by Przeworski and Teune (1970). Their lasting message is that the essence of comparative study is generalization. Successful comparative study would replace "system names" (Norway; South Africa) with "variable names" (racial homogeneity; social stratification).

Nineteen-seventy was a violent year in the United States. The Chicago Seven were on trial for their involvement in events leading to the demonstrations at the Democratic National Convention two years before. In May, Nixon's invasion of Cambodia precipitated demonstrations that resulted in the fatal shooting of four students at Kent State University by Ohio National Guard troops. These in turn brought about an uprising across the United States. Students at most universities went on strike, and university administrators obliged by shutting the universities down for the summer. Northwestern was no exception; I was given credit for the aborted spring quarter and awarded a Master's degree. My classmates and I, equipped with our newly acquired methods skills, offered our services to the Senate campaign of Adlai Stevenson III, an antiwar

Democrat. We were prepared to design and field a statewide survey, but after piloting our questionnaire, our offer was rebuffed. The campaign was in greater need of money than data.

The Political Science Department at Northwestern was self-consciously interdisciplinary, and at that historical moment, more permissive than usual. Three quarters of coursework and a research paper of publishable quality earned one a Master's degree; Ph.D. candidacy followed. We were encouraged to cross disciplinary boundaries, so when classes resumed in September 1970, I did courses on military sociology with Charlie Moskos, and one on social psychology—experimental approaches to personality, with Lee Sechrest. I was extremely fortunate to have had contact with a number of other professors within the Political Science Department, even though I did not take any of their courses. Ted Gurr and Lou Masotti had become renowned for their work on violence and civil strife. Ted's book *Why Men Rebel* (Gurr 1970) had just won the Woodrow Wilson Prize of the American Political Science Association as the best political science book of 1970. I could not have anticipated the profound effect these two were to have on my career.

My Northwestern classmates were a diverse group. We were mutually supportive and, as doctoral students should, learned a lot from each other. Some, like I, came with interests in African studies. The most common specialty was international relations. Those with whom I have remained in closest contact include Michael Stohl, who keeps me interested in terrorism (Grabosky

and Stohl 2003), and Wesley Skogan, who preceded me by three years, and whom I eventually followed into a life of crime.

Northwestern encouraged its Ph.D. students to submit their dissertations within three years of beginning graduate study, so there was no time to waste. At the beginning of my second year, I began searching for a dissertation topic. By this time, the tide of African studies had begun to turn. The Ford Foundation was winding back its African programs, and it became apparent that in a tight political science job market generally, prospects for white Africanists were slim. So I abandoned Africa, not quite knowing where to turn.

Still grappling with my military experience, I had become interested in the psychological processes that allow individuals to harm others. Relating this to political science was a minor problem, although the permissive historical moment allowed me to make the case. A chance encounter with a Philadelphia psychiatrist named Perry Ottenberg got me thinking about human destructiveness (Bernard, Ottenberg, and Redl 1965). My Northwestern supervisor, Don Strickland, whose intellectual breadth and depth was an inspiration, kept me on course. My dissertation turned out to be a *bouillabaisse* of psychiatry, theories of Marx and Simmel, the social psychology of aggression, obedience and altruism, and the obligatory multiple regression analysis of crime rates and social indicators in 50 large US cities. Readers interested in how this all fit together must approach University Microfilms (Grabosky 1973), as not one word of my dissertation was ever published. It nevertheless was the most stimulating and fulfilling episode of my career. I was about twenty years too early to catch the social capital wave.

Early Career Successes

As I was finishing up my Ph.D. thesis, I began looking for a job. The market was tight, and in April 1972, the award of a fellowship to a faculty member at Case Western Reserve University created a one-year vacancy there. I was invited for an interview, and as I was about to leave Evanston for O'Hare Airport and the short flight to Cleveland, I encountered Ted Gurr in the parking lot. I told him where I was heading; he wished me luck, and suggested that if things didn't work out in Cleveland (or even if they did), I might consider joining a project that he was about to begin with Lou Masotti. He had in mind a one year post-doctoral fellowship, about half of which would be spent in Sydney, Australia. I said I would be in touch when I got back.

I was offered the position at Case Western, but the prospect of six months in Sydney seemed much more attractive than a year in Cleveland. The project was big, and exciting. I signed on.

The "Four-City Study," as we came to call it, was a comparative study of crime and public order (and official responses thereto) in London, Stockholm, Calcutta, and Sydney. It was funded by the Center for the Study of Crime and Delinquency of the National Institute of Mental Health. The project had an interesting gestation. As noted above, the previous decade had been

extremely unsettling; the assassinations of the Kennedys and Martin Luther King, the Vietnam War, large-scale riots in scores of American cities, and a crime wave greater than anything experienced in living memory, had placed violence, crime, and disorder high on the public agenda. Marvin Wolfgang, one of the leading lights of US criminology and an advisor to NIMH, had noticed that there was little knowledge at the time about the history of crime in the United States, and even less knowledge about how other societies around the world had coped with crime waves over the previous two centuries. He inspired the project that was to involve me to an extent greater than I had anticipated.

Ted Gurr was a perfect mentor. His encyclopedic knowledge and grasp of history are daunting; his ability to generalize, masterful. Back in the 1970s he wrote prolifically on an IBM Selectric typewriter, and I would have sworn that the steady stream of typing sounds from his office in the next room really emanated from a continuous loop tape. His stream of manuscripts spoke for themselves. He always gave me as much guidance as I needed; no more, no less. From him I learned how to focus clearly on the big picture, how to write a research proposal, and how to work with a publisher. And he was very generous in offering co-authorship to his junior colleagues.

The selection of the four cities was non-random. London was chosen because, despite its reputation for disorder in the eighteenth and nineteenth centuries, it had become a paragon of civility by 1955. Stockholm was selected because Sweden was renowned as a laboratory of social reform, in stark contrast to the punitive retributivism that had been a fact of life over the course of US history. Not much was known about Sydney, except for its unusual origins as a penal settlement, and the fact that, as a British colony for over a century and given its position within the British sphere of influence since independence, Australia served as a place for the transplantation of British law and policy. Calcutta was selected because of its reputation as the worst place in the world.

Duncan Chappell, who in 1972 was at SUNY Albany, provided me with valuable contacts in Australia, and my six months in Sydney were most enjoyable. Although I was a diligent user of the Mitchell Library, I did get to the beach a fair bit, and discovered the delights of Australian beer. Most memorable, however, was the hospitality shown to me by the criminologists at the University of Sydney, Faculty of Law—Gordon Hawkins, Greg Woods, Paul Ward, and Bill Lucas. With warm feelings about Australia and Australians, and with hopes of returning there some day, I left for Chicago in April 1973, just in time for the Senate Watergate hearings. My mistrust of government and utter contempt for the Nixon Administration became even greater.

A few weeks after my return, I interviewed for a position at the University of Vermont. Luck was on my side; I received, and accepted, their offer, and spent the rest of the summer finishing up the case study of Sydney.

Vermont is a lovely place, and although I was welcomed warmly, I didn't find the Political Science Department overwhelmingly harmonious. I now recognize that this is par for the course in academia. In my experience, the student body varied widely in competence and commitment. A few students were exceptionally bright, some were abysmal, and most were there to ski and to party. After a semester I began to ask myself, "Is this what I want to do with my life?" There were the occasional high points. One night in August 1974, I sat down in a comfortable chair with a nice tall glass, an ice bucket, a bottle of gin, and a bottle of tonic, as I watched the evening's television coverage of Nixon's resignation. I loved every minute of it.

There was interesting intellectual work to be done as well. My graduate school colleague Michael Stohl asked me to contribute an essay on urban terrorism to a collection that he was putting together (Stohl 1979). The vulnerability of urban systems to terrorist activity was apparent even back then. I failed, however, to identify the potential effectiveness of suicide attacks.

In my second year at UVM my restlessness intensified. The relentless rhythms of undergraduate teaching were already becoming apparent; the Department of Political Science continued to be rancorous. Although I was on course for tenure, I wasn't sure that I wanted to spend the next 35 years teaching American politics. So I began sniffing around.

I do not remember how it came to my attention, but I applied for a Russell Sage Foundation Fellowship in Law and Social Science. This paid a modest stipend and provided entrée for the lucky recipient to a law school for an academic year where he or she would contribute to narrowing the gap between the two worlds of social science and law, a process that had begun in earnest in 1964 with the establishment of the Law and Society Association. In due course, I was advised that my application had been unsuccessful. The letter did say that the selection process had been very competitive (not the first, nor the last time I would come across those comforting words).

Meanwhile, the Four City Study had stalled. The Stockholm component had been subcontracted to a group of Swedish criminologists, who were less than enthusiastic about the enterprise. They may well have resented US prosecution of the Vietnam War; they may well have suspected an ulterior motive behind a US Government funded project that would study civil disorder in Sweden; they may well have found Americans a bit brusque. In any event, there was nothing resembling the 200-page manuscript that I had prepared on Sydney. Ted Gurr contacted me and asked if I would like to spend a month in Sweden to try to revive the project. I accepted with pleasure and spent July of 1975 in Stockholm. My maternal grandfather was Swedish, and my middle name is Nils (as was his given name). Although I had no Swedish language, I was able to trade on my ethnicity to overcome some of the resentment that had built-up over the project; with considerable help from our Swedish teammates, I completed the Stockholm study by the end of the year.

When I was nearing the end of my month in Sweden, I introduced myself to Professor Knut Sveri, the Professor of Criminology at the University of Stockholm. He mentioned in passing that he had recently received a letter from a prisoner in Arizona, who had been sentenced to two consecutive life sentences for what he claimed were non-violent sex offences with two young girls. The prisoner was curious as to what kind of sentence a similarly situated defendant would receive in a Swedish court. Professor Sveri told me that he would have to write to the unfortunate American that a Swedish counterpart would be unlikely to receive a custodial sentence, but would most likely be required to undertake some kind of psychiatric consultation. The stark difference in responses between the two societies struck me. My emerging interest in variations in the severity of penal sanctions was also stimulated by discussions with Hanns van Hofer, then a student at Stockholm University, who had compiled time series data on imprisonment in Europe, which showed a significant long term decline in rates of imprisonment beginning in the nineteenth century and continuing through the 1960s. This was also the pattern that we identified in New South Wales, Australia.

Variations in the severity of penal sanctions over time and space began to intrigue me, and I began collecting data on rates of imprisonment from a number of countries around the world, as well as from various US state jurisdictions. The work of Waller and Chan (1974) and Biles and Mulligan (1973) were benchmarks.

Having returned from Sweden for the 1975-76 academic year, I became increasingly disillusioned at the prospects of a long term future at the University of Vermont. My restlessness moved me to contact the Russell Sage Foundation to inquire about having a go at the next Law and Social Science Fellowship round. They advised that my previous application and letters of reference were on file and that I could simply reactivate them. I sent in a fresh CV with a couple of new publications, and crossed my fingers.

In the fullness of time I received a cheerful call from the Foundation, advising me that I was second-time lucky, and asking me to contact Professor Stanton Wheeler of Yale Law School to discuss where I might take up the residency. With utter delight I did so, and asked which law schools might be amenable to hosting a Russell Sage Fellow. He suggested that I would be welcome at Yale, and my quest stopped immediately.

Yale Law School was a splendid place to hang out. I sat in on quite a few courses, including Torts with Guido Calabrese, Criminal Law with Abraham Goldstein, American Constitutional Law with Charles Black, and Comparative Criminal Procedure with Mirjan Damaska. One of the most memorable was a course named Contemporary Chinese Legal Institutions, taught by a practising lawyer named Stanley Lubman. Chairman Mao died not long into the course, and we were advised that what we were learning would soon be inoperative.

In between the heavy casebooks, I continued reading penology, and began collecting statutes and prison statistics for a soon to be aborted project which I had given the catchy title "the punitive polity." I was also called back into service to help put the finishing touches on the London part of the Four City Study, by then approaching the fifth anniversary of its commencement.

Not long after I arrived at Yale, Donald Black's *The Behavior of Law* (Black 1976) was published by Academic Press. I found its ambitious sweep, its breathtaking generalization, and its grounding in anthropology to be very seductive. I introduced myself to Black, who was then a member of Yale's sociology department, and showed him a manuscript on which I had been working, which continued to explore the issue of variation in the severity of penal sanctions. The manuscript was about to be published in the (then) *Journal of Law and Society*, but Donald asked if I would recast it for publication in a new anthology which he was putting together called *Toward a General Theory of Social Control*. I was flattered by the invitation, and started work. *The Variability of Punishment*, as it came to be called, sought to explain variation in the severity of punishment across not only national and state jurisdictions, but collectivities generally (Grabosky 1984).

Professionally, I was thriving. The Russell Sage Foundation generously granted a one-year extension of my fellowship. The Four City Study, all 792 pages of it, was published in 1977 (Gurr, Grabosky, and Hula 1977). With Ted Gurr's encouragement, I had submitted a longer version of the Sydney manuscript to the Australian National University Press (Grabosky 1977). It too came out that year. But fate once again intervened, leading me in an unexpected direction.

Drastic Change

In November of my second year at Yale, I was awakened in the middle of the night by a telephone call. It was Greg Woods, with whom I had exchanged annual Christmas cards, but whom I had neither seen nor spoken to for 4½ years. He had just finished lunch with the Attorney-General of South Australia, with whom he was spending a year as a Ministerial Advisor. After seeking reassurance that I had not "bombed in New Haven,"[2] Greg got right to the point, and inquired if I would be interested in coming to Adelaide to set up an office of crime statistics and research in the Attorney-General's Department. For someone who was doing pretty well in a North American academic career, the idea seemed inappropriate. And yet, my previous experience in Australia, and the warmth of Greg's hospitality during those six months in 1972-73, were infectious. I asked him if I could think about it. It was, after all, about 3 AM in New Haven. He encouraged me to make a formal application, and offered to serve as a referee. I followed his advice.

Although I had visited Adelaide briefly in 1973, I knew little about the government, except that it was reputed to be progressive. I think Greg Woods referred to it as "One of the few social-ist governments in the free world." The prospect was intriguing.

While my application was under consideration, I came across a British

Lessons

I was offered the position, and faced a gut-wrenching decision. It seemed unwise to abandon academe when my career was just about to take off. On the other hand, Australia beckoned.

newspaper at Yale that referred to the recent dismissal of the South Australian Police Commissioner. I knew nothing of the circumstances; it turned out the Commissioner had misled the Premier, who then misled Parliament, about the existence of Special Branch files. Political surveillance was not uncommon in Australia in those days, although perhaps not on the scale of that conducted in the United States by the FBI.

In April 1978 I was flown from New York to Adelaide for an interview. Having had no experience with public service recruitment, I expected the kind of wide-ranging, free flowing discussion typical of academic interviews. At what I thought was an opportune moment, I remarked that the police commissioner had recently been dismissed, and queried how that might effect my relations with the South Australia Police. My three interviewers all appeared most uncomfortable and the senior member of the panel commented that I would have to resolve that for myself.

I was offered the position, and faced a gut-wrenching decision. It seemed unwise to abandon academe when my career was just about to take off. On the other hand, Australia beckoned. To complicate matters, when I asked Ted Gurr for his advice on what to do, he offered me yet another option—to help him spend a million dollars of US Justice Department (DOJ) money. The only condition was that it be spent in four specific US cities; aside from this we had *carte blanche*. My interpretation was that the approaching end of the fiscal year triggered a "spend it or lose it" mindset in the DOJ bureaucracy. I suspected (but never verified) that the four cities lay in the congressional districts of key members of the House Appropriations Committee. Australia's attraction proved too great however, and I landed in Adelaide in July 1978. Ted, who had a number of other projects in train, turned down the money.

The Personnel Officer for the South Australian Law Department (as it was then called) greeted me with good news and bad news. "Which do you want first?" he inquired. "Hit me with the bad news first," I replied. He advised that a hiring freeze had just been imposed across the South Australian public sector, and that I would have to do without a statistician and research officer. My office was to consist of just me, and a receptionist. "OK, what's the good news?" I then asked. "The good news is that the freeze was imposed ten minutes after your own appointment went through Executive Council, so at least you have a job." The fiscal crisis had begun to bite; it was to plague me (and provide a focus for my research) ever after.

Life in the South Australian Office of Crime Statistics was exciting to begin with. In my first fourteen months

there (July 1978-September 1979), I served (and survived) four successive Attorneys-General and two governments. My colleagues and I succeeded in establishing the first computer-based system of statistics from lower criminal courts anywhere in Australia, and I chaired an interdepartmental committee on crime victims that charted a course for victim policy in Australia. But again, I asked if there was more to life than this. After a brief period with a legal research organization in Sydney, I was recruited by David Biles, and landed at the Australian Institute of Criminology in Canberra at the end of 1983.

A Return to Research

John Braithwaite had recently left the AIC, and I inherited his office. My job was to pick up where he had left off in the study of white-collar crime. Just as I began wondering how I would ever follow an act like his, he called me from his office across town at the Australian National University and proposed a collaboration. We decided to look at regulatory enforcement. Thanks largely to his energy and vision, we succeeded in producing the first large-scale comparative study of regulatory enforcement (Grabosky and Braithwaite 1986). Other projects at the AIC included work on official misconduct (Grabosky 1989), media coverage of crime and criminal justice (Grabosky and Wilson 1989), the contribution of lawyers, accountants, and engineers to white-collar crime (Grabosky 1990), and a national commission of inquiry on violence (Australia 1990). My work was enthusiastically supported by AIC directors Richard Harding and Duncan Chappell, who returned to Australia in 1987.

After 10 years at the AIC, I was offered an opportunity to spend two years at the Australian National University looking at regulatory compliance. I spent two years working on various issues, including rewards and incentives as regulatory instruments, counterproductive regulatory interventions, and harnessing resources outside the government in furtherance of public policy (Grabosky 1994, 1995a, 1995b, 1996, 1997).

Back at the Institute of Criminology, I inherited supervisory and administrative responsibilities, eventually rising to the position of Deputy Director. My one indulgence in research on any significant scale was in computer crime. It was sparked by a newspaper advertisement early in 1995 in which Telecom Australia (now Telstra) was soliciting applications for grants for research into the social implications of telecommunications. Although I wasn't entirely sure what telecommunications was (or were), I was able to put together a proposal of sufficient credibility. What I proposed as an exploratory study of telecommunications and crime became a book, *Crime in the Digital Age* (Grabosky and Smith 1998). It was one of the first book-length overviews of computer crime.

Although much of the material on computer crime originated in the United States (and continues to do so), I was struck by some of the thorny problems arising from differences in culture, law, and policy between coun-

tries: Neo-Nazi propaganda is illegal under German law, but constitutionally protected in the United States; some countries go to great lengths to control their citizens' access to cyberspace, while others facilitate such access.

A Close Call

Meanwhile, a familiar theme returned. I began to get restless once again. A librarian at the AIC passed on to me an advertisement for a job at the US National Institute of Justice. NIJ was creating an International Center and was recruiting a Director. Had one suggested to me in 1970 that I would one day be seeking a job at the US Justice Department, I would have inquired what they had been smoking. A quarter of a century later, I had become less militant. Intrigued at the prospect, I submitted an application.

An offer was forthcoming, but at two-thirds the salary I had been led to expect. I nevertheless swallowed my pride and accepted, intending to commence work in mid-February 1998. Three weeks short of my commencement date, while still in Australia, I received an email advising me that I had been denied a security clearance, ostensibly on the grounds that I had lived continuously outside the United States for more than 5 years. I had hardly concealed this; indeed my initial application detailed every residential and employment address for the previous two decades. At the time I was invited for an interview, I was assured that my Australian citizenship would pose no bar to my appointment.

My reaction, however, was one of

relief. The realization that had I taken up the position, I would have been paid less than Linda Tripp,[3] reinforced my view that everything was happening for the better. I immediately went out and affirmed my allegiance to Australia by purchasing the biggest barbecue on sale at Barbecues Galore.

My curiosity about whether there may have been a more sinister justification for the denial of my security clearance moved me to request my FBI file under the Freedom of Information Act. After a long wait, I received a form letter advising that the FBI had no record of me. It went on to add that I was free to appeal that ruling. I found the offer momentarily tantalizing, but then decided to file the letter away for posterity, and get on with life.

My relief at having narrowly missed joining "the Bureaucracy from Hell" was revived in the months following the September 11 attacks when it became known that another branch of the US Department of Justice, the Immigration and Naturalization Service, had *posthumously* granted student visas to two of the 9/11 hijackers.

An Offer Too Good to Refuse

Committed to staying in Australia, I threw myself headlong into a second book on computer crime (Grabosky, Smith, and Dempsey 2001) and to some thinking about the impact of fiscal constraint on policing. I had also taken on a minor role in a cross-national project on restorative justice, funded by the Japanese Ministry of Education. John Braithwaite and Heather Strang were the main players; I was invited along for the ride because of my fondness for Japanese culture and my (embarrassingly unsuccessful) attempts to master the Japanese language.

Early one morning during a trip to Tokyo in conjunction with the project I was awakened by a telephone call from John Braithwaite, who suggested that I apply for a vacant chair at the Australian National University. I replied that I was disinclined to jump ship, and that in any event, Japan was not the place for me to contemplate leaving the institution to which I had devoted seventeen years of my life. Those who know John are aware that he is a persistent fellow, and the best I could do was to offer to discuss it further with him at the ASC meeting in San Francisco the following week.

John persuaded me to apply for the position. I returned to Australia via Japan, and over sushi at Kansai Airport, I drafted an application that landed me an offer. After a week of agonizing, I decided to join the ANU.

I took up the appointment in July of 2001, and since then, it has been my privilege to work closely with Clifford Shearing on a variety of issues in policing. Our basic questions relate to the empowerment of communities to identify and resolve their own security needs, and the ability of police to harness resources outside the public sector in furtherance of the police mission. These are fascinating and important issues, and highly relevant to comparative criminal justice, because they challenge my passion for generalization. I cheerfully concede that much policy is context-specific; policing arrangements which are suited to one location may be inappropriate elsewhere. What is suitable in Belfast may be inappropriate in Soweto and even less appropriate in the leafy suburbs of Canberra. So it is that when I hear people embrace the concept of "zero tolerance policing" with evangelistic fervor, I instinctively ask "in what context?"

Lessons Learned

As a former ideologue myself, I am not surprised that ideology is a powerful driver of policy. Yet it is nevertheless frustrating to see how uninterested some people are in facts.

Many tend to oversimplify. It has long been recognized that "behind every simple solution there is a complex problem." And things can go terribly wrong; the road to policy disaster is paved with good intentions (Grabosky 1996). Perhaps for this reason, I have begun to weary of evangelists. It was long ago that Justice Holmes declared that "time has upset many fighting faiths" (Abrams v. United States; Holmes J, dissent; 250 U.S. 616; 630; 1919).

As a first year graduate student in 1969, I was exposed to the work of Donald T. Campbell. His seminal article, "Reforms as Experiments" (Campbell 1969), was published earlier that year. The idea of evidence-based public policy (as it is now called) was and remains a compelling one for me. During my years in and around the public sector, I have been chronically dismayed at the "quick fix" mentality that drives much public policy. Billions of dollars have been (and continue to be) spent on programs that generate the "warm inner glow" but without any effort being made to evaluate their impact on the problems they were

Lessons
Terrorism will not disappear, and state response to terrorism is likely to become more repressive.

designed to address. Are the programs effective, and if so, at what price? Whether the taxpayers are getting a return on their investment in a given program remains a matter of great concern to me.

Global forces appear to be driving increased heterogeneity and stratification within nations. This seems likely to manifest itself in persistent crime and conflict. Terrorism will not disappear, and state response to terrorism is likely to become more repressive. Police powers are likely to increase. There will be opportunities for scholars of criminal justice to ensure that these powers are exercised responsibly; governments are always vulnerable to malevolence and blunder.

Governments everywhere will continue to be plagued by resource constraints. Pressures to improve efficiency and effectiveness in the delivery of public safety will be unrelenting. Evaluation and cost/benefit analysis will be among the more valued skills of criminologists.

I began my career at a time when elitism and competitiveness were distinctly unfashionable. Over the years, I have become resigned to the realization that prestige counts, and that the world is a competitive place. While I would encourage students to explore and to follow their interests, they should do so with open eyes. By all means, do what interests you, but bear in mind that whimsical pursuits and career interruptions may entail costs. These will not necessarily be prohibitive. Ultimately it goes into the balance against the positives of following one's passions and engaging fully with the world. In other words, there may be more to life than being a well-published comparative criminologist! And, I suspect the ones with the broader outlook on life are actually better at their jobs.

In retrospect, the spirit of adventure and professional nonchalance that persisted until I was well past my fortieth year took me to places that I could never have anticipated. I have, for the most part, not only enjoyed the ride, but thrived. Now that I am older I have become risk averse, and I would be loath to recommend to a younger student that he or she cast their fate to the wind. I have been very lucky. But then, perhaps others would be, too.

Acknowledgements

I would like to thank Bronwyn McNaughton and Michael Stohl for their editorial guidance, and for enriching my life, each in different ways. Any literary or personal shortcomings remain my sole responsibility.

Notes

1 Vince Guaraldi (1962).
2 He was referring to a theatrical term for failure in the course of a pre-Broadway tryout, and the title of a satirical piece by Joseph Heller (1968) rather than an act of urban terrorism on my part.
3 Linda Tripp was the low level employee of the US Department of Defense who befriended Monica Lewinsky and was instrumental in disclosing the latter's liaison with then President Clinton.

Selected Bibliography

Australia. 1990. *Violence: Directions for Australia*. Final Report of the National Committee on Violence. Canberra: Australian Government Publishing Service.

Bernard, V., P. Ottenberg, F. Redl. 1965. "Dehumanization: A Composite Psychological Defense in Relation to Modern War." In *Behavioral Science and Human Survival*, edited by Milton Schwebel. Palo Alto: Science and Behavior Books.

Biles, D and D. Mulligan. 1973. "Mad or Bad?: The Enduring Dilemma." *British Journal of Criminology* 13:275-279.

Campbell, D.T. 1969. "Reforms as Experiments." *American Psychologist* 24:409-429.

Garrow, D. 1986. *Bearing the Cross: Martin Luther King Jr., and the Southern Christian Leadership Conference*. New York, William Morrow.

Grabosky, P. 1973. "Dehumanization: Structural Determinants of the Abdication of Civic Responsibility." Unpublished Ph.D. Dissertation, Northwestern University.

_____. 1977. *Sydney in Ferment: Crime, Dissent and Official Reaction, 1788-1973*. Canberra: Australian National University Press.

_____. 1978. "Theory and Research on Variations in Penal Severity." *British Journal of Law and Society* 15(1):103-13.

_____. 1984. "The Variability of

Punishment." In *Toward a General Theory of Social Control*. Vol. I, edited by Donald Black. Orlando: Academic Press.

_____. 1989. *Wayward Governance: Illegality and its Control in the Public Sector*. Canberra: Australian Institute of Criminology.

_____. 1990. "Professional Advisers and White Collar Illegality. Towards Explaining and Excusing Professional Failure." *University of New South Wales Law Journal* 13(2):1-24.

_____. 1992. "Law Enforcement and the Citizen: Non-Governmental Participants in Crime Prevention and Control." *Policing and Society* 2:249-71.

_____. 1994. "Green Markets: Environmental Regulation by the Private Sector." *Law and Policy* 16(4):420-48.

_____. 1995a. "Using Non-governmental Resources to Foster Regulatory Compliance." *Governance* 8(4):527-50.

_____. 1995b. "Regulation by Reward: On the Use of Incentives as Regulatory Instruments." *Law and Policy* 17(3):256-281.

_____. 1996. "Unintended Consequences of Crime Prevention." In *Crime Prevention Studies*. Vol. 5, edited by Homel and Clarke.

_____. 1997. "Inside the Pyramid: Towards a Conceptual Framework for the Analysis of Regulatory Systems." *International Journal of the Sociology of Law* 25(3): 195-201.

Grabosky, P. and J. Braithwaite. 1986. *Of Manners Gentle: Enforcement Strategies of Australian Business Regulatory Agencies*. Melbourne: Oxford University Press.

Grabosky, P. and R.G. Smith. 1998. *Crime in the Digital Age: Controlling Telecommunications and Cyberspace Illegalities*. New Brunswick, NJ: Transaction Publishers and Sydney: Federation Press.

Grabosky, P., R.G. Smith, and G. Dempsey. 2001. *Electronic Theft: Unlawful Acquisition in Cyberspace*. Cambridge: Cambridge University Press.

Grabosky, P. and M. Stohl. 2003. "Cyberterrorism." *Reform* 82:8-13.

Grabosky, P. and P. Wilson. 1989. *Journalism and Justice: How Crime is Reported*. Sydney: Pluto Press.

Gurr, T.R. 1970. *Why Men Rebel*. Princeton: Princeton University Press.

Gurr, T.R., P. Grabosky, and R.C. Hula. 1977. *The Politics of Crime and Conflict: A Comparative History of Four Cities*. Beverly Hills: Sage Publications.

Heller, J. 1968. *We Bombed in New Haven*. New York, Alfred A Knopf.

Przeworski, A. and H. Teune. 1970. *The Logic of Comparative Social Inquiry*. New York: John Wiley.

Stohl, M., ed. 1988. *The Politics of Terror: A Reader in Theory and Practice,* 3d ed. New York: Marcel Dekker.

White, T. 1961. *The Making of the President, 1960*. New York: Atheneum.

Waller, I. and J. Chan. 1974. "Prison Use: A Canadian and International Comparison." *Criminal Law Quarterly* 17:47-71.

Chapter 2

From Air Force "Brat" to Comparativist

Philip L. Reichel

Department of Criminal Justice,
University of Northern Colorado,
USA

The easiest prediction about the future for comparative/international criminology and criminal justice is that it will continue to grow and attract attention throughout the world.

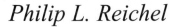

I had the fortune of growing up in a military family (the adjective *brat* is often assigned to, and accepted by, military dependents) and being reared by parents who placed a high value on diversity, equality, knowledge, and new experiences. Such values have served me well over the years and, I believe, provided a firm base for what has become a fascination with people whose lives have taken a different direction than mine, with cultures that are foreign to mine, and with social institutions that are organized and operate unlike mine. Whether by happenstance or design (probably some of each), my professional and personal life have drawn on those characteristics and today I consider myself a compartivist with specific interest in how

different countries go about achieving social control. The journey has been remarkably pleasant and I consider it quite an honor (and certainly surprising) that others may find my trek to be interesting, instructive, or both.

Developing an Interest in Comparative Studies

My father was an officer in the United States Air Force while I was growing up. Dad's changing duty assignments took the family from California, through New Mexico, Illinois, and Nebraska, to Guam, and back to Nebraska. When I left home for college, the longest I had lived in one State, was about seven years (California, from birth to age 7). I come by my *wanderlust* naturally! As with other military dependents, I learned to put down simple feeder roots in each new community so that the inevitable extraction would not be so traumatic. That meant I never really had "best friends" in the traditional sense, I often told people I had no home State, and my allegiances to schools and mascots were very flexible. On the other hand, I meet new people with relative ease, have an ability to acclimate rapidly to new surroundings, and can quickly become a fan of the major league baseball team closest to wherever I am living (much to the mortification of traditionalists like Chicago Cubs fans).

Changing schools, neighborhoods, and friends, in California, New Mexico, Illinois, and Nebraska, certainly provided the impetus to have more than the typical teenager's parochial view. By the time I was 16, I had lived in four States and traveled through at least ten others, had gone to school in both a one-room schoolhouse and more modern classrooms, and had learned to appreciate a great diversity of people, places, and ideas. All that was kicked up a notch just before my junior year of high school when Dad was transferred to the island of Guam.

Living on Guam during my junior and senior years of high school (1963 to 1965) provided me with opportunities and experiences that continued to broaden what was becoming a world view. Military dependents and Islanders attended school together and I was very fortunate to have close friends in both categories. A family vacation to Japan provided my first truly foreign experience and my interest in Japan and

> ### Lessons
>
> *Without me realizing it, the primary focus of my career was now in place— an interest in other countries and an interest in corrections.*

Japanese culture continues today.

After graduating from George Washington High School on Agana, Guam (that certainly cuts down on the high school reunions I attend), my family returned to Nebraska and I chose to attend Nebraska Wesleyan University in Lincoln. As I tell my students, I was a psychology major until I saw the light and switched to sociology. My interest in sociology in general, and in criminology more specifically, was aided by my major professor, William Cascini. Upon graduation I decided to continue my education and enrolled in the Master's program at the University of California in Santa Barbara. One of my favorite theories as an undergraduate was differential association theory and Donald Cressey, the theory's primary proponent at the time, was on the faculty at UCSB. Unfortunately, in my one class with Professor Cressey I was simply one of many faces in a large classroom and I never established more than a nodding acquaintance with him. A combination of student rioting on and near the campus in 1969 and 1970 and the pending birth of my first son encouraged me to find a full-time job. That job ended up being an institutional parole officer (similar to a classification officer with counseling duties) at the Nebraska Penal and Correctional Complex in Lincoln. Without me realizing it, the primary focus of my career was now in place—an interest in other countries and an interest in corrections.

After working a few years at the prison, I decided it was time to complete my Master's degree and did so in the sociology department at Kansas State University. I had certainly made other decisions by this point in my life that had significant impact on my eventual career (for example, leaving UCSB without having attempted to establish a closer academic relationship with Professor Cressey), but this next one was probably the first one I was making with the realization that it would be a milestone decision. I had never really considered teaching as a profession and had not, in fact, been in front of a class for purposes other than making an oral report as part of a class assignment. But, for reasons that have faded in memory, I decided I would like to try teaching for a few years so I would have a base of comparison with my two years working in the prison. Then, I would be able to better evaluate my career goals.

In 1972 it was still possible to be hired at the college level with only an M.A. degree. This was especially true in the new field of criminal justice. There were very few Ph.D. programs in criminal justice at the time, and many of us who began teaching undergraduates in this rapidly growing area had our degrees in disciplines such as sociology, political science, public administration, and others. In fact, we were teaching courses on topics that were not even offered when we were students. Augusta College (now Augusta State

University) in Augusta, Georgia was one of many schools across the country interested in offering criminal justice courses and with the start of Fall quarter 1972 I began my teaching career in the sociology department.

It did not take me more than a few quarters of teaching to realize that this was the career for me. I greatly enjoyed the students, they seemed to respond positively to me, and the job encouraged trips to conventions in cities in the Northeast and the South—areas of the country where I had never visited. The emphasis at Augusta College was on teaching more so than research, but the faculty was expected to have some level of professional activity. The encouragement to present papers at professional meetings and to submit papers for publication in professional journals actually appealed to me more than I thought it would.

The heavy teaching load (15 hours per quarter) prohibited very elaborate research endeavors, but I found that using my teaching techniques for the content, and my students as the subjects, I was able to have a few articles published in journals devoted to teaching. More important, I discovered that I really enjoyed the research and writing processes. It was also apparent, however, that if I wished to continue in this occupation I would have to return to school and get my Ph.D.

Once again it was major decision time. Having been involved in academics for several years, I knew that one's Ph.D. program has significant impact on what is learned, from whom it is learned, whom one's professional colleagues will become, and the opportunities one eventually has for research collaboration. From my perspective that meant I should try to gain acceptance in one of the more prestigious departments. But there were also more practical and immediate concerns. My wife and I now had two sons and we had the typical financial worries related to quitting our jobs and eventually finding employment after graduation. Augusta College offered to place me on two years leave of absence with partial pay if I agreed to return to Augusta College after completing my Ph.D. coursework. I could, they argued, work on my dissertation as I returned to my teaching duties. That was a very appealing offer, but it meant that Kansas State was my best option for a Ph.D. since I was assured of having all my M.A. work accepted and I already knew most of the faculty. I would be able to get in and out within the two-year window and the faculty accepted my plan to do my dissertation in absentia. In 1976, the family was off to Manhattan, Kansas and specific events and colleagues began focusing even further my interest in comparative studies.

The Role of Events and Colleagues

A few of the faculty in the Department of Sociology, Anthropology, and Social Work at Kansas State University (KSU) had criminology and deviance as interest areas, but the department was clearly better known for research activities in rural sociology and demography. It was left to me to find ways to meet my criminology/criminal justice interests in the context of courses on rural development and social change. I

have not met many colleagues over the last thirty years who point to rural sociologists as important figures in their decision to emphasize comparative crime and justice—but on reflection it makes perfect sense to me.

Two sociology faculty members at KSU encouraged my eventual comparativist focus: Cornelia Butler Flora and Jan Flora. The Floras taught courses ranging from rural development to peasant revolutions and in every course I took with either of them I was encouraged to incorporate my interest in crime and justice. One of my favorite ways to accomplish that was to draw on activities in the Union of Soviet Socialist Republics. The USSR provided opportunities to write about social change, peasant revolution, modernization theory, and a legal tradition different from the one I had been studying for ten years. I found the subject matter challenging and rewarding and I trace my continuing interest in other legal traditions to my initial fascination with the socialist legal tradition.

I completed my Ph.D. coursework in 1978 and returned to Augusta College where I picked up my teaching responsibilities in addition to researching and writing my dissertation. Somehow (and I certainly do not recommend this to budding academics) I was able to complete my dissertation while doing a reasonably good job of teaching three classes, five days a week. I received my Ph.D. in Sociology in 1979 and stayed at Augusta College until 1983 when I accepted a position at the University of Northern Colorado (UNC). Although UNC also emphasizes teaching, there are increased expectations for professional development and a more reasonable teaching load (nine hours per semester) that allows for greater involvement in research and writing.

Shortly after arriving at UNC, I decided I would try my hand at writing a textbook. It would be a new challenge and allow me to combine my interest in finding information, organizing it in a meaningful way, and writing it in a way I hoped others would find enjoyable to read. My "peculiar twist" (publishers want something to make your book "special" from others on the same topic) was to include in an introductory criminal justice book some boxed items that would describe aspects of the criminal justice system in other countries. It would, in other words, give a cross-national perspective to the standard coverage of American criminal justice. The publisher was intrigued with the idea but reviewers, in 1986, did not think it would be especially informative or interesting. Deferring to the wisdom of the reviewers, the publisher declined to publish the book.

After the initial disappointment of rejection (not the first time my attempts at publishing were turned down, but that doesn't mean it gets any easier to accept), I decided that I was most disappointed that my interest in adding a comparative aspect to traditional courses was not being received enthusiastically. So, I decided to take a different approach and work on a textbook that was specifically designed for a course on comparative criminal justice systems—but I needed to gain a broader background and identify a structure for the book. As fortune would have it, this

was about the time for my first sabbatical leave at UNC.

In the mid-1980s, my interest in the socialist legal tradition had resulted in a correspondence-only acquaintance with Professor Andrzej Rzeplinski (currently the Dean of the Faculty of Applied Social Sciences and Resocialisation) at Warsaw University. Professor Rzeplinski and I collaborated on a research project that assessed the views held by our respective students about the justice system in each other's country (Reichel and Rzeplinski 1989). When I began searching for sabbatical leave opportunities, I decided to see if I could arrange something in Poland. The sabbatical proposal, written in 1989 for study in 1991, submitted a plan to conduct research on the socialist legal system as it operated in Poland. By the time I actually took the sabbatical leave, world events meant that I would instead be studying a legal system in transition as Poland moved from socialism to democracy.

The changing political nature of central Europe in the early 1990s encouraged me to include in my plans a trip to Austria where I would gather information about the civil legal tradition as a contrast to my knowledge of the socialist tradition. I had no contacts in Austria, so I called the Austrian Consulate in Denver to ask for suggestions. I was provided with the name of a law professor at the University of Vienna who had an interest in international law and occasionally taught classes at a law school in Texas. Professor Frank Höpfel was kind enough to agree to visit with us in Vienna.

With Professor Rzeplinski as our

host in Warsaw, my wife, Eva, gathered information about her area of academic and professional interest (gerontology) as I learned about policing and prisons. Rzeplinski's colleagues Zbigniew Lasocik and Monika Platek arranged tours of the police academy and two prisons, then allowed me to present several guest lectures in their classes. I had brought with me some slides of State and Federal prisons in America and my presentations occasioned considerable interest among the students.

From Warsaw we went to Vienna and met Professor Höpfel. A friendship was struck that remains today and includes several cooperative publishing efforts. On this first trip to Austria I was not able to conduct any research nor gather more than rudimentary information about the Austrian justice system. However, I returned to Colorado with a renewed interest in comparative studies and an enthusiasm about writing a textbook for a course on comparative criminal justice—interestingly, a course I had never taken as a student nor taught as a professor.

In 1992, Prentice Hall editor, Robin Baliszewski, decided to take a chance on a new author and a relatively new subject matter. At that time there were few textbooks devoted specifically to comparative criminal justice systems—the most notable being by Richard Terrill (2003). But, world events and academic activities were indicating that things were about to change. The Academy of Criminal Justice Sciences began discussing the formation of an International Section, more courses on comparative justice were popping up around the country, and students were

Lessons
But, world events and academic activities were indicating that things were about to change.

expressing greater interest in world affairs. Professor Terrill's book was an excellent source of information about the criminal justice system in specific countries (seven countries in the book's current edition), but I wanted my book to have a different approach. One that reflected my teaching philosophy and research orientation.

A Teaching Philosophy and a Research Orientation

I am a strong believer in the teacher-scholar model that encourages college professors to use research to inform their teaching. As a result, many of my journal articles over the years have resulted from topics I was covering in class and about which I, or the students, wanted more information. Examples include the history of slave patrols (Reichel 1988 and 1992) and media coverage of executions (Reichel and Munden 1989). On other occasions, my research topic resulted from my desire to incorporate specific material into my courses—for example, comparative justice (Reichel 1980; Reichel and Rzeplinski 1989; and Reichel 1992). But regardless of the topic covered, I hold fast to the belief that professors should teach rather than preach.

My academic training in sociology encouraged a value free orientation wherein the investigator's personal values are not allowed (hopefully) to influence social research. There is considerable debate about whether that is a possible or even desirable approach to social research, and I certainly do not want to involve myself in that debate here. However, I believe attempts at maintaining a value free (or at least value neutral) orientation has served me well in my research, teaching, and writing. Value neutrality allowed me to approach the socialist legal tradition with minimal bias (value neutrality is a goal rather than an accomplishment). It also serves me well when trying to understand, appreciate, and explain to others, the Islamic legal tradition. Some of my most cherished feedback over the years has come from students and colleagues who, having personally experienced and studied socialist and Islamic legal traditions, have found my analysis and explanation to be reasonably fair and accurate.

I believe that if value neutrality is appropriate for research it is also appropriate when teaching. I have always taught at schools that emphasize the teaching role—while also encouraging research in the teacher-scholar tradition. In addition, I have always taught undergraduate students (with a few exceptions when asked to serve on a thesis or dissertation committee) and I will be perfectly happy if at my retirement that statement remains true. Nothing against graduate students, of course, but I truly enjoy watching students develop from freshman espousing black and white truths to seniors who are not only questioning their own assumptions but are doing so by using

knowledge and information gained in my classes and from those taught by many of my colleagues. Satisfying examples include a student who wrote a paper as a sophomore that was titled *Why prisoners have too many rights* (a perspective that is considerably short of the value free goal), then as a senior was participating in class discussion by arguing that discussion of prisoners' rights must be conducted in the context of constitutional guarantees. I get similar satisfaction when, during the first week of class, students in my comparative criminal justice systems course are proudly proclaiming the superiority of the United States criminal justice system. Then, by the middle of the course, many of the students are wondering aloud if there may be something to learn from how Canada approaches the exclusion of evidence or how the day fine system operates in Europe. Maybe Americans do not have all the answers and maybe all countries can learn from one another. I sleep well after such days.

If I was to approach teaching with the belief that I must convert students to the values and beliefs that I hold to be true, I may just as well have become a preacher. Instead, I see my job as providing students with enough information about various topics to allow them to develop their own informed opinion and, importantly, to be able to clearly explain why they hold that opinion. One of my most satisfying teaching experiences occurred while teaching a course on the death penalty. At the beginning of the semester I required each student to state their position (for, against, undecided) but explained that I would not divulge my position until the end of class. Over the remaining weeks we reviewed arguments for and against the death penalty and I often found myself taking and supporting a position that was held by no one else in the class. Sometimes I was arguing what I actually believed, and other times I was arguing something on which I was actually in opposition. During the last week of class I asked the students, via an Internet poll, to identify my position on the death penalty. There was no consistent response as students assigned me, about equally, to either an abolitionist or retentionist perspective. I enjoyed that class all the more because the students received information about an important topic in a way that allowed them to clarify, change, or develop an opinion based on research and theory rather than on what the teacher says they should believe.

I try to accomplish the same goal when writing textbooks—which is the direction my research and writing has taken over the last ten years. A textbook, from my perspective, simply allows me to expand the number of students I reach. But that also means that I refrain from taking a specific perspective in a textbook. I do not provide a critical analysis of legal systems nor do I show how modernization theory can best explain the occurrence of crime and the structure of the justice system. Instead, I would like my contribution to the field of comparative/international criminology to be understood as having provided a more organized and efficient way to describe and analyze criminal justice systems around the world. And this returns me to my comment above

that I wanted to approach comparative justice studies in a different manner than what was being done at the time. Specifically, I believed that comparative justice studies could be presented in a manner similar to the way courses and textbooks cover our own justice system. That is, instead of teaching comparative justice through separate description of the system in different countries, I would compare and contrast systems while covering topics of policing, courts, and corrections. That idea was not unique in comparative research, but is unusual for a textbook. The result was my comparative criminal justice systems book (Reichel 2002), which provides a descriptive account of justice systems around the world by progressing through the law, police, courts, and corrections stages of the criminal justice process.

Things Learned

I am a sucker for a good quotation and when asked to offer advice or suggestions to students I often rely on phrases that have impacted me. Occasionally I will even try my own hand at composing a succinct phrase.

As for me, all I know is that I know nothing. And when I want to know something, I look it up in books—their memory never fails (Arturo Perez-Reverte, *Club Dumas*).

As the years go by, I become increasingly confident in the maxim that a scholar is not someone who has all the answers, but instead is someone who knows where to find them. I am more comfortable today, than I was earlier in my career, in responding to tough questions from students (and colleagues) by saying that I don't know the answer. But, I am also confident that someone, somewhere, has found or is working on the answer. Only after I am convinced that the question has not been addressed do I consider whether I should undertake the necessary research project myself. For those of you who are writing term papers this sounds like an interpretation of academic life as a constantly recurring review of the literature. If that sounds like a horrible way to spend one's day, you will likely find a career in academics to be rather burdensome. If it sounds like an intriguing challenge with unending opportunities to learn new things you may as well purchase your mortarboard now.

A man's feet must be planted in his country, but his eyes should survey the world (George Santayana, *The Life of Reason*).

As an undergraduate in sociology classes I became familiar with the concept of ethnocentrism. I learned how functionalist theories explain that this belief in the superiority of one's own culture has both positive (e.g., patriotism) and negative (e.g., racism and stagnation) aspects; but it always seemed to me that the negatives clearly outweigh the positive. I suspect that my frequent moves, numerous "home" locations, and variety of friends, during my younger years have something to do with my perspective. But even without that bias of socialization, I am convinced that no one can successfully engage in comparative studies without having—or soon developing—an appreciation for diversity of people, opinions, and institutions.

Similarities are seldom discovered while concentrating on difference.

Social theorists, Emile Durkheim especially, who consider order and disorder as two sides of the same coin have provided a very useful concept for comparativists. Most of my research and writing on justice systems in a variety of countries concentrates on the differences among those systems. That seems to be the easier approach to take and it also provides a contrast by which my audience (which essentially are students in the United States) can understand better their own system. However, by concentrating on the *differences-side* of the coin, both my students and I overlook the equally intriguing and important *similarities-side* of the world's justice systems. I do not believe I am alone in doing this since so much of the comparative justice literature concentrates on contrasts. I hope that the future brings a greater number of journal articles and books that identify and explain things in common amongst the world's justice systems.

What's Next?

The easiest prediction about the future for comparative/international criminology and criminal justice is that it will continue to grow and attract attention throughout the world. More difficult to predict, are the specifics of that expansion. Two changes, however, seem especially likely to me: A greater interest in transnational crime will precede greater attention to comparative justice, and comparison will become more common than description.

Interest in comparative justice systems seems initially to rely on a "what can it do for me" type attitude. The first several classes of my comparative criminal justice course are spent convincing students that it is important for them to understand and appreciate the justice system in other countries. Whether they find careers in law enforcement, the courts, or corrections, it is increasingly likely that they will have occasion to work on a crime-related issue with a foreign agency. And that is not simply true for people working in large metropolitan agencies. Sheriffs' deputies in my own rural county in Colorado have worked at least two murder cases that required them to understand, and rely upon, the Mexican criminal justice system. After the September 11, 2001 terrorist attacks in New York City and Washington, D.C., this argument was not such a hard sell.

My research endeavors during the last several decades had convinced me that justice professionals around the world were likely to appreciate the need for cooperative efforts among justice agencies in different countries. This was especially true in law enforcement

as shown in the success of INTERPOL and, more recently, EUROPOL. Recognition of the importance of such cooperation was lagging, however, in the media and among the citizens— more so in the United States than in many other countries. Increased attention on terrorism seems also to have brought increased attention to other transnational crimes such as trafficking in humans, illicit trade in cultural artifacts, and environmental crime. As citizens in general, and criminology and criminal justice students more specifically, become more interested in transnational crime the importance of understanding how criminal justice operates in other countries will become increasingly apparent.

As concern with combating transnational crime drives greater interest in comparative criminology and criminal justice, it is reasonable to expect greater cooperation among the world's justice agencies. Greater interest in regional cooperation among law enforcement agencies should result in more EUROPOL-type arrangements to supplement the international work of INTERPOL. Similar arrangements at the court level are already occurring as the International Criminal Court becomes fully operational. When the United States finally chooses to participate—which seems inevitable to me— it will join other countries of the world in an increasing effort to combat transnational crime through international cooperation. Similar cooperative efforts in the broad area of corrections seem less likely to me. Maybe there will someday be "border prisons" operated by two or more countries, but more likely there will be cooperative efforts wherein one country monitors prisoners and enforces sanctions imposed by another country.

Regardless of the specific format taken, I believe we are clearly heading toward greater cooperation among the law enforcement, courts, and corrections agencies in countries throughout the world. Increasing transnational crime motivates that cooperation but, I hope, good will and common sense will perpetuate it.

I have argued elsewhere (Reichel 2002) that comparative study of justice systems should begin with a descriptive approach. This seems most reasonable to me since it would be impossible to determine similarities and differences amongst people, places, or things without first having them described. Related to the importance of description is the more complicated issues of what should be described. Is it better to know how something is supposed to work (e.g., in Foreignland the police should not stop, question, and detain citizens without very good reason to believe those citizens were involved in a crime) or how it actually works (e.g., in Foreignland the police are constantly stopping, questioning, and detaining citizens without any justification). Clearly, both the *law on the books* and the *law in action* must be discerned before Foreignland's system can be accurately described. However, it seems to me that we must start with a description of the model before we can understand how practices vary from that model.

In its beginning stages, comparative justice studies have mostly provided descriptive accounts of the criminal justice system—as it is supposed to operate—in a variety of countries throughout the world. This is the necessary first ingredient toward a scientific inquiry into comparative justice studies. As with any necessary ingredient it should never be omitted as other important ingredients are added. But, it is probably now time to start adding those other ingredients. Specifically, we must move beyond simple description to more complete comparison. For example, how close to the model do different countries actually carry out their procedures?

Possibly most important, description must be accompanied by theoretical analysis. Comparative criminology has more successfully applied theory to an understanding of how and why crime rates differ across countries than has comparative justice applied theory to understand how justice agencies operate in different countries. Acceptance as a legitimate field of study, and eventually an academic discipline, will require comparative justice studies to prepare hypotheses about the differences in, for example, police practices or adjudication processes; then conduct research relevant to those hypotheses; and then to analyze the results of that research in the context of theories that are adapted from other disciplines and that are developed within comparative justice studies itself.

If You Are Intrigued

Possibly, even hopefully, the musings provided by authors in this compilation will intrigue some readers to pursue a career that has a comparative aspect. If you are amongst those people who see this as an exciting and important area of study, the following suggestions may be helpful.

Find a mentor. Notable by its absence in my autobiographical account is any mention of a particular professor whom I consider to have been my mentor. I make no claims to have accomplished on my own whatever success I have had. In fact, such colleagues as Leanne Fiftal Alarid, Jay Albanese, Adam Bouloukos, Harry Dammer, Frank Höpfel, Matti Joutsen, Bob McCormack, Hedi Nasheri, Graeme Newman, Ursula Smartt, Richard Terrill, and Prabha Unnithan, have each played an important role in the opportunities I have had and in any recognition I may have received. But, were I to do it again I would seek out a specific professor with interests similar to mine at the time and for whom I had respect and a desire to maintain a long-term relationship. Much of that is determined by one's choice of graduate schools (see my next suggestion), but I suspect that at least one professor at most any university will meet your criteria. Of course, mentoring is a two-way street. You must show yourself to be a good investment for the mentor's time and effort. As Frank Cullen (2002) explains, a student might show "worthiness" by doing well in the potential mentor's courses, expressing appreciation for the professor's time spent with the student, and working assiduously on assignments. In return, the student will benefit from the mentor's knowledge, experience, and contacts—not just while in school but for years after.

Carefully choose your graduate school. My decision to take the path of least resistance in getting my Ph.D. at

---

Lessons

Interested in pursuing a career that has a comparative aspect?

· *Find a mentor*
· *Carefully choose your graduate school*
· *Learn at least one other language.*

Kansas State University was a mixed blessing. On one hand I truly believe I would not have developed an interest in comparative studies were it not for my courses in social change and rural development. On the other hand, I did not have fellow graduate students, nor professors, who shared my particular interest in criminology/criminal justice. As a result, I do not have reunions with my graduate student cohort nor with old professors when I attend criminology and criminal justice conferences. In recent years some of the Rutgers University and Sam Houston State University faculty and alumni have been kind enough to let me "hang out" with them, but I do miss having colleagues with whom I shared graduate school experiences. So, I encourage you to choose carefully your graduate school program. The program that is most convenient geographically, provides the quickest completion, or is the least expensive, may not provide the greatest returns over the long haul. Consider instead, the course offerings, the research interests of the faculty, the closeness of fit between your interests and the program itself, and try to get a feel for the camaraderie among the current graduate students.

Learn at least one other language. One of my great disappointments in the area of personal achievement is my failure to have ever learned another language. Sure, I took some Spanish classes in high school and struggled with a few semesters of French in college, but other than recognizing occasional food or drink items in Mexican and French restaurants I am clearly monolingual. Some of my colleagues in comparative studies believe it is not even possible to be a comparativist if one does not speak the language of the country being studied. I understand, appreciate, and mostly agree with that perspective. However, I believe there is still a role to be played by us "language dullards." Thankfully, if embarrassingly, English is commonly spoken by academics around the world. My research activities in Austria, Germany, and Poland were hindered— but not impossible—by my very limited knowledge of German and my complete absence of knowledge of Polish. Self-paced learning with German language media (and being married to someone fluent in German) prior to a sabbatical leave helps, but I certainly wish I had taken the opportunity to learn another language while younger.

Parting Words

I greatly appreciate the opportunity to participate in this project and I look forward to reading the personal accounts provided by my colleagues in comparative/international criminology and criminal justice. Because this is a relatively small area of academic interest, most of us know (or know of) each other and the opportunities to collaborate on projects is unending. Should you wish to pursue comparative justice studies as an academic career, learn more about comparative studies because of your current research activities, or desire to make contacts with practitioners in other countries, you will find the scholars and practitioners currently involved in the field to be encouraging, accommodating, and always willing to welcome new converts to this exciting field.

Selected Bibliography

Cullen, F.T. 2002. "It's a Wonderful Life: Reflections on a Career in Progress." In *Lessons of criminology*, edited by G. Geis and M. Dodge. Cincinnati, OH: Anderson.

Dammer, H.R. and P.L. Reichel, eds 1997. *Teaching About Comparative/ International Criminal Justice: A Resource Manual.* Highland Heights, KY: Academy of Criminal Justice Sciences International Section.

Mukherjee, S., and P.L. Reichel. 1999. "Bringing to Justice." In *Global Report on Crime and Justice*, edited by G.R. Newman. New York: Oxford University Press.

Reichel, P.L. 1980. "Teaching About Crime in Communist Societies." *Teaching Sociology* 7:141-162.

_____. 1988. "Southern Slave Patrols as a Transitional Police Type." *American Journal of Police* 7(2): 51-77.

_____. 1992a. "The Misplaced Emphasis on Urbanization in Police Development." *Policing & Society* 3(1):1-12.

_____. 1992b. "Poland's Prison System." *American Jails* 6(4):74-78.

_____. 1997. "Criminal Justice in Other Countries." In *Introduction* to *Criminal Justice: Theory and Practice*, edited by D.H. Chang and M.J. Palmiotto. Wichita, KS: MidContinent Academic Press.

_____. 1999. *Global Bibliography of Prison Systems (2.0)*. United Nations Centre for International Crime Prevention. Retrieved October 25, 2003 (www.uncjin.org/country/GB OPS/gbops.html).

_____. 2002. *Comparative Criminal Justice Systems: A Topical Approach*, 3d ed. Upper Saddle River, NJ: Prentice Hall.

Reichel, P.L. and L. Munden. 1989. "The New York Times' Coverage of Executions." *Journal of Contemporary Criminal Justice* 5(4):220-232.

Reichel, P.L. and A. Rzeplinski. 1989. "Student Views of Crime and Criminal Justice in Poland and the United States." *International Journal of Comparative and Applied Criminal Justice* 13(1):65-82.

Terrill, R. 2003. *World Criminal Justice Systems: A Survey*, 5th ed. Cincinnati, OH: Anderson.

Chapter 3

Harnessing Criminology and Victimology Internationally

Irvin Waller

Department of Criminology,
University of Ottawa,
Canada

My time has been dominated by my passion for using criminological and victimological knowledge to improve public policy in Canada and across the world.

I live in Canada where I have been a full professor of Criminology at the University of Ottawa since 1982. I am a public speaker and a consultant to governments across the world on crime reduction and victim rights.

My forty years in criminology have included traditional academic appointments focused on teaching and major research publications, but my time has been dominated by my passion for using criminological and victimological knowledge to improve public policy in Canada and across the world.

In the 1960s, I taught and researched at the University of Toronto. In the 1970s, I left academe to head the Canadian equivalent of the National Institute of Justice. In the 1980s, I returned to academe, but combined it with consulting and advocacy for governments and nongovernmental groups in Canada, France, and elsewhere. In the 1990s, I was the founding executive director of the International Centre for Prevention of Crime—an agency associated with the United Nations (UN) to promote effective crime prevention. In 2000, I returned to academe and now combine these pursuits with advising governments and nongovernmental groups.

From my first appointment to a government task force in 1973, I have been a direct consultant to more than 8 Canadian ministers and 8 ministers on other continents. I have advised as many as 100 countries on crime prevention and victim rights, including the summit of the European Union on crime prevention and 5 UN Congresses. I have influenced directly the content and acceptance of two international standards on victims and crime prevention.

In order to be more effective in these endeavors, I perfected my French and learned Spanish, but more than anything I learned that the problems of crime and justice across the world have more in common than people realize and that innovation in one country will inspire innovation in other countries.

The Origins of My Interest in Criminology

Some of my earliest memories involve my father and his penchant for starting debates at the dinner table about court cases in which he was involved. This started my interest in justice, fairness, and crime.

My father was a barrister in northeastern England who earned a good living fighting for justice both as a prosecutor and a defense lawyer. He was passionately involved in his work. He was also a part-time judge in several northern cities, deciding how long robbers, rapists, and thieves would spend in prison.

By the age of seventeen I had spent ten years in private boarding schools, but I had never been out of the United Kingdom. I took six months to see the world before going to university. I joined the crew of an ocean-going freighter bound for the United States and Australia. My fellow seamen had been brought up in modest circumstances in the slums of London or Liverpool. They were running away

from violent families, school failure, and unemployment. Street fighting and drinking were a normal part of their lives. They seemed to be tough and had little fear. They were frightening to me.

After going through a hurricane, the freighter pulled into the port of Philadelphia in the United States—the land of milk and honey. The captain gave strict orders that we were only to go ashore in groups of three to cross the twelve blocks of slums to reach the affluent parts of the city. Little did I know that four years later I would be at a lecture by Marvin Wolfgang at Cambridge where he analyzed those blocks of Philadelphia and the extraordinary high rates of murder and violence.

Philadelphia was where I saw, for the first time, guns used for the protection of civilian property. Coming from England, it was amazing to see banks guarded by private security men with guns and shops selling a full range of firearms. In England, no one had guns or saw any need to have guns—least of all police officers.

The freighter picked up merchandise from several east coast cities in the United States then set off for Australia through the Panama Canal. Violence on board was rare when we were at sea, but in port, fights were common both on shore and on board. Crossing the date line, I had my first near-death experience when I was bullied viciously by a couple of the trainee officers who did not like my fortunate origins.

There were many factors in these fights, but I was most struck by the deep anger and pre-disposition to cruelty among some of my colleagues. The violence erupted around disputes over women, after excessive alcohol and challenges from crews from freighters of different nationalities.

In Melbourne, Australia, the seaman who sat next to me at meals murdered the seaman who sat opposite me in a fight over a record player. This left a major impression. It made me question how it was possible for someone to kill with such an unlikely motive.

When I started at Cambridge, I was going to do nuclear physics. I could speak Russian well. I was being trained to be a pilot by the Royal Air Force (RAF). But the experience with those seamen changed my life. I joined other undergraduates who would visit Hollesley Bay Borstal—made famous by Brendan Behan's book *Borstal Boy*.

After my first year, I changed to Sociology and Economics because I wanted to understand more about why men were violent and also what criminal justice was about. After graduating, I decided to do a post-graduate degree in Criminology. I worked a summer for the Family Development Study in working class London. This was an empirical study of children growing up to determine the precursors of their involvement in delinquency. My supervisor was Donald West, a psychiatrist who wrote about juvenile delinquency. It was West and Gibson who initiated the project. Later, David Farrington, who had done his Ph.D. thesis in psychology, shifted domains to make his international reputation from the analysis of this study (Farrington 2002).

Professor Leon Radzinowicz was the founding director of the Institute of Criminology at the University of Cambridge. His criminology was a policy science, where research and theory were not ends in themselves but ways to improve the world in which we lived. His life was one of academic writing combined with advising ministers in England and the United States on what to do about crime.

He had brought together a team that included Roger Hood and Richard Sparks, who were committed to empirical evaluations of crime policies. They had undertaken evaluations of the Borstal schemes and then the detention centers. They had worked on prediction systems, invented originally by Leslie Wilkins. And, they published an influential book, *Key Issues in Criminology* (Hood and Sparks 1970). With my background in math, I enjoyed the quantitative studies. With my background in economics, I was fascinated by the efforts to evaluate outcomes from correctional programs.

It was a natural development then to apply for a job in Canada to evaluate the penitentiary and parole system.

Criminology at the University of Toronto

John Edwards was the founding director of the Centre of Criminology at the University of Toronto who also believed that criminology was to be applied. He was a lawyer interested in the role of Attorney General in the commonwealth.

He was interested in large-scale studies in criminology, which were policy relevant. These typically combined quantitative and ethnographic methods. John Hogarth completed his unique study of *Sentencing as a Human*

Process (1971). I worked with funds from the Ford Foundation and the Canadian government to evaluate and propose solutions for prison and parole in Canada. *Men Released from Prison* (Waller 1974) confirmed that retributive justice was expensive and ineffective! It identified the classic social causes of offending and recidivism.

This book brought me acclaim on the front page of Canada's national newspapers. Disappointingly, the managers of prison systems, even in Canada, have still not forged the policies to confront those facts. However, it led to my first taste of influencing criminal policy. I was selected by the Solicitor General of Canada to be one of three members of a national task force on the sentencing and parole system of Canada with Mr. Justice Jim Hugessen. We visited every major federal prison in Canada, but also learned from top policy makers in Washington and London. We recommended a sentencing and parole system whose decision-makers would be drawn from judges, police chiefs, criminologists, and victim groups, but would be influenced by quantitative data providing predictions on which categories of offenders were likely to commit serious offenses.

The report became a blueprint for revisions that Canada made (Hugessen 1973). Today many of the characteristics of the parole system date from that report. Even so, it failed because bureaucrats, defending the status quo, blocked the data system that was essential.

Denis Szabo had invited me several times to meetings of the Quebec

> ## Lessons
>
> *This book brought me acclaim on the front page of Canada's national newspapers. Disappointingly, the managers of prison systems, even in Canada, have still not forged the policies to confront those facts.*

Society of Criminology, because I understood some French. In 1971, he recruited me to spend six months at a center of criminology that he had initiated on the Ivory Coast. This was my first experience of Africa. It was also my first exposure to the partie civile system, where victims were represented in court and able to claim reparation. It was also a chance to immerse myself in French.

In 1972, the Canada Council agreed to fund the development of a victimization survey instrument for Canada as well as an examination of what both victims and the public wanted and how crime would be prevented and victims assisted. It was eventually published as *Burglary: The Victim and the Public* (Waller and Okihiro 1978) from which I still receive royalties! This demonstrated that victims' main expectation from the criminal justice system was reparation not retribution. It demonstrated ways to prevent burglary and how to respond to victims.

It made the front page also but government policy-makers did not act on the facts and so burglary rates doubled in the following decade before declining marginally in the 1990s.

This project led to an invitation

Lessons
Facts and examples from other juris-dictions were used to convince Canadians to abolish the death penal-ty, control firearm use, and tackle vio-lence. Money was allocated to provide pilot projects and data to prevent crime and violence in Canada.

from Emilio Viano to an institute in Bellagio, Italy that was to become a major theme of my life (1976). The meeting was on victimology. He brought together academics and practitioners. Among the 50 attendees at this meeting were several people who have influenced me—Lynn Curtis, Eric Kibuka, Koichi Miyazawa, Hidemichi Morosawa, Leroy Lamborn, Murray Strauss, Gerd Kirchhoff, John Dussich, and Ezzat Fattah.

I undertook an international comparison of rates of incarceration that showed the different levels of incarceration between nations (Waller and Chan 1977). It underlined the importance of ensuring that comparisons between countries must be based on data that describes the same thing rather than similar words. This short article has been reproduced in more than 100,000 copies, including French. It also became the foundation for a fascination that I have with international comparisons of levels of crime, policing, justice, and prisons, and underlies a significant amount of my advocacy for what is right, whether in Canada (1982), the United States (Donziger 1996), or the UN (Newman 1999).

Criminology Inside Government

In 1974, I went to work at a senior level for the Canadian government, believing that bureaucracies would face facts to forge modern policies. Indeed, for a short time, this was true in the government led by Pierre Elliot Trudeau.

Canada established a research center that would be relevant to crime policy. The British and the Dutch were particularly interested in our way of doing things. Facts and examples from other jurisdictions were used to convince Canadians to abolish the death penalty, control firearm use, and tackle violence. Money was allocated to provide pilot projects and data to prevent crime and violence in Canada. I had the privilege of hiring many distinguished criminologists, one of whom—Chris Nuttall—I brought from the Home Office Research Unit and with whom I shared the love of quantitative criminology and policy.

But after the legislation was adopted, the bureaucracies used the money elsewhere and so they continued to do what they had always done—retributive justice and meeting the needs of their employees. No clear goals for reducing crime were set, no plan instituted to achieve the goals, and no data organized to hold the bureaucracy accountable to those goals.

In 1975, Canada was interested in connections with Europe to counterbalance its dependence on the United States. The Council of Europe was interested in getting Canada involved. I became the front person to participate in the Committee of Crime Problems of the Council of Europe. Besides the immediate challenges, this introduced me to a network of Europeans, many of whom were directors of government research centers and some interested in the victim issue.

I also enjoyed exchange visits with European government centers devoted to criminology, such as the Home Office Research Unit and the Dutch Research and Documentation Center. It was in the latter that I met Jan Van Dijk (also presented in this anthology) for the first time as he was conducting some of his first victimization surveys. I have shared with Van Dijk a common interest in quantitative research, victims, and crime prevention, as well as in contributing to policy.

In 1978, Hans Joachim Schneider (1982) came to visit me in Ottawa in preparation for his International Symposium on Victimology that was set to take place in Munster. I presented two papers, both of which were selected for publication in English, German, and French. During that meeting, the World Society of Victimology was founded and I was elected to its first executive committee. I also met Marlene Young, who had also submitted two papers. I was surprised and flattered to be invited by her to join the board of the National Organization for Victim Assistance (NOVA) in the United States.

These appointments crystallized a major part of my career, which was to bridge the scientific knowledge of victimology with the promotion of policy to respect victims of crime, particularly through the insights and inspirations to which I had access internationally.

Paul Rock wrote about my role in the development of victim policy in his book analyzing the development of policy on victims in Canada. He described me as "a moral entrepreneur in a classical guise, who was inspired by the victims' movement and imported into the core of" the government department. I "constructed social networks, disseminated ideas, and seized lines of action as they developed forcing them together" (Rock 1986:380; see also Chapter 4).

In 1979, I was invited to the School of Criminal Justice at the State University of New York in Albany, which had become the peak of criminal justice studies internationally. I was shoulder to shoulder with Michael Gottfredson, Michael Hindelang, Travis Hirschi, Graeme Newman, Lawrence Sherman, Margaret Warren, and the unique Leslie Wilkins with whom I lived during the week.

They were interested in my experience in influencing criminal policy through criminological research (Waller 1979). I discovered their compulsory course on planned change. It was exciting to know that other criminologists were thinking about the process to bring about change in criminal policy.

Criminology and International Advocacy

In 1980, I resigned my influential job in the Canadian government to move to the University of Ottawa. The media were very interested as to why I was leaving. I was reported as saying:

> Members of parliament are more interested in yesterday's *Globe and*

Mail than in information...In criminal justice, we take up the symbolic issues and avoid the major ones...if we ran the economy like that...in 1977 every Canadian was taxed $112.16 for criminal justice services of which only 27 cents went to compensate victims...lack of attention to victims and heavy emphasis on imprisonment...more emphasis should be placed on prevention...rehabilitation should at least be tried...by setting goals, sticking to them, and not changing direction every year, it is possible to control crime. It's a question of will and priorities. (*Globe and Mail,* July 5, 1980)

They continued to use me as a critic of what the government was doing about crime for the next decade. I did countless interviews for radio, television, and newspapers, promoting the importance of crime prevention as well as rights and services for crime victims.

At that time, the criminology program at the University of Ottawa was taught at the graduate level in an English and a French section by professors with many years of experience in practice. It was a wonderful environment because my classes were only at the graduate level with people who had already worked and knew why they were there.

Moral Entrepreneurship for Victims of Crime

In 1981, with assistance from a graduate student, I wrote a booklet called *Rights and Services for Crime Victims*

for the Canadian Council for Social Development (1981). I brought NOVA to Toronto for their annual conference. I organized a one-day course for U.S. and Canadian Legislators with the Canadian Centre for Parliamentary Exchange. The Ministry of the Solicitor General premiered a short educational movie called "Victims: A View from the Shadows," which I still use in my classes today.

My work on the Board of NOVA brought me into contact with the leaders of the victim movement in the United States. In 1982, President Regan set up a Presidential Task Force on Victims of Crime. Marlene Young, executive director of NOVA, was closely associated with crafting the report with Lois Height Herrington, the chairperson. This report demonstrated the lack of attention given to victims by the police and criminal justice personnel, but called for services from a broad range of sectors, including schools, churches, and the rapidly growing victim assistance movement. It was also the origin of a proposal to provide rights for victims in an amendment to the U.S. Constitution.

I was also on the Board of the Canadian Church Council on Justice of Corrections, where much of the seeds for the international restorative justice movement were sown in debates with Dave McCord, Frank Miller, Hans Mohr, and Dave Worth.

The UN has a commission on crime prevention and criminal justice based in Vienna. This provides a forum for ministers of justice, and interior and foreign affairs to meet once a year and adopt strategies to deal with crime. It is this commission that has adopted a series of standards on juvenile justice, rehabilitation, preventing torture, and so on.

Inspired by the work of Marlene Young and NOVA in the United States, I became interested in promoting similar successes in Canada and internationally. At the International Symposium on Victimology in Tokyo-Kyoto, I proposed to Marlene Young and Leroy Lamborn that we develop a United Nations Declaration on Rights for Crime Victims. Leroy Lamborn was a professor of law at Wayne State University in Detroit and the only other academic on the NOVA Board.

As a Board member of NOVA and Executive Member of World Society of Victimology (WSV), I was in a unique position to develop the necessary momentum. Denis Szabo referred me to a woman working for the UN secretariat in New York named Irene Melup, a brilliant UN official devoted to human rights and reform. She was to be my professional partner, cajoler, and guide to the UN system. She was as energetic, networking, and committed to victims as me, but wanted a broader definition of victims that would include victims of abuse of power.

Irene Melup and Leroy Lamborn were to be my close partners in a unique life experience—getting the UN General Assembly to adopt, within a record period of three years, a human rights instrument called the Declaration on Basic Principles of Justice for Victims of Crime and Abuse of Power.

It was an exciting three-year sprint of:

- Drafting the basic paragraphs from an analysis of the NOVA Legislative

Lessons
The extended family of the WSV...provides a growing and strong network of persons committed to research, service, and advocacy for victims...In recent years, it has been joined by www.victimology.nl, which is a web site maintained for the WSV and the UN by the Dutch Ministry of Justice. This is a rich library and source of information on victim issues.

Directory as well as academic papers presented at the International Symposia on Victimology in Munster (Schneider 1982) and Tokyo-Kyoto (Miyazawa 1986).

- Working with the boards of the World Society of Victimology and NOVA.
- Meeting with experts from across the world connected to the network of Irene Melup. Interesting non-governmental groups, such as Amnesty International and the Society for Post-Traumatic Stress Studies.
- Collaborating with the Canadian and French governments, including for a UN Expert meeting that took place in Ottawa.
- Working with Paul Separovic in meetings in Dubrovnik and particularly the 5th International Syposium on Victimology organized in tandem with the UN Congress in Milan.
- Lobbying and orchestrating the WSV members who were members of national delegations to the UN

Congress on Crime Prevention and Criminal Justice in Milan in 1985, which eventually adopted the Declaration.

- Advising the Canadian and French governments to assist the General Assembly to approve the resolution that adopted the Declaration on the Basic Principles of Justice for Victims of Crime and Abuse of Power in November 1985.

The extended family of the WSV has been a rich source of friendship, encouragement, and inspiration. It provides a growing and strong network of persons committed to research, service, and advocacy for victims. It was instrumental in getting several other actions from the UN to implement the Declaration, including a manual for practitioners and a guide for policy makers. In recent years, it has been joined by *www.victimology.nl,* which is a web site maintained for the WSV and the UN by the Dutch Ministry of Justice. This is a rich library and source of information on victim issues. Its material on most countries is better than can be found in their own libraries.

Moral Entrepreneurship for Crime Prevention–Gilbert Bonnemaison

In 1983, with assistance from a couple of my graduate students, I wrote a booklet called *Crime Prevention through Social Development* (1983) for the Canadian Council for Social Development and the Canadian Criminal Justice Association. I received assistance from Dick Weiler. At the time, the Solicitor General of Canada had made some progress on crime prevention, particularly through a national crime prevention week, but the tendency was to focus too exclusively on situational crime prevention.

In preparing this booklet, we came across some exciting new developments in France, inspired by the Mayor of Epinay sur Seine, a working class suburb of Paris. Gilbert Bonnemaison was to be my professional partner in the next phase of my life devoted to getting governments nationally and locally to invest in prevention.

Gilbert Bonnemaison had chaired a task force of mayors in France who were concerned about youth violence and disorder in cities. They had recommended action to deal with the social causes, the physical design factors, and the lack of sensitivity of policing to local concerns (Bonnemaison 1983).

Gilbert Bonnemaison provided them with a vision by calling for intelligent solutions to crime. He thought his vision was common sense. But as we know common sense is not so common, particularly when it comes to reacting to crime. He saw that crime would be solved by the agencies that could tackle the causes of crime. His praxis lead to solving crime by mobilizing schools, housing, social services, police, and justice around a shared analysis of the local crime problems. He set in place structures that would generate some of the reform that was needed.

I got to know Bonnemaison while on a sabbatical at the University of Aix en Provence. Bonnemaison worked tirelessly with me outside of his country to mobilize a vehicle to foster that change.

He had the political acumen, practical insights, and prestige. He had been very close to the center of political power in France. He had a media profile. I had the academic access to criminological knowledge, the ability to write, and an international network of contacts that was basic to reform outside of France. I also was fluent in French.

In 1987, Bonnemaison, with the Council of Europe, organized a major meeting for mayors on urban safety in Barcelona. It was here that he launched the European Forum on Urban Safety to which I became scientific advisor.

In 1989, I organized with him the first European and North American Conference on Urban Safety and Crime Prevention in Montreal. We witnessed Ed Koch, then Mayor of New York City, debate methods of reducing crime with the female mayor of Strasbourg in France—Rambo vs. Snow White—but we also debated what were the causes of crime, what had worked, and what should be done.

Our venture was jointly organized by the big city mayors from the United States (The United States Conference of Mayors), the leaders of local government in Europe (European Forum on Urban Safety), and the municipal leaders from Canada (Federation of Canadian Municipalities).

Among the conclusions in the final declaration (European Forum for Urban Safety 1989) are:

- We must go beyond a response by our criminal justice system—police, courts and corrections—if we are to prevent crime in our cities. Our response must be part of a long-range approach, yet be responsible to immediate needs.
- Crime prevention must bring together those responsible for housing, social services, recreation, schools, policing, and justice to tackle the situations that breed crime.
- Elected officials at all levels must exert political leadership and assume responsibility to prevent urban crime. Without this, our belief in community, the quality of life in our cities, and human rights can be threatened.

Two years later in Paris, the same group of organizations arranged an even more successful conference, entitled the Second International Conference on Urban Safety, Drugs and Crime Prevention. This endorsed the same messages but stressed the need to establish national crime prevention agencies such as that in Sweden, city crime prevention boards such as those now established across England, and test projects that prevent crime with evaluation built-in to improve the projects and inform the public about their advantages over classic criminal justice solutions.

Our working relationship helped launch the ICPC (International Centre for Prevention of Crime). This was a specific recommendation from that Paris Conference which was organized in tandem with a political summit to reorganize the UN crime program. This summit made crime prevention one of the three priorities for the UN and endorsed the need for the ICPC, which was to work with the UN, developed, and developing countries and expert organizations to reduce crime, violence, and insecurity by sharing best practices.

Criminology Inside International Agencies

In 1994, I started the first of eight years as the founding director general of International Centre for Prevention of Crime (ICPC). I learned much about how governments on different continents operate.

Much of my time and energy was occupied by finding funds to maintain the ICPC. To get governments to commit funds, I developed a case for prevention building on my vision statement to open the Paris conference (Waller 1991). This was refined as I participated on commissions in Canada (Quebec 1993), South Africa (1997), and the United States (Donziger 1996).

At the ICPC, I insisted that we produce a digest on the arguments for crime prevention, which pioneered and developed the arguments that crime costs in police and prison expenditures, but in addition is associated with huge costs of trauma and loss to victims. In response, it demonstrates that successful crime prevention includes programs that will assist teenagers at risk by mentoring or helping them to complete school; works with families in difficulty to help their children or tackling bullying in schools; and assists victims with information on how to reduce opportunities for crime and limiting accessibility to firearms (International Centre for Prevention of Crime 1999a:18-50; US Department of Justice

2001). In addition, successful crime prevention is more cost effective than adding police officers or incarcerating more offenders; is successful when it is based on a diagnosis of the problem by the entities—schools, parents, sports, and local government—that are able to tackle the multiple social causes of crime and violence; is focused on social situations such as dropping out of school; and, ultimately, provides other social benefits.

The International Centre for Prevention of Crime brought together 100 descriptions of prevention programs to inspire action (International Centre for Prevention of Crime 1999b). These provide easy access to examples for all levels of officials.

During my time before and during the ICPC, I was particularly influenced by the strong beliefs in prevention of activists such as:

- Michel Marcus, chief executive of the European Forum for Urban Safety and of the French Forum for Urban Safety. He is a Magistrate and was an Advisor to the French Commission of Mayors on Safety in the early 1980s, Deputy General Delegate of the National Crime Prevention Council from 1984 to 1987 and General Secretary of the National Council of Cities between 1989 and 1994.
- Nigel Whiskin, chief executive of Crime Concern from its launching in 1988 to a 300 person agency with several regional offices engaged in capacity development with communities to reduce crime through prevention in the United

Kingdom. He was a probation officer, then launched a victim assistance program and later worked to create jobs for ex-offenders on a national scale.

- John Calhoun, Executive Director of the National Crime Prevention Council of the United States. He is internationally recognized as a "mover and shaker" in the fight against crime through prevention. He has served on national boards and commissions, he has pioneered comprehensive programs for youth development, and was appointed by a United States President to serve as the Commissioner, responsible for the U.S. government's policy for child abuse, Head Start, child welfare, and domestic violence.
- Claude Vézina, previously principal adviser on public safety to the head of local government. He is a low-profile facilitator, who gets crime prevention to happen in Canada and Africa at the local government level.

Criminology and Advocacy–Next Steps

In 2001, I resigned from my senior job at the International Centre for Prevention of Crime because I wanted to spend more time with my family. I had also learned Spanish and wanted to enjoy opportunities in Latin America.

I co-chaired the organizing committee for the 10th International Symposium on Victimology in Montreal with the head of the Quebec victim assistance organization. This attracted 1,300 people from over 61 countries and reminded many of the importance of the UN Declaration on rights for crime victims, of crime prevention, and of the work needed to create a better world (Gaudreault and Waller 2001).

At the time of preparing this contribution, I am back teaching at the University of Ottawa. I have to teach third-year, fourth-year, and master's level students. Most of the students come to my classes without any real knowledge of crime rates, victimization studies, and the costs of crime, let alone victim rights or crime reduction. Few have any real experience with police, courts or corrections, crime prevention, or victim rights. A new doctoral program at the school will attract some students with experience interested in crime victims and crime prevention.

However, I continue to be consulted by governments and nongovernment agencies, particularly in Latin America on these issues. I also enjoy teaching the international courses offered by the World Society of Victimology in Dubrovnik, El Salvador, and Caracas.

In 2002, the Soros Foundation asked me to prepare a guide for activists—such as the local Soros Foundation offices—interested in improving rights and services for crime victims. The European UN Institute published the report in English and Russian (Waller 2002). The Soros office in Mongolia hired me to spend two weeks with their police agency, justice department, and violence prevention nongovernmental group accelerating efforts to get better services for victims at the police level and nationally.

I am working with Defense for Children International in their efforts to launch a global campaign to reduce the number of children and youth behind bars. Their interest in me is that I can articulate for them the crime prevention message, but I also have fun dealing with comparative crime and incarceration statistics.

I am on the board of the International Bureau for Children's Rights, which has recently produced Guidelines for Child Victims and Witnesses (2002), which they are considering promoting as a new international norm that might be adopted by the UN General Assembly.

I have worked on an operational guide on victims and witnesses for the International Criminal Court, which is particularly interesting because of the extent to which the Statute of Rome provides real rights for victims and because the numbers and horror of the victimization is so immense (Waller 2003).

I have collaborated with the World Health Organization on the implementation of their World Report on Health and Violence. I have participated with others in efforts to define a World Report on Crime and Victimization that might be produced by the UN Office on Drug Control and Crime Prevention.

In 2002, I was a friend of the chair for the UN Expert meeting to develop guidelines for crime prevention. By July 2002, a new human rights instrument entitled the Guidelines for Prevention of Crime had been accepted by the General Assembly (UN 2002). These clarify that governments have a responsibility to reduce crime through prevention and state ten essential elements. The guidelines start with the following assertion: "There is clear evi-

dence that well-planned crime prevention strategies prevent crime and victimization" (UN Economic and Social Council 2002).

This clear evidence had already been brought together and agreed upon by national commissions, such as those completed for no less influential bodies than the Home Office and Treasury, UK (Goldblatt and Lewis 1998); the International Centre for Prevention of Crime (1999a); and the White Paper on Safety and Security (South Africa 1998).

The essential elements include:

* Governments must establish a responsibility center to spearhead efforts to implement crime prevention. These centers must be permanent and with the technical and financial resources necessary to sustain prevention. Such centers already exist in Scandinavia and Australia.
* Governments must make use of the international knowledge base about the multiple causes of crime and promising and proven responses. The UK government's investment in the Youth Justice Board and the Effective Crime Reduction strategy are examples of this.

In 2005, the UN will hold its next Congress on Crime Prevention and Treatment of Offenders. Likely it will take place in Bangkok and will include a major theme on the implementation of standards and norms. The innovations by the British government on pre-crime prevention for youth offenders and local government leadership in crime prevention, combined with the current strength of interest of the UNODCP, WHO, UNICEF, and Habitat provide fertile terrain for multiple implementation of strong crime reduction policies. I hope to be there as the Chair of the UN Liaison Committee of the World Society of Victimology.

Conclusions for Young Criminologists

My criminology is focused on criminological and victimological knowledge to influence public policy on crime prevention and victim empowerment. While every country has its charm and its problems, the government response to crime is within the same paradigm across the world. They all harbor the vain hope that more police and prisons will make it go away.

Governments must, at some time, realize that they cannot incarcerate or "police-officer" their way out of the crime problem, particularly when the evidence and recent UN instrument demonstrates that effective and well-planned crime prevention actually reduces crime at a fraction of the cost. The International Criminal Court shows that most governments across the world believe that victims should have standing to participate, be represented, and get reparation.

So it is a good time for young criminologists to find out about these areas. You can participate in an international course on victimology sponsored each year by the World Society of Victimology where you would meet faculty and students from other countries as well as your own. You can take courses such as those at the University of Ottawa on

---

> *Lessons*
>
> *UN Guidelines on Crime Prevention build on clear evidence that well-planned crime prevention strategies prevent crime and victimization. So it is a good time for young criminologists to find out about careers devoted to public policy on crime prevention and victim empowerment.*

---

crime prevention or victim rights. You can do placements during the summer with UN agencies such UNODCP or WHO.

You can learn or use a foreign language. Spanish is particularly useful for Latin America where economic disparity go hand in hand with staggering levels of violence that are unaffected by cops, courts, and corrections. Mandarin Chinese will be useful for those wanting to counter the crime wave developing in the location where one in five people live.

You can use the Internet to visit sites such as those maintained at *www.victimology.nl*, *www.crime-prevention-intl.org* or the Youth Justice Board. You can go to conferences where you can meet those from other countries and learn of other Internet sites. You can go to the next UN Congress on Crime in Bangkok.

You can use evidence, particularly comparative knowledge, about what works, what is intelligent, and what meets international standards, to make a world that is better for your children. A world where there are far fewer victims of crime and abuse of power and where those that are, will have rights, respect, and reparation in all criminal justice systems.

Selected Bibliography

Bonnemaison, G. 1982. *Face à la Délinquance: Prévention, Répression, Solidarité–Rapport au Premier Ministre*. (Rapport Bonnemaison). Paris, Premier Ministre: Documentation française.

Canada. 1982. *Le Droit Pénal Dans la Société Canadienne/The Criminal Law in Canadian Society*. Ottawa.

Canadian Council for Social Development. 1983. *Crime Prevention Through Social Development*. Ottawa.

Canadian Council on Social Development. 1981. *Rights and Services for Crime Victims/Les Droits et les Services pour les Victimes d'actes Criminels*. Ottawa.

Donziger, S. 1996. *The Real War on Crime: The Report of the National Criminal Justice Commission*. New York: Harper.

European Forum for Urban Safety. 1992. *Safety in the City: The Prevention of Crime, Recidivism and Drug Abuse/ Villes en Sécurité: Prévention de la Délinquance, des Drogues et de la Toxicomanie*. Paris.

European Forum for Urban Safety. 1989. *Agenda for Safer Cities: The Declaration of the European North American Conference on Urban Safety and Crime Prevention*. Paris.

Farrington, D. 2002. *Key Results from the First Forty Years of the Cambridge Study in Delinquent Development*. New York: Kluwer/ Plenum Press.

Gaudreault, A. and I. Waller. 2001. *10th International Symposium: Selected Symposium Proceedings*. Montreal: Association Québécoise Plaidoyer-Victimes.

Globe and Mail. 1980. "MPs Aren't Addressing Real Problem of Crime, Resigning Official Says." Toronto, July 5 p. 16.

Goldblatt, P. and C. Lewis. 1998. *Reducing Offending: An Assessment of Research Evidence on Ways of Dealing with Offending Behavior*. London: Home Office, Research and Statistics.

Hogarth, J. 1971. *Sentencing as a Human Process*. Toronto: University of Toronto Press.

Hood, R. and R. Sparks. 1970. *Key Issues in Criminology*. New York: McGraw Hill.

International Bureau for Childrens' Rights. 2003. *Guidelines on Justice for Child Victims and Witnesses*. Montreal.

International Centre for Prevention of Crime. 1999. *Crime Prevention Digest II: Comparative Analysis of Successful Community Safety*. Montreal.

International Centre for Prevention of Crime. 1999. *100 Crime Prevention Programs to Inspire Action Across the World*. Montreal.

Le Devoir. 1989. "L'entrevue du Lundi: De la Victimologie à la Prévention du Crime," Décembre.

Miyazawa, K. 1986. *Victimology in Comparative Perspective*. Tokyo: Seibundo.

Newman, G. 1999. *Global Report on Crime and Justice*. New York:

Oxford University Press.

Quebec. 1993. *Pour un Québec plus Sécuritaire: Partenaires en Prévention: Sommaire du Rapport de la Table Ronde sur la Prévention de la Criminalité 1993.* Sainte-Foy: Gouvernement du Québec, Ministère de la Sécurité publique.

Rock, P. 1986. *A View from the Shadows: The Ministry of the Solicitor General of Canada and the Making of the Justice for Victims of Crime Initiative.* Oxford: Clarendon.

Schneider, H. 1982. *The Victim in International Perspective.* New York/Berlin: Walter de Gruyter.

South Africa: Minister of Safety and Security. 1998. *White Paper on Safety and Security: In Service of Safety 1998-2000.* Pretoria.

United Nations General Assembly. 2002. *Guidelines for the Prevention of Crime.* New York.

United Nations General Assembly. 1985. *Declaration of Basic Principles of Justice for Victims of Crime and Abuse of Power.* New York.

United States. 1982. *President's Task Force on Victims of Crime: Final Report.* Washington.

US Department of Justice, Bureau of Justice Assistance. 2000. *Investing Wisely in Prevention: International Experiences.* Washington, DC: Monograph, Crime Prevention Series #1.

Viano, E. 1976. *Victims and Society.* Washington, DC: Visage.

Waller, I. 2004. "Solving Crime." Book manuscript in preparation.

_____. 2003. *Crime Victims: Doing Justice to their Support and Protection.* Helsinki: HEUNI.

_____. 2003. "Operational Guide for International Criminal Court on Victims and Witnesses." Ottawa. Unpublished manuscript.

_____. 2002. *International Trends in Crime Prevention: Key Aspects for Canada.* National Crime Prevention Centre Canada: Manuscript.

_____. 2001. "Europe Working Towards Crime Prevention." In *Conferencia de Alto Nivel Sobre a Prevençao da Criminalidade.* Lisbon: Ministerio da Justiça, Gabinete para as Relaçoes Internacionais.

_____. 1979. "Organizing Research to Improve Criminal Justice Policy: A Perspective from Canada." *Journal of Research in Crime and Delinquency* July:106-217.

_____. 1974. *Men Released from Prison.* Toronto: University of Toronto Press.

Waller, I and Norm Okihiro. 1978. *Burglary, the Victim and the Public.* Toronto: University of Toronto Press.

Waller, I. and J. Chan. 1977. "Prison Use: A Canadian and International Comparison." In *Correctional Institutions,* 2d ed., edited by L.T. Wilkins and D. Glazer. New York: J.B. Lippincott.

Chapter 4

Comparative Research in a Government Environment

Pat Mayhew

Home Office
London, England

*International comparative work is not
for the feint hearted.*

There is historical accident in all our lives (if I had missed *that* party, I would not have met the person I have shared three decades with). It also applies to professional careers—at least it did to mine. At secondary school, I had one of those teachers who shape subsequent paths. He had a daughter at the London School of Economics (LSE), teaching Sociology. His vision for me was shaped by her success and interest in social science. I went along with his suggestion to follow a similar path, not having much vision of my own. In 1963, I got into LSE (to do a B.A. (Hons.) in Sociology and Economics) mainly because I took heed from the interviewee before me who emerged in tears having been told, "if she was interested in people, why did she not become a bus conductress." Looking back, if I had had more confidence and vision of my own, I would have tried to be a weather forecaster. Therein lies historical accident.

Although LSE was heavyweight on teaching standards and course content, I did not like it socially. I would have been happier at a less metropolitan "campus" university, campaigning about mini-skirts, rather than the earnest issues on which LSE students spent their time. Criminology was one of the course options (demography another). It seemed focused, and I thought it might be an easy ride. In the event, it genuinely came to inspire me, as a subject about which there was more to learn than I thought. And I soon saw it as a potential career choice— pulling together a topic of academic weight with the chance of using it in the confines of applied research.

But I did not enter criminology on graduating. Instead, another historical accident took me to northern Argentina (to a province no one has ever heard of), where I was part of a team of U.K. professionals (I was barely one of course) looking to develop low-cost housing for indigenous South Americans. As the demographer, I mainly counted legs and divided by two. Perhaps there was a seed of interest sown in other cultures nonetheless.

Entering Criminology

On returning to the United Kingdom in 1967—short of money and other plans—I pursued a job offer I had been given whilst at LSE to become a government social researcher. My first choice had been a placement at the Home Office, the department responsible for criminal justice (and some other things besides). More or less, I have spent my whole working career there. (I did mention lack of vision....)

I cut my teeth on a variety of things unrelated to international comparative research. I did work on Children's Departments, responsible for children in care (they have long ceased to exist); prison escapees (why they escaped— though one might think the answer not very taxing); and other things. The formative leap forward was to be assigned to work in the 1970s under Professor Ron Clarke, who subsequently "brained-drained" to the United States. He had no particular interest in comparative studies. Indeed, he was rather impatient with the intricacies and limitations of large international data-sets. Nonetheless, he mentored me in painstaking data analysis, hypothesis testing, "getting to the point"—and all those skills one should have under one's belt (one lesson he tried to instill was to have ready in advance of writing a paper, the table(s) one would use and a clear summary of conclusions. I have never quite mastered this).

I worked with Ron Clarke on situational crime prevention research— looking at the dynamics of, and successful interventions against, burglary, vandalism, and car thefts, amongst other things. Oscar Newman's "defensible space" theory during the 1970s was hot at the time, and although U.S. born, it had general applicability to urban design, which we put to good effect.

One piece of work Ron Clarke and I did together, however, had a more deliberate comparative focus than most. This was in relation to suicide, which we saw as providing critical ammunition to the "displacement" challenge to situational crime prevention—i.e., if crime is made harder, then offenders simply displace their activities (in time, space, or method). We brought together studies from several countries that undermined the argument that suicide was hard to prevent (it was seen commonly seen, of course, as behavior determined by strong internal motivation, and thus highly prone to displacement). The strongest example was the very substantial decline in the *overall* suicide rate in England and Wales between the mid-1960s and the mid-1970s. We showed this to be the result of the detoxification of gas, as natural gas replaced coal gas. Denied their "favorite" accessible, painless, and non-disfiguring suicide method, very many people left it at that (Clarke and Mayhew 1988).

The British Crime Survey

My next career leg, which was to last some time, was to help develop the British Crime Survey (BCS), which is now over two decades old. I attended the 1980 International Symposium on Victimology in Muenster (Germany), where I was presenting on defensible space as I recollect. There were several papers on the U.S. National Crime Survey (as then called), and it seemed clear to me that national victimization surveys were the "must have." In early 1981, others in the Home Office and myself promoted the idea of a national survey as an alternative way of measuring levels of crime, and the nature of "ordinary" risks. Ron Clarke and Mike Hough played key parts.

Costs were an issue, as well as the political snares of exposing high estimates of unrecorded crime. But we won the day, with a case largely resting on the value to policy-makers of having at least a rough guide to the extent and shape of the problem that the criminal justice system was intended to tackle.

Another persuasive argument was the survey's promise as an antidote to public misconceptions about crime levels, trends, and risks. A survey-based index of crime could demonstrate the possibility that an index of crime based on offences recorded by the police might be subject to "statistical inflation" by virtue of changing reporting and recording practices. Information on crime risks was also expected to demonstrate the comparatively low risks of *serious* crime, and perhaps puncture inaccurate stereotypes of crime victims.

With the benefit of hindsight, it is easy to interpret the outcome in terms of changes in the climate of law-and-order politics—in particular the shift of emphasis at the time from offenders to victims—a new political entity. It may be that the idea of a national victim survey was simply one whose time had come, although those of us involved certainly did not feel that we were buttressed by the weight of historical inevitability.

NIJ Fellowship

I worked actively on the BCS for many years. It honed my knowledge of survey methodology and analysis, which proved central to my getting involved in the development of the International Crime Victimization Survey (ICVS). But before that, work on the BCS led to my first serious inroad into comparative criminology, with a fellowship at the National Institute of Justice (NIJ) in Washington DC. Here, my self-appointed task was to look at the BCS, and the U.S. and Canadian national surveys, to see what they told us about the level and nature of burglary in the three countries, and whether survey conclusions challenged the picture from police figures.

The potential of victimization surveys for comparative purposes had not gone unnoticed at the time. They promised an alternative to police figures, widely seen as being contaminated by differences in police recording practices and possible differences in levels of reporting to the police. National surveys also offered the potential for comparing the cost, impact, and characteristics of criminal incidents across a country, as well as comparisons of which groups faced highest risks (about which police figures say rather little).

That was the principle at least. What my work at NIJ showed, as did other attempts to compare independently mounted surveys, was that survey figures have measurement problems rivaling those of police figures. For those of us who started to dabble in comparative analyses, it soon became clear that there were substantial technical problems in handling independently organized surveys that, though similar in measurement aims, forged their own ways to achieve these. Differences in survey design and administration severely undermined comparisons, influencing both the amount and type of victimization measured (my work at NIJ showed that the differences revolved around counting "series" incidents; offence definitions, respondent eligibility, mode of interview, "screening" methods; recall periods; weighting for non-response—to list only some).

With the three surveys I was working with, I made "hard" adjustments through data reanalysis to account for

---

Lessons

What was clear was that the distribution of risks was similar in the three countries (a finding later endorsed by the ICVS across a broader range of countries).

---

the first three design differences above, and this alone halved (published) differences in rates of burglary between the U.S. and Britain. Only "soft" adjustments—in effect based on informed guesswork—were possible to account for other survey differences. In truth, I made a rod for my own back by including the U.S. survey as one of the three. Its distinctive features (its panel design for instance) made it particularly difficult to compare.

I came up with rather few substantive conclusions about burglary in the United States, Canada, and England and Wales (Mayhew 1987). Police figures in the early 1980s showed U.S. rates were higher than in England and Wales and Canada (although this would not hold now with the substantial drop in police rates since then in the United States and Canada). The survey picture, even after adjustments, did not show the same. U.S. survey rates were higher (though they too fell subsequently) than in Canada, with survey rates in England and Wales the lowest. There seemed more "walk-in" burglaries in the United States, and proportionately more "completed" burglaries than attempts—possibly due to differences in residential layout and household security. These conclusions were packed with caveats. What was clear was that the *distribu-*

tion of risks was similar in the three countries (a finding later endorsed by the ICVS across a broader range of countries). Thus, for instance, risks were related to income in much the same way (highest for the most and the least wealthy); were lowest for elderly households; lower for houses than apartments; and higher when houses were left unoccupied.

A number of other survey analysts attempted similar comparative exercises, though none went to quite the tortuous lengths that I did (I had the luxury of a year's fellowship to do nothing else). Most work was done in the 1980s, but little after. Analysts soon learned the same hard lessons, and the advent of the ICVS of course promised a less backbreaking way forward.[1]

The International Crime Victimization Survey (ICVS)

My NIJ work clearly demonstrated to me that if international comparisons were to go anyway other than through police figures, it had to be by means of a standardized survey in which the same questionnaire, survey administration, and analysis methods were used to produce equivalent results.

It was a harnessing of shared interests between myself, Jan van Dijk (then at the Research and Documentation Centre of the Dutch Ministry of Justice—also presented in this reader) and Martin Killias (University of Lausanne) that led to the first ICVS. Neither Martin nor I (nor indeed anyone else subsequently involved) would challenge Jan's dominance as its main driver. He had connections that left Martin and me standing. And he had

vision certainly greater than mine. The success of the ICVS is in very large part due to Jan (currently head of the United Nations' Center for International Crime Prevention in Vienna).

It is as well to say that the ICVS was not quite the first initiative of its kind. Standardized questionnaires had been used in a few places—though not always identically administered. Marshall Clinard did one in Zurich, Switzerland (Clinard 1978), and a later one was done in Stuttgart (Kirchoff and Kirchoff 1984). A survey in Scandinavia in the early 1970s dealt mainly with violence (e.g., Aromaa 1984). The Organization for Economic Co-operation and Development (OECD) recommended uniform surveys to measure accidents and criminal harm (OECD 1976), but after some pilot work the initiative flagged. The Max Planck Institute fielded companion mail surveys in the early 1980s in Germany and Texas (Teske and Arnold 1982), later replicated in Hungary and Zurich (Schwarzenegger 1989). Gallup included some victimization questions in polls in 22 countries in 1984 (Gallup International 1984), but as far as I know has not done so since.

The ICVS was on another scale. It is now a far-reaching standardized survey monitoring experience and perceptions of crime in a very large number of countries. The International Social Survey Programme (ISSP) (http://www.issp.org/info.html), and the World Values Survey (http://wvs.isr.umich.edu/index.html) are in the same league, although neither takes up criminal justice matters (the ISSP looks at such things as social inequality, gender roles, work orientation, the environment, and national identity. The most relevant module is religious and moral values). The World Values survey is focused on similar socio-cultural and political attitudes, and like the ISSP has repeated questions over time.

The first ICVS took place in 1989, the second in 1992, the third in 1996, and the fourth in 2000. Its scope expanded in 1992 with the involvement of UNICRI (the United Nations Interregional Criminal Justice Research Institute), which developed surveys— usually at city level—in countries in transition (Central and Eastern Europe), and the developing world. Ugi Zvekic and, in particular, Anna Alvazzi del Frate have been leading lights in taking the ICVS outside industrialized countries.

The methodology and administration of the ICVS is well documented (see, e.g., van Kesteren et al. 2001). Suffice it to say that samples are relatively small (usually about 2,000 people or fewer in the city surveys). Interviews are mainly done by telephone, in industrialized countries at least. Response rates are variable.

At the time results from the 2000 survey were reported for the industrialized countries, ICVS standardized surveys have been carried out in 24 industrialized countries since 1989, and in 46 cities in developing countries and countries in transition. (The ICVS questionnaire has also been used in several other countries, albeit not in a fully standardized way.) My most direct involvement has been with respect to industrialized countries.

It requires little imagination to see the difficulties of getting the ICVS to run. There was an initial Working Group comprised of Jan van Dijk, Martin Killias, and myself, which soon expanded to involve UNICRI. For the fourth sweep, Gerban Bruinsma and Paul Nieuwbeerta of the Netherlands Institute for the Study of Criminality and Law Enforcement in Leiden took part. So, too, did John van Kesteren, who has done most of the data management of the ICVS to date.

The ICVS has had enlightened financial backing from the Dutch Ministry of Justice and UNICRI (although most countries paid their own fieldwork costs). It also needed country coordinators to get involved in tedious technical oversight to ensure consistency. There were problems about ownership of results, and how and when these were released (crime "league tables" are sensitive). It was not an easy ride in the early days. By now, though, the ICVS has its own momentum. Its value is reflected in the interest that key international organizations take in it—for instance the World Health Organization, and the European Commission (EC), which is now providing funds for the 2004 surveys in European Union member states.

As someone closely involved throughout, it is difficult to be objective about the ICVS. Some of the methodological criticisms (see, e.g., Travis et al. 1995; Bruinsma et al. 1992) undoubtedly carry weight. Some are perhaps overstated. For instance, there is a general consistency in country positions across sweeps for countries that have participated more than once, which suggests a degree of reliability. Also, the claim that respondents in different countries could have different cultural thresholds for defining certain

```
┌─────────────────────────────────────┐
│                                     │
│            Lessons                  │
│                                     │
├─────────────────────────────────────┤
│                                     │
│  The ICVS provides a wealth of data for │
│  researchers interested in the patterns, │
│  contours and effects of victimization in │
│  both developed countries and others.  │
│                                     │
└─────────────────────────────────────┘
```

behaviors as crime is belied by results that show that most victims hold strikingly similar views about the relative seriousness of different offence types.

ICVS results have in many instances provided balance to what has sometimes been ideologically slanted national discourse on crime and criminal justice. The move into Eastern Europe countries, in transition from centrally guided to free market economies, provided crucial information on changes in experience and perceptions of crime in the transitional period. In several countries, ICVS participation evolved into fully-fledged national crime surveys. The ICVS has had a similar influence in Africa, Asia, and Latin America, and its potential here is likely to grow more.

The ICVS provides a wealth of data for researchers interested in the patterns, contours and effects of victimization in both developed countries and others. Its main findings are covered in all the main reports. In addition, a number of useful secondary analyses are reported in Nieuwbeerta (2002), the result of a workshop for analysts organized by the Netherlands Institute for the Study of Criminality and Law Enforcement in June 2001.

Life After the ICVS

My ICVS "hat" earned me several jobs in the Home Office with a comparative focus. One of the most fraught was presenting the international evidence on behalf of the Home Office on the relationship between guns and crime for Lord Cullen's Enquiry into the massacre in March 1996 of 16 small children and a teacher in the small Scottish town of Dunblane. Here, it was a matter of trying to be objective about a research base that was extremely ideologically cast, and often partisan. The thrust of my argument—that many sources of evidence suggested a link between gun ownership and gun crime, suicides, and accidents—came under heavy fire from the U.K. "gun lobby" (Munday and Stevenson 1996). It also placed the then Conservative U.K. government in an uneasy position, strongly aligned as it was to rural (gun-using) constituents. Nonetheless, the evidence highlighted the value of comparative analysis, in this case widening the evidence base on gun control beyond the heated confines of North America argument.

Australian Institute of Criminology

Between September 2001 and March 2003, I was consultant criminologist at the Australian Institute of Criminology (AIC) in Canberra. It was a happy and interesting time. I ventured into several new pastures: farms, building sites, and retail sites (victimization levels therein).

One of the main pieces of work I did at AIC, the costs of crime in

Australia (Mayhew 2003a), had little comparative focus (I made some effort, soon thwarted by the lack of any common costing approach). It was a technical nightmare, and I am trying to forget the bill.

Three other pieces of work had more comparative content. One was on differences in attitudes to punishment in different world regions, using an ICVS question on what respondents recommended as an appropriate sentence for a recidivist burglar (Mayhew and van Kesteren 2002). The most evident polarization was the support for imprisonment *versus* community service. Community service was the most favored sentencing option in West Europe and Eastern and Central European (ECE) countries—worth emphasizing given that political rhetoric is fuelled by the notion of unshakeable and widespread public support for "locking 'em up." There was more support for imprisonment in countries lower on the UN Human Development Index. Taking West Europe and the New World together, support for imprisonment has generally increased in the 1990s, whereas it has generally fallen in ECE countries—possibly the result of "Westernization." There was some similarity in the social and demographic correlates of punitiveness in different countries and regions (e.g., the younger and less well educated being harsher). But few key variables carried the same weight everywhere, suggesting that some cultural divergence remains essentially unmeasured.

Another thrust of work was looking at data from 54 countries in Europe and North America who replied to the Sixth United Nations Survey as regards the level of criminal justice personnel and indicators of output (e.g., convictions achieved). I also made use of results from the ICVS. Issues of comparability severely uncut the reliability of the comparisons of how the different criminal justice system operate, and I am not sure that a great deal of major import emerged (see Mayhew 2003b). A couple of results are worth mentioning though. First, I looked at whether the ICVS gives a different picture of relative crime levels to figures of crimes recorded by the police—possible for 34 countries. Only a third (11) fell into the same quartile on both crime measures (i.e., they might have been in the "worst" quartile as regards both the ICVS and police figures, or in both of the "best" ones). Other countries were in different quartile placements (for instance, Finland had very high crime on police figures but low crime according to the ICVS; in the Russian Federation and the Ukraine the opposite applied). When ICVS results were restricted to crimes reported to the police, there was much more correspondence between the survey and police figures. The broad conclusion, then, is that police-recorded crime may be a fair guide to the level of reported crime, but is less indicative of the everyday experience of crime. This confirms the validity of the ICVS for the purpose of international comparisons of crime levels.

Secondly, there was no clear association between a measure I constructed of overall system productivity and the level of crime in different countries. This may be because countries that appear to be performing badly in terms of the volume of crime (i.e., they have

Lessons

My final effort at AIC was attempting to explain a fairly consistent downward trend in crime in many industrialized counties in the 1990s; a criminological phenomenon that I feel has been woefully ignored.

high crime levels) simply have more capacity to record it, or more opportunities for it provided by comparatively affluent conditions. It may also signify that criminal justice systems play a minor part in determining crime levels compared to social, political, and economic dynamics.

My final effort at AIC was attempting to explain a fairly consistent downward trend in crime in many industrialized countries in the 1990s; a criminological phenomenon that I feel has been woefully ignored. (The "crime drop" in America had received attention of course, e.g., Blumstein and Wollman 2000.) But this had been mainly in terms of "local" U.S. explanations— e.g., gun control, the decline of crack cocaine, increasing imprisonment rates—with the usual myopic American disregard of trends anywhere else, even Canada.

The ICVS results played some part in documenting falling crime rates. But my analysis was based mainly on police figures. I looked at indexed *trends*, discounting countries where there were evident breaks in series. Let me say up front that I failed to bring this work to any published conclusion (though I touted my wares at a number of

Australian conferences and seminars). This was in part because the "trends" work was driven more by my own interest than AIC's agenda for me (many Australian criminal justice stakeholders, though, were intrigued enough by Australia—not New Zealand incidentally—lagging somewhat behind the overall trend in other Westernized countries).

But the main reason for an unsuccessful conclusion was the difficulty of *explaining* the downward trends. My ruse (somewhat mischievous) was to brigade all the explanations criminologists had used to explain the *rise* in crime (e.g., more opportunities for theft; weaker parenting through family fragmentation; more leisure activities taking people away from home; more drug taking; the breakdown in social cohesion; decreasing risk of sanctions; etc.). I then turned these explanations on their head to see whether improvements (as it were) provided a plausible explanation of falling crime. It did not work of course. There are now more lovely things to steal; more single parents; more health clubs; arguably more drugs taken; and so on. In other words, criminological insights into rising crime did not serve well explanations of falls in crime in the 1990s. I came up with some ideas—difficult to test rigorously with firm comparative figures. For instance, there might have been an improvement in security protection and policing, although the case would have to be for a "step change" here, because both improved in the 1980s when crime rose. Demography may have some effect, with fewer in the "high risk" age group, and a greater dominance of middle-aged values. Generally favorable economic climates are undoubtedly a factor. More fanciful hunches were that greater cannabis use has left youths too "stoned" to bother with nicking and fighting; or that changes in youth lifestyles and aspirations have "civilized" those at the margins, with a steady income rather than misbehavior now the fashion. I would like more time to bring the "fall in crime" work to conclusion. In the meantime, I defend myself with the excuse that as criminologists never explained the crime rise well, it was a tall order for me to explain the stabilization or falls!

Theoretical Orientation

What has been my theoretical orientation to international comparisons? The highbrow answer would be to say it was to build a theory about crime levels in the world that withstood sound empirical test—or at least examine existing theories (e.g., modernization (Shelley 1981); civilisation (Elias 1982); opportunity theory (Cohen and Felson 1979); cultural theory (Lynch 1995); strain (Bennett 1991); or social disorganization (Bursik 1988)). But, in truth, I have had more of a practical orientation than a strictly academic one. This is clearly influenced by working in a government research environment where "applied" criminology is in greater demand than theoretical. Thus, I have seen no reason not to be responsive to the interests of criminal justice practitioners who simply seek indicators of their own performance, want to be told what preventive lesson can be drawn from elsewhere, and tend to be impatient with

the answer that few are available. Comparisons with other countries are newsworthy (whether as regards crime levels or crime prevention novelties), but many are appallingly badly grounded, with not only journalists at fault, but also many academics. Getting the right facts clear seems to me a reasonable endeavor.

Having said this, I have learned some lessons. Let me mention just one. Testing or building theory with police figures may have had its hay day. The social and economic factors that might be associated with crime levels are also associated with the *amount* of crime recorded by the police. Thus, ICVS results confirm notable differences in reporting levels across a country, to which can be added known differences in police recording patterns. There are now several analyses of ICVS results that have focused on explaining differing levels and profiles of survey-measured crime in different countries. One key result to emerge, for instance, is that, *lower* affluence is significantly associated with *higher* property crime risks. This goes against modernization theory, which proposes that less developed countries have lower property crime levels, which probably simply reflects lower reporting rates and less well-developed police recording systems. A job that seems to me worth doing is to set ICVS conclusions on the macro and micro determinants of crime alongside those from other meta-level studies based on police figures. There has been little effort made to do this (though see Kangaspunta 2000; van Dijk 2001; and, notably, Howard and Smith 2003). Some of the best ICVS analyses, by the way, are van Dijk (1994); van Dijk and Kangaspunta (2000); van Dijk and Nevala (2002); and van Wilsem et al. (2002).

Advice to Comparative Researchers

International comparative work is not for the feint hearted. Even work on a limited front (taking three or four countries for instance) requires detailed knowledge of country systems and data. It is ideal to work with others *in* the countries concerned, but one should at least aim to liaise with those who know about the police or administrative criminal justice data. This increases the chances of getting what one wants, rather than what is routinely collected.

There are a number of wide-ranging compilations of international figures on crime that can be used for comparative analyses. I register some views about them.

The Interpol figures are not, to my mind, worth pursuing, although for a time they were widely used in comparative research, in the absence of much else. There is a long run of figures, covering a number of offences categories. But the explanation of the figures is poor and there are inconsistencies across time. The Interpol volumes actually come with a warning against using their figures in comparative work.

The *European Sourcebook of Crime and Criminal Justice Statistics* used country advisors to collect figures and explain definitions, counting rules, etc. It provides a good source of information on police figures, prosecution statistics, conviction data, and prison populations (Council of Europe 1999). The initiative was started in 1993 with data collected for 1990-1996. The second Sourcebook is in hand with data for 1996-2000 for 40 countries.

The international figures compiled by Cynthia Tavares and Gordon Barclay in the Home Office are also useful (Barclay and Tavares 2003). There is not the same attempt made to explain coverage differences as in the *Sourcebook,* but major breaks in series are noted. Figures are given on total recorded crime, homicide, homicide in selected cities, violent crime (lots of different definitions), domestic burglary, theft of motor vehicles, drug trafficking (not very reliable), and prison populations.

The *UN Survey on Crime Trends and Operations of Criminal Justice Statistics* is now a major source of information that is difficult to ignore. It is wide in scope, with seven surveys done to date, covering about 30 years (data for the seventh survey is downloadable at http://www.unodc.org/un

odc/en/crime_cicp_survey_seventh.ht
ml). A data request for the eighth survey was issued to about 190 countries
in August 2003, though not all will
reply with anything like complete figures. Data quality has improved sub-
stantially since the early surveys,
although "health warnings" are still
substantial. There is additional social,
demographic, and economic information added. Graeme Newman edited a
comprehensive report on the Sixth
Survey (Newman 1999), and there is a
recent report of the figures for Europe
and North America (Aromaa et al.
2003). These are essential reading for
comparative analysts, if only to know
what has been done. As with the
Sourcebook, the UN survey figures on
prosecutions, convictions, and sentencing are especially problematic for comparative analyses because system differences mean like is usually far from
like.

The comparability of homicide figures from different sources is more
problematic than one might think
because of such things as the treatment
of attempts and manslaughter. The
World Health Organization's (WHO)
figures on homicide from mortality
records are useful in having wide coverage, although they tend to be lower than
from police figures (WHO 2002).
WHO also has data on war-related
deaths and suicides.

These compilations only cover
"conventional" crimes. For topics such
as money laundering, organized crime,
etc., the uphill task is even steeper.
Leaving this aside, the potential range
of comparative work is immense—so
advice here can only be partial. For
work involving data from a large num-

ber of countries (rather than limited
jurisdictional studies) I would underline
just four points. First, do not bother trying to compare victimization surveys
that have been independently mounted.
And if messages from *standardized* surveys and police statistics conflict, there
is good reason to calibrate from the former, since they bypass differences in
reporting and recording practices.
Second, be realistic: recognize that firm
conclusions from comparative research
will be stymied by data limitations (of
which sampling error in the ICVS is
one). Third, get on top of the major
sources mentioned above, and know
what analyses have been done, and with
what results. Fourth, think creatively
about additional secondary analysis.
The scope is enormous. Testing out
what circumstances and conditions foster or inhibit offending is fine. But
there is also plenty of basic work to be
done to improve the data first.

Notes

1.   For historical record, some of the
     comparisons of existing surveys
     (though without many adjustments)
     are: Braithwaite and Biles (1980–
     U.S. and Australia); Van Dijk and
     Steinmetz (1983–Canada, U.S. and
     The Netherlands); Hough (1986–
     U.S., Canada, The Netherlands, and
     England); Breen and Rottman
     (1985–England, Eire, U.S., and
     The Netherlands); Killias (1989–
     Switzerland, The Netherlands,
     England, Canada, Australia and
     U.S.). Studies in which survey
     data was manipulated to improve
     comparability were more limited.
     Richard Block did much of the

work (e.g., Block 1984), concentrating mainly on United States, England and The Netherlands. Some standardization was also usually built into the few comparative studies that looked at the correlates of victimization, principally lifestyle factors (e.g., Maxfield 1987a, 1987b; Block 1987).

References

Aromaa, K., S. Leppä, S. Nevala, and N. Ollus. 2003. *Crime and Criminal Justice Systems in Europe and North America 1995-1997*. Helsinki: HEUNI.

Aromaa. K. 1984. "Three Surveys of Violence in Finland." In *Victimization and Fear: World Perspectives*, edited by R.L. Block. Washington D.C.: Bureau of Justice Statistics, U.S. Department of Justice.

Barclay, G. and C. Tavares. 2003. "International Comparisons of Criminal Justice Statistics 2001." *Home Office Statistical Bulletin* 12/03. London: Home Office.

Bennett, R.R. 1991. "Development and Crime: A Cross-National Time Series Analysis of Competing Models." *Sociological Quarterly* 32:343-363.

Block, R.L. 1987. "A Comparison of Victimisation, Crime Assessment and Fear of Crime in England/Wales, the Netherlands, Scotland and the United States." Paper presented at American Society of Criminology Meeting, Montreal, November 1987.

Block, R.L., ed. 1984. "Victimization and Fear of Crime: World Perspectives." Bureau of Justice Statistics: U.S. Department of Justice. Washington, D.C.: Government Printing Office.

Blumstein, A. and J. Wollman. 2000. *The Crime Drop in America*. Cambridge: Cambridge University Press.

Braithwaite, J. and D. Biles. 1980. "Crime Victimization in Australia: A Comparison with the U.S." *Journal of Criminal Justice* 3:95-110.

Breen, R. and D. Rottman. 1985. "Criminal Victimization in the Republic of Ireland." The Economic and Social Research Institute, Paper No. 121. Dublin: The Economic and Social Research Institute.

Bruinsma, G., H.G. van de Bunt, and J. P.S. Fiselier. 1992. "Quelques Rèflexions Théoriques et Methodologiques à Propos d'une Recherché Internationale Comparée de Victimisation." *Deviance et Societé* 16(1): 49-68.

Bursik, R.J. 1988. "Social Disorganization and Theories of Crime and Delinquency." *Criminology* 26: 519-552.

Clarke, R.V.G. and P. Mayhew. 1988. "The British Gas Suicide Story and its Criminological Implications." In *Crime and Justice*. Vol. 10, edited by M. Tonry and N. Morris. Chicago: University of Chicago Press.

Clinard, M.B. 1978. *Cities with Little Crime: The Case of Switzerland*. Cambridge: Cambridge University Press.

Cohen, L.E. and M. Felson. 1979. "Social Change and Crime Rate Trends: A Routine Activity Approach." *American Sociological Review* 44:588-608.

Council of Europe. 1999. *European Sourcebook of Crime and Criminal Justice Statistics*. European Committee of Crime Problems (CDPC). PC-S-ST (19) 8 REV Strasbourg: Council of Europe.

Elias, N. 1982. "The Civilizing Process." Vol. 2: *Power and Incivility*. New York: Pantheon Books.

Gallup International. 1984. *International Crime Study*. Gallup Poll, November, 1984. Poll conducted for the *Daily Telegraph.*

Hough, J. M. 1986. "Victims of Violent Crime: Findings from the British Crime Survey." In *Re-orientating the Justice System: From Crime Policy to Victim Policy*, edited by E. Fattah. London: Macmillan.

Howard, G. and T. Smith. 2003. "Understanding Cross-National Variation in Crime Rates on Europe and North America." In *Crime and Criminal Justice Systems in Europe and North America 1995-1997*, edited by K. Aromaa, S. Leppä, S. Nevala, and N. Ollus, Helsinki: HEUNI.

Kangaspunta, K. 2000. "Secondary Analysis of Integrated Data Sources." In *Surveying Crime: A Global Perspective*, edited by A. Alvazzi del Frate, O. Hatalak, and U. Zvekic. Rome: Instituto Nazionale di Statistica (ISTAT).

Killias, M. 1989. *Les Suisses Face au Crime*. Grusch, Switzerland: Ruegger.

Kirchhoff, G.F. and C. Kirchhoff. 1984. "Victimological Research in Germany." In *Victimization and Fear: World Perspectives*, edited by R.I. Block. Washington D.C.: Bureau of Justice Statistics, U.S. Department of Justice.

Lynch, J.P. 1988. "A Comparison of Prison Use in England, Canada, West Germany and the United States: A Limited Test of the Punitive Hypothesis." *Journal of Criminal Law and Criminology* 79:180-217.

Maxfield, M.G. 1987a. "Household Composition, Routine Activity, and Victimization: A Comparative Analysis." *Journal of Quantitative Criminology* 3:301-320.

———. 1987b. "Incivilities and Fear of Crime in England and Wales and the United States: A Comparative Analysis." Paper presented at American Society of Criminology Meeting.

Mayhew, P. 2003. "Operation of the Criminal Justice System." In *Crime and Criminal Justice Systems in Europe and North America 1995-1997*, edited by K. Aromaa, S.Leppä, S. Nevala, and N. Ollus. Helsinki: HEUNI.

———. 2003. "Counting the Costs of Crime in Australia." *Trends and Issues in Crime and Criminal Justice*, No. 247. Canberra: Australian Institute of Criminology.

———. 1987a. "How are We Faring on the Burglary Front? A Comparison with the U.S. and Canada." *Research Bulletin*, No. 23. London: Home Office Research and Planning Unit.

Mayhew, P. and J. Van Kesteren. 2002. "Cross-National Attitudes to Punishment." In *Changing Attitudes to Punishment: Public Opinion,*

Crime and Justice, edited by J.V. Roberts and M. Hough. Cullompton, Devon: Willan Publishing.

Munday, R.A.I. and J.A. Stevenson. 1996. *Guns and Violence: The Debate before Lord Cullen*. Brightlingsea, Essex: Piedmont Publishing.

Nieuwbeerta, P., ed. 2002. *Criminal Victimization in Comparative Perspective: Results from the International Crime Victims Survey, 1989-2000*. The Hague: Boom Juridische uitgevers.

Newman, G. ed. 1999. *Global Report on Crime and Justice*. United Nations Centre for International Crime Prevention. Oxford and New York: Oxford University Press.

Organisation for Economic Co-opera tion and Development (OECD). 1976. *Data Sources for Social Indicators of Victimisation Suffered by Individuals—With Special Reference to the Potential of Victim Surveys*. The OECD Social Indicator Development Programme. Special Study No. 3. Paris OECD.

Schwarzenegger, C. 1989. "Zurcher Opferbefragung Fragestellung, Vorgehen und erste Resultate." *Kriminologisches Bulletin de Criminologie* 15:5-29.

Shelley, L. 1981. *Crime and Modernisation: The Impact of Industrialisation and Urbanisation on Crime*. Carbondale: Southern Illinois University Press.

Teske, R. and H. Arnold. 1982. "Comparison of the Criminal Statistics of the United States and the Federal Republic of Germany." *Journal of Criminal Justice* 10:359-374.

Travis, G., S. Egger, B. O'Toole, D. Brown, R. Hogg, and J. Stubbs. 1995. "The International Crime Surveys: Some Methodological Concerns." *Current Issues in Criminal Justice* 6:346-361.

Van Dijk, J.J.M. 2001. "Does Crime Pay?" In *Forum on Crime and Society* 1(1) (February). Vienna: United Nations Office for Drugs Control and Crime Prevention.

———. 1994. "Understanding Crime Rates: On the Interactions Between the Rational Choices of Victims and Offenders." *British Journal of Criminology* 34:105-121.

Van Dijk, J.J.M. and K. Kangaspunta. 2000. "Piecing Together the Cross-National Crime Puzzle." *National Institute of Justice Journal* January 2000. Washington, DC: National Institute of Justice.

Van Kesteren, J., P. Mayhew, and P. Nieuwbeerta. 2001. *Criminal Victimisation in Seventeen Industrialised Countries: Key Findings from the 2000 International Crime Victims Survey*. The Hague: Ministry of Justice.

Van Dijk, J.J.M. and S. Nevala 2002. "Intercorrelations of Crime." In *Criminal Victimisation in Comparative Perspective: Results from the International Crime Victims Surveys 1989-2000*, edited by P. Nieuwbeerta. The Hague: Boom Juridische uitgevers.

Van Dijk, J.J.M. and C. Steinmetz. 1983. "Victimization Surveys: Beyond Measuring the Volume of Crime." *Victimology: An International Journal* 8:291-301.

Van Wilsem, J., N. Dirk de Graaf, and K. Wittebrood. 2002. "Variations in

Cross-National Victimization." In *Criminal Victimisation in Comparative Perspective: Results from the International Crime Victims Surveys 1989-2000*, edited by P. Nieuwbeerta. The Hague: Boom Juridische uitgevers.

World Health Organization. 2002. *Global Atlas on Violence and Health*. Geneva: World Health Organization.

Selected Bibliography

Mayhew, P. 2000. "The State of Crime: Local, National and International Victim Surveys." In *Doing Research on Crime and Justice*, edited by R.D. King and E. Wincup. Oxford: Oxford University Press.

———. 1993. "Research Issues in Relation to the International Crime Survey." In *Understanding Crime and Experiences of Crime and Crime Control*. UNICRI Publication No. 49, edited by A. Alvazzi del Frate, U. Zvekic, and J.J.M. Van Dijk. Rome: UNICRI.

———. 1992. "Crime and the Law." In *The Economist Atlas of Europe*. London: Economist Books.

———. 1990. "Opportunity and Vehicle Crime." In *Policy and Theory in Criminal Justice: Contributions in Honour of Leslie T. Wilkins*, edited by D.M. Gottfredson and R.V. Clarke. Aldershot: Avebury.

———. 1987b. "Residential Burglary: A Comparison of the US, Canada and England and Wales." Report to the National Institute of Justice, Washington, DC.

Mayhew, P. and L.J.F. Smith. 1985. "Crime in England and Wales and Scotland: A British Crime Survey Comparison." *British Journal of Criminology* 25(2):148-159.

Mayhew, P. and J.J.M. van Dijk. 1997. *Criminal Victimisation in Eleven Industrialised Countries*. The Hague: Ministry of Justice, Research and Documentation Centre.

Van Dijk, J.J.M. and P. Mayhew. 1993. *Criminal Victimisation in the Industrialised World: Key Findings of the 1989 and 1992 International Crime Survey*. Ministry of Justice: the Netherlands.

Van Dijk, J.J.M., P. Mayhew, and M. Killias. 1990. *Experiences of Crime Across the World: Key Findings of the 1989 International Crime Survey*. Daventer, Netherlands: Kluwer.

Chapter 5

On the Victims' Side

Jan J.M. van Dijk

United Nations,
Vienna, Austria

Go "glocal"...think globally and act locally.

1. The First Years

Shortly after I was born in Amsterdam in 1947, my father decided to return to Indonesia (the former Dutch Indies) where his family had lived for several generations. It was an unfortunate move since Indonesia in those years was in a post conflict situation. Crime was rampant and Dutch nationals were no longer welcome. My mother suffered from the tropical heat and from anxiety about the safety of her children. In the mid-fifties all Dutch nationals were requested to repatriate and our family traveled back to The Netherlands. My father's sister, aunt Ida, who worked as a pediatrician in an Indonesian hospital, was among the last Dutch nationals allowed to remain in Indonesia. When she was finally expelled, she joined the World Health Organization which took her to The Philippines, Nepal, and Sri Lanka. As a child I entertained a regular correspondence with her and we remained close till her death.

My aunt was a hard-nosed idealist, more interested in delivery of services to people than political ideology and with an open mind for the relative merits of the socialist model in health care. Politically, she was to the left of my parents, unsentimental about the colonial past of The Netherlands and a strong supporter of the movement of non-aligned countries, of which Indonesian President Sukarno was one of the leaders. On her death, she bequeathed to me a Jewish candelabrum, a gift of one of the many Jewish children she had saved during the German occupation by smuggling them into liberated Belgium. This tough-minded, unglamorous lady was for many years my main window to the world outside The Netherlands. Writing this mini-biography I came to realize that she has been, more than anybody else, the key role model of my professional life.

2. My First Job at Nijmegen University

In the final year as law student at Leiden University I took several courses in other faculties to prepare myself for a position as a criminological researcher. On joining the Criminological Institute of the University of Nijmegen in 1971, I was asked to take over the office, teaching obligations, and research portfolio of my predecessor. In the drawers of his desk I found tables with basic information on the victims of violent crimes which were taken from court files. The information on the victims' side of the story, as recorded by the authorities, was too rudimentary to merit publishing. In order to salvage the work, I decided to interview a small sample of victims of recently committed crimes of violence myself. In line with the victimological notions of my professor in Leiden, Willem Nagel, my main interest was whether victims who had somehow precipitated the crime by their own behavior would be more lenient in their views on the appropriate sentence for the offender. The results of the study were inconclusive on this issue. But the face-to-face interviews with recently victimized persons taught me something else.

Many victims were vulnerable people, ill-equipped to cope with the effects of crime. Many were keen to talk about their experience and obviously in need of support. Few had received compensation. Many had been treated rudely by the police. Although I did not realize it at the time, the agenda of my professional career had been set.

My second research project, in the 1970s, sponsored by the United Nations Interregional Criminal Justice Research Institute in Rome, focused on the impact of criminological research on decision-making. The main conclusion was that in-house research has more impact on decision-making in government than research conducted by outsiders. In the same year, crime and fear of crime emerged as key political issues in The Netherlands. In response to criticism of its conservative-legalistic approach, the Ministry of Justice decided to import a group of young social scientists to strengthen its profile and knowledge base. I was among those invited to join the newly established Research and Documentation Centre of Ministry of Justice. Other recruits included Dato Steenhuis, Josine Junger-Tas, and Cyrille Fijnaut who all would make their names in international criminology. I personally had some misgivings about leaving the university with an unfinished Ph.D. thesis on violent crimes on my desk but decided to take the plunge. The Dutch Parliament had just started to discuss state compensation for victims of violence. Political parties of the left were asking for a new, proactive approach to crime. The opportunity to influence emerging criminal policies from the inside seemed too good to miss.

3. Working for the Dutch Government

Upon arrival in 1975 we, the new recruits, embarked on an ambitious program of empirical, policy-oriented research. The cornerstone of the program was the launching of a National Victimization Survey. This survey, using colloquial rather than legal terminology, intended to reveal the true volume and nature of crime and helped to put the new Centre on the political map. The Centre's mission to inject fresh data into the political debate on crime control was duly picked up on by the media. We advocated focusing future criminal policies on volume crime such as vandalism, pick pocketing, and household burglary rather than on traffic offenses, family-related homicides or drugs offences. I persuaded the Ministry to submit grants to three NGOs offering support to victims of crime and helped to draft detailed guidelines for better treatment of victims by police and prosecutors. In the drafting committee I learned to appreciate the practical approach of Dutch prosecutors who readily agreed that better treatment of crime victims would require changes in their own attitude rather than in the law.

Apart from large-scale surveys, the Centre specialized in policy-evaluation studies and field experiments. Concepts like team policing, victim support, community service orders and treatment programs for drug addicts were pilot tested locally, using semi-experimental designs. In this type of research an international orientation is obviously useful. A well-staffed documentation unit was tasked to monitor the international literature on similar projects elsewhere in the world. The "nothing works" theory on offender treatment and the famous Kansas City police patrol experiments became household words at the Ministry. We had set ourselves the goal to base Dutch criminal policies on international *best practice* and to test out promising, cutting-edge ideas in our country.

At a time that university-based criminology showed more interest in historical than in cross-national studies, "administrative criminology," as our type of work was sometimes disparagingly called, looked across national borders for inspiration and support. Partly in response to cold shoulders from former peers at the University-based institutes, we enthusiastically reached out to like-minded in-house research centers in Europe, North America, and Australia. Although our mandate was to assist national and local policies, our outlook had soon become distinctly international.

In the years that Josine Junger-Tas and I headed the Centre, the international outlook became an official institutional priority. Staff was admonished to take an active part in international conferences such as those organized by the Council of Europe and the United Nations (UN). The Centre twinned itself with the Home Office Research Unit and the Criminological Centre in Oxford. English criminologists like Pat Mayhew (presented in this reader), and Joanna Shapland became regular visitors. The Centre later initiated a series of seminars of policy-oriented European research centers and regularly invited North American or European scholars as visiting fellows. The list of fellows include: Daniel Glaser, Wes Skogan, Irvin Waller (also included in this anthology), Richard and Becky Block, Menacheim Amir, Marcus Felson, Martin Killias, and Michael Tonry. Each of these visitors effectively contributed to the Centre's research agenda in those years.

4. Society and Crime

The most striking achievement of the Centre in those early years was the collective drafting of a comprehensive policy plan against crime, *Society and Crime,* adopted by the Dutch government in 1985. This policy plan, largely drafted by Steenhuis, Junger Tas, Fijnaut, and myself proposed a differentiated approach towards volume crime and organized crime respectively. The steady increase of crime as measured by our annual victimization surveys was ascribed to the weakening of intermediary structures, exercising informal social control and the commercialization of the public domain. A three-pronged prevention strategy was designed, focusing on integration of youth at risk, situational crime prevention and the strengthening of semi-formal surveillance. Organized crime was analyzed as the result of The Netherlands' unique geographical position as the "Gateway to Europe." To counter this new international threat the plan announced the establishment of specialized investigative units and new legislation regulating special investigative techniques.

This policy plan with its clear criminological approach to crime and its control soon received all-party support in Parliament. It would lay down the intellectual foundations of Dutch crime

> ## Lessons
>
> *The steady increase of crime as measured by our annual victimization surveys was ascribed to the weakening of intermediary structures, exercising informal social control and the commercialization of the public domain.*

policies for over two decades. As key author of the plan I was incrementally drawn into policymaking and managerial functions, eventually as head of the directorate of crime prevention. I would advise a succession of four Ministers of Justice, representing four different political parties, on their crime prevention policies. In the spirit of the unforgettable TV series "Yes Minister" I wrote official papers and speeches for all of them, thus ensuring continuity in Dutch policy in the area of criminal justice.

To promote crime prevention a generous fund was set up for demonstration projects to be carried out by municipalities. In line with our recommendations ten percent of the budget was set aside for monitoring and evaluation by independent researchers. Most successful in the final analysis appear to have been instances of situational crime prevention and well-structured projects targeting youth at risk. Crime prevention in The Netherlands in the eighties and early nineties was generously funded. Its main implementation obstacle proved to be institutional jealousies, or more precisely the refusal to maintain a powerful centre responsible for crime prevention at the Ministry of Justice. As in many other countries, responsibility for crime prevention was eventually scattered over several institutions with no real overall commitment for crime prevention and little political clout.

Lasting achievements of the original plan include the institutionalization of youth sanctions and of victim support—both administered by independent, specialized organizations—and of different forms of semi-formal surveillance (for example, more surveillance in public transport and city guards recruited from the long-term unemployed in the inner cities). Our initiative to issue an annual Award for the most successful crime prevention project proved its worth as a generator of free publicity for community-based crime prevention. The first winner was Patty Deconinck, who successfully reintegrated delinquents in a neighborhood of Rotterdam with funding from the local business community (Ministry of Justice 1997). Her successes were in the media for weeks. The Award became a model for similar awards in Belgium, the UK, and eventually the European Union. Another achievement that has survived the years was the co-financed partnership with the business sector to tackle special crime problems such as commercial robberies, car theft, and cyber crime. We involved not only the criminal justice elite but also several CEOs of the leading companies of the country by organizing early dinner meetings chaired by the Minister of Justice.

5. Promoting Victim Support

The new, non-legalistic crime strategy offered excellent opportunities for effective lobbying for a comprehensive reform agenda on behalf of victims. In my free time I became the founding president, of the Dutch National Association of Victim Support. This association which started in 1987 on a shaky financial basis with three employees is now offering assistance to over 100,000 victims per year. Together with my successor as president of the association, Marc Groenhuysen, I also lobbied for improvements in the role of victims in criminal procedure. Dutch law offered victims the opportunity to request a civil law verdict for compensation from the criminal tribunal adjudicating the criminal case. In practice less than 3 percent of relevant victims ever obtained such a verdict and received compensation from the offender at the end of the day. Discussions with Joanna Shapland of the UK brought me to the idea to give teeth to the largely ineffectual adhesion provisions through the introduction of a criminal "compensation order," to be enforced as a fine. Through a torrent of books, articles, interviews, and participation in several committees Groenhuysen and I achieved the introduction into Dutch criminal law of the restitution/compensation measure. Marc and I followed up with a series of training seminars for prosecutors and judges during which participants were engaged in role-playing sessions, alternatively playing the role of interviewer and victim. The sessions sometimes became so emotional that we had to break them off.

Twenty years after our first efforts to introduce the new sentencing option, the majority of victims in relevant categories of crime obtain a compensation measure. Most offenders faced with such orders actually pay up. The payment of compensation to the victim has become a common feature of criminal trials in The Netherlands. In a recent Ph.D. thesis by Brienen and Hoegen at Tilburg University, studying compliance of 22 European countries with the Council of Europe's (1985) Recommendations on The Position of the Victim in Criminal Law and Procedure, Dutch policies ranked first.

6. Leiden University and the International Crime Victimization Survey (ICVS)

While I spent most of my time in the nineties on politics and administration, I pursued my career as criminological scholar as part-time professor at Leiden University. I taught several criminology courses including for first year law students and law students from abroad and I continued to publish regularly on crime prevention and victim assistance. In the meantime I enjoyed my ongoing contacts with international colleagues. On several occasions I had daydreamed at conferences with Wes Skogan, Irvin Waller (presented in this reader) and other friends about the conduct of a fully standardized victimization survey among a large sample of different countries. The proposal found its way into several resolutions of bodies of the Council of Europe and UN but neither of these organizations possessed the institutional capacity to put it into practice. When I heard about the new technologies of computer-assisted telephone interviewing (CATI) and random digit dialing (RDD) being pilot tested

across Europe by a Dutch polling company, I decided the time for such survey had come. I invited Pat Mayhew of the UK and Martin Killias of Switzerland, who had both worked on their own national crime surveys, modeled after the Dutch survey, to assist me in this endeavor. The preparation of the survey was facilitated by Martin and me, as continental Europeans, speaking several languages (I speak four and Martin five or more). Some months later I sent out invitations from the Dutch Ministry of Justice to Ministries of Justice across the Western world with the invitation to join our survey at their own cost (a Dutch treat). Ten Western European countries as well as Canada and the USA finally accepted the invitation. At that time the only communist country which regularly attended Council of Europe conferences on crime problems was Poland. My Polish counterparts agreed to also take part, a unique decision in the Soviet era where police figures were considered state secrets. I also arranged the piloting of the survey in the city of my childhood, Surabaja (Indonesia), by Prof. Sahetapy, currently chair of the Indonesian Parliamentarian Commission on Legislation.

The ICVS was conducted for the first time in 1987 in fourteen countries. Results were published the next year. Following a meeting at the UN Crime Congress in Cuba, Ugi Zvekic and Anna Alvazzi del Frate of UNICRI joined the working group. Thanks to their imagination and hard work the survey was subsequently also carried out in all Eastern and Central European countries and in a sample of countries from other world regions. In several countries including Poland, Argentina,

Lessons

The ICVS has at present been officially carried out once or more in over eighty countries among a total of over 250,000 respondents.

and South Africa , the ICVS was adopted as the national crime survey. The work on the ICVS engaged me in decades long collaboration with literally hundred or more fellow criminologists across the world. As recognition for these efforts the University of Tirunelveli in Southern India awarded me an honorary doctorate in law in 2002 where my Indian counterpart Prof. Chockalingam had become Dean.

The ICVS has at present been officially carried out once or more in over eighty countries among a total of over 250,000 respondents. In 2003 the European Commission decided to fund the conduct of the survey in the Union's Member States as proposed by the international working group. The continued replication of the survey in the future now seems assured. Its questionnaire has become the *de facto* world standard for such surveys.

Somewhat surprisingly The Netherlands, the United Kingdom and, more recently Switzerland show relatively high rates on the survey, certainly not lower than the United States. In my own view this finding shows that high levels of many forms of crime can be both opportunity and poverty-driven. Vandalism, drugs-related theft and alcohol-related violence are poverty-driven in developing countries but they belong to

the downside of affluence in the West. Some commentators, including many British and Dutch criminologists and politicians, did not accept this. They could not understand how some of the world's most affluent and integrated societies can suffer from relatively high rates of volume crime. They therefore suspected that the survey's instruments were somehow biased against the home countries of their designers. Although the questionnaire indeed possesses a Eurocentric slant, this cannot really explain the high British, Dutch or Swiss rates. When rates for bicycle theft and vandalism are, for example, discarded the Netherlands and the UK still show relatively high rates, high enough to give honest politicians—and criminologists—cause for concern.

7. More International Networking

My interest in crime prevention and victim policies of other countries led me to play a supporting role in the establishment and development of the European Forum on Crime Prevention. As president of the Dutch Victim support organization I convened a preparatory meeting in Geldrop, The Netherlands of what would later develop into the European Forum on Victim Support. From the outset I was much engaged in the World Society of Victimology (WSV). I represented my country at the founding meeting in Munster in 1979 where I became acquainted with the late M. Mendelsohn, founding father of victimology, who expressed his great respect for my professor at Leiden, Willem Nagel. At the official meeting I ventured to express doubts about the need for a special organization, independent from the International Society of Criminology. Surely criminologists would not contemplate studying criminal victimization disconnected from offenders? My theoretical and ideological concerns were not heeded. Gilbert Geiss, an American professor explained to me, tongue in cheek, that the new organization would at any rate offer extra opportunities for criminologists to add an international function to their CV.

Despite of my initial reservations I became a regular participant of the Society's international symposia and summer courses, delivering keynotes and lectures on numerous occasions. Later, in 1997, I organized the Symposium in Amsterdam. Unlike most international conferences the symposium was truly international with a significant participation from non-western countries and a Nigerian fair. Most memorable for me was the workshop on the recently committed genocide in Srebrenica, organized by Paul Separovic and some professors from Sarajewo. As follow up a WSV related NGO was established in Sarajewo. We organized an international conference in war-torn Sarajewo on "Screbrenica and its aftermath," back-to-back to the society's annual summer course in Dubrovnik, Croatia. Bosnian participants ventilated against me as Dutch national for the failed peace-keeping mission of our army and against our American students from Dubrovnik for showing lack of respect with their casual attire. Our NGO later carried out a needs assessment for repatriated victims but it failed to find a sustainable place in the myriad of donor-driven, post-conflict initia-

tives. I learned that in the delivery of technical assistance good intentions and some funds are not enough to make a difference. The Society simply lacked the expertise for such initiatives.

After the Amsterdam event, I was elected president of the WSV (and, as Geiss had premeditated twenty years before, duly updated my CV). My presidential priorities were the revitalization of the society's research committee, the launching of a website on victimology and the restyling of our newsletter. Canadian victimologist, Joanna Wemmers, one of my former Ph.D. students in Leiden, took charge of the newsletter and made it into one of the society's greatest assets. The website, www.Victimology.NL, launched and maintained by the Ministry of Justice, continues to be the best on the web in its domain.

In 2004 the Society awarded me in Stellenbosch, South Africa, the Hans von Hentig Award for lifelong achievements in victimology, after having received earlier at the Dutch Embassy in Washington the Stephen Schafer Award of the USA based National Organization for Victim Assistance.

8. Working for the UN

In 1998, I accepted the invitation of the Italian sociologist Pino Arlacchi, author of several books about the mafia, to join him at the UN Office on Drugs and Crime as director of the crime program. In our first conversation, he thanked me profusely for my readiness "to work for him." In his view, apparently, I had not agreed to join the UN as an institution but to become a member of his personal coterie or court. On joining the organization I found most of the crime-colleagues in a state of shock about the authoritarian and often arbitrary regime exercised by Mr. Arlacchi. I decided to keep my distance from the fourteenth floor, as the court was generally called, and to focus my energies on the negotiations of the convention against transnational organized crime and the launching of technical assistance programmes against organized crime, trafficking in persons and corruption. I recruited a dozen staff members with strong academic and professional qualifications and tried to introduce a hands-on, non-bureaucratic work culture. The daily intrigues of Arlacchi, however, made my efforts to launch a professional crime program into an uphill battle. To my personal dismay Arlacchi was adamantly opposed to the continuation of the ICVS. Arrangements were made for the continuation of the ICVS from Leiden University.

Six months after joining I started to suffer from serious stress-related health problems from which I have fortunately fully recovered but which thoroughly spoiled the fun of working for the UN. The government of The Netherlands decided as the only donor country to discontinue its funding of the drugs program, in protest against Arlacchi's mismanagement. My position in the Office became very difficult. When an internal oversight investigation was finally started into Arlacchi's management style, I silently handed over a detailed report about my experiences to under secretary-general, S. Nair from Singapore. My input reportedly contributed to Arlacchi's forced resignation a few months later. One of the first

things I proposed to Arlacchi's successor, the Italian banker Costa was renewed attention in the crime program for victim support and for the ICVS. To my relief he welcomed these priorities. He also fully backed my policy line of focusing the crime program on the delivery of technical assistance.

In December 2000 the General Assembly adopted the UN Convention against Organized Crime. On the day before the signing ceremony in Palermo I accompanied Pino Arlacchi to the grave of Judge Falcone, a dedicated anti-mafia judge whom I had once met in Rome, killed by the mafia in 1992. Arlacchi had worked closely with him and assisted him in unraveling the mafia's organizational structure. Since the rest of the UN company was somewhere stuck in the Palermo traffic, we spent some silent minutes alone, standing before the grave, observed by the Italian press. I was moved by the occasion, in spite of my mixed feelings towards Arlacchi in his UN position.

In Palermo, that week, I was accompanied by Samuel Gonzalez-Ruiz, former head of the anti-mafia unit of the Mexican prosecutorial office who had recently joined my team. He introduced me to Leoluca Orlando, Mayor of Palermo and another of the many Italian heroes in the fight against the Mafia. Orlando's rule as Mayor of Palermo demonstrates the importance of a preventive, victim-oriented approach to mafia-related crime problems. In later years he would help us to elaborate the UN Guidelines for the Prevention of Crime in which we incorporated his concept of a "culture of lawfulness." The fight against the Mafia requires, according to Orlando, both law enforcement and the mobilization of civil society against crime. Fighting the Mafia without a preventive program supplementing repression is like riding a Sicilian cart with just one wheel: no real progress can be made.

I look back with satisfaction to having serviced from beginning till end the elaboration of the Palermo Convention, although my substantive role in the drafting process has been modest. At critical moments I was able to play a bridging role between emerging negotiating camps, for example by organizing a high-level seminar in Bangkok, where we brought together in more than one sense the key negotiators of the United States, Latin America, and Asia. I think I was generally respected as an "honest broker" and received an unusual warm round of applause when the chair welcomed me back at the podium after a sick leave of three months. At a crucial moment in the negotiations on the marking of firearms, I invited some key delegates from the United States and China to my room at two o'clock in the morning for a final attempt to agree on a compromise text. When one of the negotiators from Beijing lashed out to me, the ambassador's wife, attending the meetings as a member of the Chinese delegation, exclaimed: *"Please gentlemen, Mr. Van Dijk's heart!"* Our collective efforts and mutual goodwill were to no avail. At four o'clock we had to admit defeat. It would take a full new round of negotiations before a watered down protocol against the illicit manufacturing and trafficking of firearms was finally adopted. It has in the meantime been duly ratified by China but not

by the United States (yet?).

In two areas I indulged in clandestine lobbying behind the scenes for the inclusion of my own substantive ideas. In cahoots with the very active and effective Dutch delegation during the negotiations, I managed to insert a strong and innovative provision in the Convention on the prevention of organized crime. The article reminds State Parties that law enforcement against organized crime groups must be supplemented by measures to ensure professional integrity of legal professions, raise awareness among the public, protect young people at risk, rehabilitate offenders and prevent reinvestment of criminal assets in the legitimate economy. In order to smooth out the initial opposition of the US delegation against the Dutch proposals, I distributed copies of Jim Jacobs's book on the successful application of preventive action against La Cosa Nostra in New York under Giuliani. The American negotiators had never heard of this success story and were duly impressed. The Dutch draft of the prevention article remained largely intact and is now often mentioned as one of the more imaginative parts of the Convention.

I also took a special interest in the provisions on victims in the Convention. Already in the first drafts these provisions largely complied with the UN Victims Declaration of 1984 and didn't seem to need my special attention. Less satisfactory and more controversial were draft provisions for rights of victims of trafficking in persons. The protocol is clearly victim-oriented and does introduce several legal guarantees for the victims of trafficking. However,

Lessons

However, both the United States and the majority of the European Union countries refused to grant victims of trafficking residential status which would allow them to testify in court against their traffickers or exploiters.

both the United States and the majority of the European Union countries refused to grant victims of trafficking residential status which would allow them to testify in court against their traffickers or exploiters. They also refused to make the provision of specialized support for victims such as shelters as a treaty obligation. I lobbied discreetly with the ambassador of Pakistan and some other negotiators from the developing world for language more generous for victims. In the final round the minimalist position of the destination countries prevailed. Within two years after the protocols were finalized both the United States and The European Union would themselves adopt legislation on the rights of victims of trafficking which go even beyond our proposals. If the protocol would be negotiated now these victim-friendly proposals would have been readily accepted. With our ideas for a better deal for the victims of human trafficking we had unfortunately been just two years ahead of the curve.

9. The Human Security Dimension

In the years after Arlacchi's departure, the operational crime program took off with a vengeance. The number of operational projects jumped from a handful in the late nineties when I joined the program to over fifty in 2004. The budget increased from less than a million U.S. dollars to ten million per year. Technical assistance projects in capacity building against trafficking in persons and judicial corruption are now spanning countries across the world. These global programs have more recently been supplemented by projects on juvenile justice, victim support, and urban security. A major project assists the transitional government of Afghanistan in the reconstruction of its criminal justice system. Following past practice in the Netherlands, I volunteered to draft the speech of the minister of Justice, Karimi, for an important donor conference, which he accepted in good humor.

Under the new management, I finally found peace of mind to work with a small team of colleagues on the collection of data on organized crime groups and on the development of a composite index of organized crime/ corruption, using a dozen existing indicators of mob-related criminal activities. With this index and the ICVS results it should now be possible to paint a more comprehensive crime map of the world.

As a delegate for The Netherlands I have campaigned for years with Matti Joutsen (presented in this reader) of Finland in the UN Commission for Crime Prevention and Criminal Justice for the establishment of a United Nations Fund for Victim Support. Resolutions asking for such initiative go back more than fifteen years. Over the years few issues have frustrated me more than the failure to turn this obviously worthwhile project into reality. It is a source of great satisfaction that in 2004 with my UN colleagues, Kristtiina Kangaspunta and Jo Goodey, we finally managed to raise sufficient funds to award grants to twenty NGO's to promote victim support in developing countries. We hope there will be many more of such grants in future years and that these will prime the pump for victim support globally.

In 2003 the crime and drugs programs of the UN have been fully merged. The Branch headed by myself, responsible for substantive backstopping of operational projects, is called the Human Security Branch. In its terms of reference the Branch is defined as a centre of excellence on drugs control and crime prevention, *focusing in particular on the impact of drugs and crime problems on people* (italics mine). As I explained to staff, with these words the victimological orientation is firmly anchored in the mandate of the new Branch. Drugs and crime-related problems are to be fought with a view of reducing damage to real people. Since the ultimate success of its activities is to be measured in terms of human security, law enforcement will always have to be supplemented by (evidence-based) prevention. One of the Branch's future priorities will be the prevention of crime and drugs abuse, including the spread of HIV/Aids as well as promoting victim support.

10. Dealing with the Media

One of the interesting aspects of being a criminologist, certainly in The Neth-

---

> ### Lessons
>
> *Unwilling to engage in the usual white-washing of bad "marks" which is typical for small countries, I stipulated on prime time television that ours apparently was a "degenerate" society (een verloederd land).*

---

erlands, is ample media exposure for one's ideas. The downside of this ego-pleasing exposure is that one's public image as a criminologist is largely based on statements made during media interviews. In my own case this involves several media-hypes about me having flaunted politically incorrect opinions. On the occasion of the release of the first results of the ICVS I had to explain to journalists why The Netherlands had come out on top of the crime league in Europe. Unwilling to engage in the usual white-washing of bad "marks" which is typical for small countries, I stipulated on prime time television that ours apparently was a "degenerate" society (*een verloederd land*). This sound bite triggered a full-fledged Parliamentary Debate. It also caused, unsurprisingly, a furor of strident criticism from fellow criminologists, some of whom still saw crime problems as a social construction of the right wing press. Although much of the criticism was unfair, I plead guilty for having provoked it. On later occasions I came to the defense of an older colleague slandered to be a Nazi doctor for having proposed socio-medical studies of chronic delinquency, hailed the expansion of the private security industry as a positive trend, criticized the leakage of development aid due to corruption in developing countries, and warned against the silent infiltration of the Dutch Bar by mob lawyers. On these and other occasions my uncompromising and perhaps slightly provocatively formulated statements caused storms of moral indignation and angry questions from concerned Parliamentarians.

In Adelaide, Australia I was once interviewed in a chat show on a popular TV channel about the high level of assaults in the country. I linked this finding to Australia's equally unrivalled national rates of beer consumption. This interpretation caused a media riot and on the next day the channel sought responses from the locals in Adelaide's pubs. The friendliest theory was that the professor must be one of those awful wine snobs. Upon my return to The Netherlands the first appointment was with a member of the executive board of Heineken International Ltd. He was not amused either. Had I been a wiser man, I would have saved myself, as on other occasions, much trouble by being more discrete.

11. Theoretical Underpinnings

The essence of a criminologist's contribution to the discipline is to be found not in his sound bites or reports on empirical studies, but in the growth and development of his theoretical views. In a recent review of my work on the ICVS the Belgian criminologist Patrick Hebberecht (2001) qualifies Ron Clarke and me as main architects of neoliberal criminal policies, originating in the UK and The Netherlands in the eighties and increasingly adopted elsewhere as well.

Neoliberal policies help states to legitimize their reduced roles by focusing on the control of security risks through situational measures. In his view the ICVS has been the main vehicle of the global advance of neoliberal criminal policies.

Hebberecht probably exaggerates the political impact of my work on the ICVS but is right in pointing out my affinity to situational crime prevention theory of Ron Clarke as well as to the underlying theory of rational choice. The idea that crimes can—and should—be prevented by making them more difficult and less profitable for potential offenders has indeed always appealed to me. Hebberecht overlooks, however, my special commitment for advancing the interests of potential and actual crime victims. The point of departure, of my theoretical ideas, is identification with the victim's side. Without this element my theoretical position within criminology and its development cannot be properly understood.

A discourse on crime which sincerely takes the victim's suffering as its point of departure will, first of all, not easily evolve in a radically anti-governmental or relativist direction. In my early years I was briefly tempted by critical criminology but the idea to totally abolish the criminal justice system—a very popular notion among Dutch and Norwegian professors in those days—never really appealed to me. The victim's suffering presented itself to me not as a social construction by state agencies or special interest groups but as an authentic human experience with near universal features. Unsatisfactory as the police response to victims might be, the idea that victims would be better off without a police seemed unconvincing. I had probably spoken with too many real victims early in my career to be attracted by so called radical criminology. In my view the criminal justice system ought to be reformed with a view to better servicing the interests of victims but not abolished.

The victimological policy agenda is not limited to promoting services and rights for crime victims. Potential and actual victims must also be advised on the best ways to prevent victimization or revictimization by crime. For me this is as obvious as the need for preventive medicine. In reality few victimologists share my affinity with situational crime prevention theory. Their reservations towards situational crime prevention are not difficult to understand. It comes from justified reluctance to blame victims for their misfortune. It is all too common for bystanders, shocked by the commission of a crime in their midst, to blame the victim for his/her misfortune as a way to reassure themselves that cautious citizens have nothing to fear. This kind of instinctive victim-blaming is grossly unfair and must be categorically rejected. It is unfortunate, though, that these irrational forms of victim-blaming have made the victim's own role in the acts leading to a crime into a taboo subject for victimological research. Victims, like offenders, should not be seen as mere objects of their life histories and circumstances. They are subjects invested with free will who can in many cases, or at least within specific margins, influence the extent of their risks to be victimized. In fact, by realizing their own possible mistakes and

capacity to take better preventive action against future victimization, victims may put themselves in a better position to regain confidence and a feeling of control over their lives than by being told they had nothing to do with what happened to them.

In 1994 I published an article in the *British Journal of Criminology*, titled "On the interactions between the rational choices of victims and offenders." In this article rates of property crimes are analyzed as the outcomes of interactions at the macro level between the rational decisions of potential offenders to commit crimes, and of potential victims to protect their property. In this model offenders are seen as greedy consumers of criminal gains and victims as reluctant investors in their own protection. Both parties are optimizing their net gains. The model predicts stabilization of the level of property crimes at a point where neither party can collectively better its position. As known, property crimes have indeed shown a remarkable stabilization over the past ten years in most Western countries. In my view not so much due to the efforts of law enforcement but the collective investments of victims in their own security have brought about this success. The champions of this success story in crime fighting are not the Giuliani's of this world but the citizens as potential victims themselves.

In my view it is essential for governments to increase the transparency of local crime so as to inform citizens better about their risks. Honest crime information should be as readily available as food or water safety information. Much more needs to be done in this respect such as the collection and

---

> ### *Lessons*
>
> *At the trial, victims should, with due regard for the rights and interests of both parties, be allowed to present their side of the story and to claim compensation.*

---

dissemination of better information on the crime risks of certain professions or of foreign travelers. I do also think that on both economical and humanitarian grounds, governments should financially promote the use of crime prevention measures by disadvantaged groups, including recently victimized citizens or small shopkeepers. My favorite crime prevention programs consist of the large-scale funding of better security for repeat victims, for inhabitants of poor, crime-ridden neighborhoods and for the elderly in the UK.

My preference for situational crime prevention does not as Hebberecht suggests mean that as director of crime prevention or otherwise I have ever opposed conventional, offender-oriented preventive measures such as early intervention projects or projects supporting youth at risk or job placement projects etcetera. In fact most of the available budgets under my supervision went to such welfare type projects. I have always argued for a balanced, two-sided crime prevention program investing in interventions on both sides of the criminal equation, supporting (potential) victims and (potential) offenders.

To sum up, then, the following are my theoretical views. Victims should be seen as subjects who have been at the receiving end of a morally wrongful act. It is the duty of the state to bring the offender to justice on behalf of the legal community, including the victim. At the trial, victims should, with due regard for the rights and interests of both parties, be allowed to present their side of the story and to claim compensation. If relevant their own possible role in the chain of events culminating in the crime should be addressed. Victims also have a vital role to play in the prevention of crime. Crime reduction cannot be achieved with more police and longer sentences alone. It requires well-funded crime prevention, striking a balance between victim- and offender-oriented measures; always involving civil society.

These are not, I admit, conventional socialist ideas about crime and its control but whether they can appropriately be labeled neoliberal remains to be seen. Most of what I have promoted in terms of victim support or crime prevention requires more social interventions by the welfare state. Since I have been a lifelong member of the Dutch Labor Party and an occasional consultant for the Labor government of the UK, I would prefer to be associated with the crime prevention policies of new Labor.

12. With Hindsight

Reflecting on the development in my criminological publications over three decades, I am struck by the similarity between my first article about victims of violence in the *Dutch Journal of Criminology* in 1975 and the article in the *British Journal of Criminology* of

1994. The latter publication seems almost a remake of the original with the focus broadened from the individual to the collective level. Even the title of the later article—*on the interactions between rational choices of offenders and victims*—echoes the earlier one—*actions and reactions of victims*. While writing this article, it also dawned on me how much my work builds on the seminal publications on victimology of my teacher and predecessor in Leiden, Willem Nagel. Nagel published in 1964 an English article on "The Victimological Notion in Criminology." In this and other articles he argues for an interactionist criminology which understands the commission of serious crimes as the outcome of derailed interactions between offender and victim. He saw the criminal trial as a forum for the closure of such derailment. This seems to sum up the thrust of my own work pretty well too.

Nagel did not only influence my thinking along the usual academic lines of being my teacher, thesis supervisor, and senior colleague in the early years. Under his literary penname, J.B. Charles, he published his experiences as former leader of the Dutch resistance movement against the German occupation. In these best selling books he expressed bitter disenchantment with a post war Europe divided between a right wing NATO camp, condoning the speedy rehabilitation of former Nazis, and the communist bloc, oppressing and murdering dissidents. The ideals of the anti-fascist struggle had in his view been completely forgotten in post war Europe. For people unfamiliar with recent Dutch history, it may be difficult to fully appreciate the deep imprints these books have made on the political conscience of Dutch intellectuals of my generation. In a biographical essay which I published in the seventies in a literary journal, I interpreted Nagel's victimological agenda as criminologist against the background of his wartime experiences. Offenders must be held accountable for their misdeeds and potential evildoers must not be condoned or appeased but confronted head on. I also expressed my deep admiration for his attitude of rugged individualism in politics, eternally in opposition to the politically correct opinions of the day. The worst crimes according to Charles are always committed by groups feeling good about themselves. It is the intellectual's duty to spoil the party.

13. Lessons Learned

The single most decisive choice in my career was to join the Ministry of Justice in 1974, never to return full time to academia, as it turned out to be. How do I look back at this career move? On the downside of life in administration I see an endless series of hopelessly long, excruciatingly boring meetings. Frustration with delayed action, due to rampant bureaucracy is another sore point. On the minus side I also count the nagging, guilty feeling of playing truant, while reading a book or writing an article, such as the present one. On the plus side I remember the many occasions of real team play with colleagues in getting things done and, of course, the opportunity to directly influence policy decisions or legislation, nationally and internationally, in line with one's views.

Any specific lessons learned, worth sharing with younger colleagues? Working in the trenches of bureaucracy can be a lonesome and at times trying experience but the opportunity to help shape new responses to newly emerging crime problems from the inside made it worthwhile for me. Working in or for the government seems equally challenging and potentially rewarding nowadays for young criminologists in Latin America, Russia or Africa and, considering the global nature of crime, probably elsewhere as well. Crime has become more organized and society's responses should become much more organized as well. Criminological advice how to do this is urgently needed.

In my view criminology is by the nature of its subject matter policy- and action-oriented. A criminologist who shuns advisory work for the government resembles a medical doctor who refuses to work in a hospital. For me it is strange to be a specialist in the study of avoidable human suffering without at least an occasional interest in finding and testing ways of reducing it.

The most disappointing aspect of senior positions in administration in the long term may be the lack of real feed back from practical experiences about the validity of one's ideas. Policy-making at the central government level or an international organization is simply too far removed from activities in the real world to have much learning value. From working on the inside one learns how to promote criminological ideas— timing for example is important—but not very much about how these ideas work out in practice. In order to test out one's criminological ideas a position in local government would probably be

more rewarding. The career of British criminologist Ken Pease, discoverer of the phenomenon of "repeat victimization," is a case in point. He combined teaching criminology with advising the local police on crime prevention. At one point he even swapped his room at University for a room at the local police station. Ken's formula, then, may be ideal for executing the mission of victimological criminology as I see it: to design and test out in a local setting international best practices to reduce criminal victimization. In short, I advise young criminologists to go "glocal": to think globally and act locally.

Selected Bibliography

Brienen, M. and E. Hoegen. 2000. *Victims of Crime in 22 European Criminal Justice Systems,* Nijmegen, WLP.

Dijk, J.J.M. van and A. G. Dumig. 1975. *Acties en Reacties van Geweldslachtoffers; Enige Uitkomsten van een Victimologisch Onderzoek* (Actions and reactions of victims of violent crime; some results of a victimological study), April, pp. 63-73. Nederlands Tijdschrift voor Criminologie.

Dijk, J.J.M. van, P. Mayhew, and M. Killias. 1990. *Experiences of Crime Across the World: Key Findings of the 1989 International Crime Survey.* Deventer: Kluwer Law and Taxation.

Dijk, J.J.M. van. 1991. *Criminaliteit als keerzijde* (Criminality as downside), Inaugural Address University of Leiden, 5 maart 1991. Gouda Quint, Arnhem.

Dijk, J.J.M. van and J. de Waard. 1991.

"A Two Dimensional Typology of Crime Prevention Projects; with an Extensive Overview of the Literature." *Criminal Justice Abstracts*, pp. 483-503.

Dijk, J.J.M. van. 1994. "Understanding Crime Rates. On the Interactions Between the Rational Choices of Victims and Offenders." *British Journal of Criminology* 34(2).

Dijk, J.J.M. van. 1999. "The Experience of Crime and Justice." In *Global Report on Crime and Justice*, edited by G. Newman. Oxford: Oxford University Press.

Dijk, J.J.M. van., Ron van Kaam, and Joanna Wemmers, eds. 1999. *Caring for Crime Victims*. Selected Proceedings of the 9th International Symposium on Victimology, Monsey.

Dijk, J.J.M. van. 2002. "Empowering Victims of Organized Crime: On The Concurrence of the Palermo Convention with the UN Declaration on the Basic Principles of Justice for Victims." *International Review of Victimology* 9:15-30.

Hebberecht, P. 2001. "De International Crime Victims Survey in een Theoretische, Methodologische en Breed Maatschappelijke Context" (The ICVS in a Theoretical, Methodological and Broad Social Context). *Tijdschrift voor Criminologie* 43:192-201.

Jacobs, J.B. 1999. *Gotham Unbound, How New York was Liberated from the Grip of Organised Crime*. NYP University Press.

Ministry of Justice. 1997. *Pioneering Crime Prevention. The History of the Hein Roethof Awards, 1987-1996*. Ministry of Justice, The Netherlands.

Nagel, W.H., C.I. Dessaur, F. Denkers, J.J.M. Van Dijk, and H. Willemse. 1972. *The Impact of Criminological Research, First Interim Report*, Universities of Leiden and Nijmegen, UNSDRI, Rome.

Orlando, L. 2001. *Fighting the Mafia; and Renewing Sicilian Culture*. San Francisco: Encounter Books.

Chapter 6

Reflections on a Cross-National Criminological Career

David P. Farrington

Professor of Psychological Criminology, Cambridge University, England

Choose your collaborators carefully.

School

I was born in 1944 and brought up in Ormskirk, which is a small town in the North of England. My family was poor; we had an outdoor toilet and no indoor bathing facilities in our old rented house. Baths were in a tin bath in front of the fire on a Friday night! However, my mother and father never pressured me to go out to work to assist the family economy or (unlike other local families) to leave school at the earliest possible age, which was 15 years old. They were happy for me to stay at school until I was nearly 19, because they wanted to give me every possible opportunity. When I walked past the men in boiler suits going to work in the Brass Foundry a hundred

yards from our house, I always thought "there but for the grace of God go I."

Luckily, I was born clever. I went to the local state schools, which had rigid streaming (tracking) from a very early age. In the primary school, certainly before age 10, our seating position in class each week was determined by our performance on the test at the end of the previous week. We were streamed into 4 classes: A, B, C and D, each of about 40 children, and I was usually top of the A stream. I passed my 11+ examination (the teachers told me in advance that it would be a miracle if I failed! Presumably, they were not hoping for such a miracle) and went to the local grammar school. Only about 20 percent of the graduating students in state schools at that time went to grammar schools; the other 80 percent went to secondary modern schools, from which it was almost impossible to get to university.

The grammar school, of course, had rigid streaming, again into A, B, C and D classes, but this enormously benefited me, because I was always competing with, and stimulated by, the most intelligent children from the area. In Ormskirk at that time, few people were rich, and so few children went to private schools. The grammar school teachers were of high quality; many had graduated from Oxford or Cambridge. Along with two classmates, I achieved some notoriety at age 14 by representing the Manchester region on television in the Inter-Regional Quiz of Great Britain. We had to go down to London for our TV appearances, which were a great adventure on the train. We reached the final of this competition but were beaten by a team from the Bristol region.

Ormskirk Grammar School succeeded in getting one student a year, on average, into Oxford or Cambridge, which is a widely accepted criterion of school success. However, in my year, three of us got into Cambridge, which was great. Five of us were successful in obtaining State Scholarships, which were given to the top 2,400 children in the country (of whom about 800 went to Cambridge—out of an undergraduate intake of 2,400—700 to Oxford, 400 to London University, and 500 to all other British universities).

University

Being an undergraduate at Cambridge University was wonderful. I can recall lots of stimulating discussions with other undergraduates in my college (all males, since the colleges were not co-residential at that time) until the early hours of the morning, sometimes fuelled by alcohol! Because I came from a poor family, I had a full grant (and all fees paid), so I could manage very well financially. Few students had to work to earn money at that time. I even saved up enough money to embark on a hitchhiking tour of the United States from New York to Los Angeles and back in 1964, at the end of my first year. This was quite an adventure, as I had never been abroad before.

The greatest feature of Cambridge was the supervision system, where a university teacher met once a week with one or two undergraduates. I learned far more from supervisions than from lectures. Supervisions were very demanding, because the supervisor would be quite challenging. I started off at University doing math, physics, and chemistry (math was my best subject at school) but eventually graduated in psychology. All of these subjects were in the Natural Sciences Tripos, so it was easy to move between them.

I had always been interested in psychology and always intended to do math and psychology at university. When I was 16, I had our local library order many of Freud's books and I read them avidly: *The Psychopathology of Everyday Life, The Interpretation of Dreams* (of course I kept a notepad next to my bed and tried to write down my dreams when I woke up!), *Civilization and its Discontents, The Future of an Illusion,* etc. Public libraries were great! Eysenck's books also inspired me: *Sense and Nonsense in Psychology, Uses and Abuses of Psychology,* and so on. Sad to say, Cambridge focused very much on experimental psychology and indeed the scientific method, and so I was soon taught that these idols had feet of clay!

The greatest influence on my undergraduate career was a Lecturer in psychology by the name of Alan Watson. He supervised me in psychology and very conscientiously went through all my essays line by line. In supervisions, he would constantly say "How does this follow from that?" and "What do you mean by this?" He would challenge me to write more clearly and be more explicit about what I wanted to say. Under his tutelage, my writing style and clarity improved enormously. Cambridge was great for me as an undergraduate because it enormously expanded my intellectual abilities.

After graduating in Psychology in 1966, I applied to do a Ph.D. degree in Cambridge and, fortunately, was accepted. Alan Watson agreed to supervise my Ph.D., which tried to test different theories of human learning, focusing on the ability of Cambridge undergraduates to learn three-digit numbers. I had a very good memory for numbers myself and had always been good at mental arithmetic. The model of the Cambridge Ph.D. was very much one of Master and Apprentice, and again I learned a great deal from Alan Watson about conducting and writing up experiments, reviewing the literature, and other skills.

My Ph.D. thesis described 12 experiments that I had carried out with Cambridge undergraduates as subjects. My meetings with Alan Watson were very stimulating, because we would take stock of the results obtained in the last experiment, then talk about the loose ends and new questions raised, and then plan the next experiment to address these new hypotheses. Actually, it was very reminiscent of the logical deductive methods I had used in chemistry, for example, in trying to discover what an unknown substance was. It was very much the model of an experimental science.

Unfortunately, Alan Watson was very busy. He was a very clever man indeed, but he was Acting Head of the Psychology Department in the mornings and Senior Tutor (Chief Executive Officer) of Fitzwilliam College in the afternoons and evenings. Consequently, our meetings were often in the Psychological Laboratory at 7.00 a.m. or in Fitzwilliam College at midnight. He read most of my drafts (and much else) in the middle of the night. Because he spent most of his time in teaching and administration, he rarely published anything and the one thing he did not do was teach me how to publish. Consequently, although my Ph.D. thesis was accepted with no changes (a rare event) in 1969, I never published any of the 12 experiments in journals, which I should have done eventually.

Over to Criminology

As I was coming to the end of my Ph.D., I was becoming more disillusioned with experimental psychology. Much of it seemed rather irrelevant to real life, and I wanted to do something more socially relevant. At that time, I was interested in sociology and believed that it might have something to offer. Consequently, when I saw an advertisement in the Psychological Laboratory for someone to work as a

Research Officer on a longitudinal study of delinquency, based in Cambridge, I applied for it, and was offered the job by Donald West in 1969. It suited me to stay in Cambridge, and I knew enough about longitudinal studies to know that they were unusual and interesting.

I knew nothing about criminology at the time. However, Donald West appointed me because of my statistical and computing skills. When I started my Ph.D. in 1966, Alan Watson had encouraged me to learn Fortran programming, and so I knew how to analyze data using the computer, which was a fairly new thing at the time. I wrote lots of subroutines, inspired by a book by Donald Veldman—as did Irvin Waller, by the way, who was very much a contemporary of mine in Cambridge. The only other thing I did for my Ph.D. thesis that has ever proved useful since is to learn all about ROC curves!

Professor Zangwill, Head of the Psychological Laboratory, was not pleased that I had defected to criminology. He had arranged one Lectureship in Psychology for me, at the University of Sussex, and I was offered another at the University of Leeds. However, I had irrevocably burned my boats with experimental psychology.

Criminology was an alien environment. In 1969-70, British criminology was dominated by sociologists who were stridently anti-empirical and anti-scientific. They talked in impenetrable jargon and were very critical of the Cambridge Study in Delinquent Development, which they regarded as an atavistic throwback to the work of the then-hated Gluecks (who were later revived by Sampson and Laub 1993).

Lessons
Whereas many criminologists accepted positive results rather uncritically, any positive results in psychical research were strongly challenged so that it was important to be careful and to think of, and try to test, alternative explanations.

However, I enjoyed working with Donald West on this survey and thought it really fascinating. Donald was a very careful researcher. Like many psychiatrists, his first question was: "What is the evidence for that?" and of course I liked this very much. I think Donald's previous career as a psychical researcher had made him unusually careful. Whereas many criminologists accepted positive results rather uncritically, any positive results in psychical research were strongly challenged so that it was important to be careful and to think of, and try to test, alternative explanations.

I worked on soft money for five years, until I managed to get a university job in 1974. I really enjoyed the research but the financial uncertainties were troubling. Also, Professor Radzinowicz, the Director of the Institute of Criminology, wanted all results published in books in the Cambridge series that he edited, not in journals. Even more troubling, he regarded researchers such as myself as the lowest form of pond life and did not want us to be co-authors of the books (even though we might have done most of the work). Interestingly, when I eventually became a Professor in 1992, he

<table>
<tr><td>*Lessons*</td></tr>
<tr><td>*I believed that criminology should become more of an experimental science.*</td></tr>
</table>

said "Now you are a Professor, I would like to invite you to dinner" and after that he pestered me with dinner invitations every time he was in Cambridge!

Happily, I was appointed to a university teaching post in 1974, and so was no longer dependent on soft money, but unhappily I then became Director of the M. Phil. Course in Criminology from 1975 to 1978. During this time period, I shouldered a heavy burden of university teaching and administration and also did a lot of college teaching to supplement my derisory salary (because I had three small children to support and a wife at home looking after all of us). None of this was conducive to publishing journal articles, although I continued to work on the Cambridge Study, and we published another book in the Cambridge Series (West and Farrington 1977).

I also embarked on a series of randomized field experiments on dishonesty (Farrington 1979a). For example, we left unsealed, stamped, apparently lost letters on the streets of London containing cash and different notes (e.g., indicating that the money was for a Senior Citizens' outing or for *Yachting Monthly*) for unsuspecting members of the public to pick up and either return or steal. This was very much using my training in experimental psychology, and I believed that crimi-

nology should become more of an experimental science. However, nobody liked these experiments. For example, when I tried to get funding from the Home Office, they argued that stealing in this kind of an experiment could encourage people to embark on a life of crime! So, I gave them up.

Also in this time period, I helped to found the Social Science Research Council Law and Psychology Group (Farrington et al. 1979) and the British Psychological Society Division of Criminological and Legal Psychology. I thought that it was essential for psychologists to join together to support each other and to stimulate each other by exchanging information about research. In criminology, psychologists seemed to be a beleaguered minority, and I believed that there was strength in numbers. Unlike many British sociologists, British psychologists believed in science and empirical research.

Ottawa and Washington

Two sabbaticals changed my life. After I finished my stint as Director of the M. Phil. Course, I spent a year (1978-79) in Ottawa in the Solicitor General's Department working on the Young Offenders Act. For this I have Irvin Waller to thank. I also carried out my first real cross-national comparative research, comparing the Cambridge Study with Marc LeBlanc's longitudinal survey of Montreal adolescents (Farrington et al. 1982). When I went to Ottawa, I had published very little: a couple of books and about a dozen articles. In my year in Ottawa I wrote 15 articles and, for the only time in my life, caught up with all the things that had been hanging around for years. From then on, I was able to learn from Alan Watson and publish a lot and avoid administration like the plague.

The Solicitor General's Department was a large bureaucracy. On the first day, one of the people I met said, "Welcome to the Titanic." My contract had been held up until the last minute because one Solicitor-General (who was in favor of the *Young Offenders Act*) had to resign because he forged his girlfriend's husband's signature in order to get her an abortion, and then the next Solicitor-General (who was worried about "a criminal code for juveniles") didn't want to have anything to do with this proposed Act. While I had had quite a bit of previous contact with the Home Office, it was very interesting to be close to the political and policy-making process.

Every month, I went to Montreal to collaborate with Marc LeBlanc, who is a brilliant researcher. I stayed at the entrance to St. Joseph's Oratory and had to struggle up the hill to the University of Montreal to collect my computer printouts. In the winter, with the temperature around -30°C and with 60cm of snow on the ground, it felt like climbing Mount Everest! I also struggled to read most of the excellent reports that Marc and his colleagues had written, since they were almost all in French at that time. I had done French at school and could read French to some extent, but I spent a lot of time puzzling over tables (mainly I read the tables!) with the aid of a French dictionary. Still, I learned a great deal from this happy collaboration.

One of the papers I finished in Ottawa was my review of longitudinal studies in crime and delinquency that was published in volume 1 of *Crime and Justice* (Farrington 1979b). This was a very important publication, because it brought me to the notice of key American researchers such as Al Blumstein and Al Reiss, who gave me detailed comments on the first draft that greatly improved the final version. It brought me into contact with Michael Tonry and Norval Morris, who also proved to be very important in fostering my career. In particular, it massively expanded my knowledge of American longitudinal and criminal career research. Also during my year in Ottawa, I traveled widely in the United States and visited leading American researchers who had previously been in Cambridge such as Jim Short, a wonderful man.

I soon decided that being on sabbatical was the best possible state, and so I applied for another sabbatical in 1981 to be a Visiting Fellow in Washington at the National Institute of Justice (NIJ). While at NIJ, I began my collaboration with Patrick Langan (Langan and Farrington 1983) and further expanded my knowledge of American criminological research and researchers. I was a great admirer of brilliant empirical researchers like Al Blumstein and Al Reiss, and learned a lot from them. NIJ in 1981 was initially rather demoralized by various threats of laying-off staff by the new administration, but in fact the tenure of Chips Stewart as Director of NIJ proved to be the golden age of American criminological research in my opinion.

It was a golden age especially for longitudinal and experimental research, both of which I strongly advocated.

<table>
<tr><td>

Lessons

The great thing about Americans is their optimism that everything is possible.

</td></tr>
</table>

While I was at NIJ, I completed a second *Crime and Justice* chapter on randomized experiments in criminology (Farrington 1983), which proved almost as influential as the first. NIJ funded many randomized experiments (Sherman 1992). However, the 1980s were mainly memorable to me for the exciting development of longitudinal and criminal career research in the United States.

The great thing about Americans is their optimism that everything is possible. When I advocated longitudinal and experimental research in the United Kingdom, the reaction was very negative: "you could never do it." Instead of thinking about all the problems, the reaction of American researchers was to say, "let's go for it." That is why I was delighted to be involved in so many exciting American research activities in the 1980s.

Longitudinal and Criminal Career Research in the 1980s

During the 1980s, the most influential American criminologists (at least with the federal government and leading foundations) were Al Blumstein, Norval Morris, Lloyd Ohlin, Al Reiss, James Q. Wilson, and Marvin Wolfgang. Happily, they all advocated longitudinal and criminal career research. I was delighted to be a member of the National Academy of Sciences panel on criminal career research (chaired by Al Blumstein) from 1983-85, along with Morris, Reiss, Wilson, Wolfgang, and other luminaries such as Del Elliott, Rolf Loeber, and Lee Robins (Blumstein et al. 1986). I really felt that we were developing an exciting new paradigm and that we were pushing back the frontiers of knowledge (although Pat Langan always chided me that I should say pushing forward the frontiers of knowledge!).

In 1982, the MacArthur Foundation decided that it wanted to advance knowledge about crime and set up a committee chaired by Norval Morris (and containing Lloyd Ohlin and Jim Wilson). This committee advised the Foundation to mount new longitudinal studies. The Foundation then set up a kind of architectural competition in which 20 researchers were invited to send in designs for a new longitudinal study. I was one of three persons who evaluated the 13 designs submitted. Three designs were chosen as "winners" to be discussed at a meeting in Chicago in 1983, but unfortunately the Foundation also invited the "losers" to the meeting, some of whom proceeded to lambaste the "winners." The Foundation then decided that if researchers could not agree among themselves, it would not be funding a new study.

Norval Morris saved the day in 1984 by persuading the Foundation to commission Lloyd Ohlin, Jim Wilson, and myself to write a book outlining the design of a new study (Farrington et al. 1986). We advocated a multiple-cohort longitudinal experimental study.

In 1984-85, the Office of Juvenile Justice and Delinquency Prevention (OJJDP) funded a series of "executive sessions" on juvenile justice and juvenile delinquency organized by Mark Moore and Jim Wilson (e.g., Wilson and Loury 1987). It was on the plane home from one of these sessions that Jim Wilson persuaded OJJDP that they should mount some new longitudinal studies. OJJDP put out a solicitation in 1986 and selected three new studies for funding, in Denver, Pittsburgh, and Rochester. Happily, I was (and have continued to be) a co-investigator of the Pittsburgh Youth Study, along with Rolf Loeber and Magda Stouthamer-Loeber (see Loeber et al. 2003). This has been a wonderful collaboration for me, as the Pittsburgh Youth Study and the other two studies have really advanced knowledge in numerous ways. And I have come to realize that "Beautiful Pittsburgh" is not an oxymoron!

On my many visits to Pittsburgh, Al Blumstein and his wife Dolores have been kind enough to put up with me. Their hospitality has been very warm and generous. Al has undoubtedly had a great impact on my professional life, and he has been a wonderful role model and mentor. He is an inspiring and stunningly brilliant researcher with an amazing ability to work up to about 4.00 a.m. on a regular basis. I once emailed both Al and Rolf at 9.00 a.m. in England (4.00 a.m. in Pittsburgh) and both responded at once! At that time, Al was just coming to the end of his shift and Rolf (who is a very early riser) was just beginning!

Sad to say, NIJ was rather upset when OJJDP mounted these three studies. There was always rivalry between the two agencies, and NIJ always regarded itself as superior. However, these three high profile studies—often described as the "jewel in the crown" of OJJDP's research program—threatened this assumption of superiority. Consequently, NIJ decided to collaborate with the MacArthur Foundation (who was now receptive to the idea, after our 1986 book) to mount a bigger and better longitudinal study.

NIJ and MacArthur funded the Program on Human Development and Criminal Behavior, led by Michael Tonry, Lloyd Ohlin, and myself, from 1987 to 1989. We set up various working groups to plan a new longitudinal study and had numerous stimulating meetings culminating in the book *Human Development and Criminal Behavior* (Tonry et al. 1991). Incidentally, this and many other key books of that time period were published in a Springer-Verlag series edited by Al Blumstein and myself and masterminded by a former student of mine, Bob Kidd. This was, again, a very happy collaboration. The 1991 book proposed a bigger and better multiple-cohort longitudinal survey with 7 cohorts beginning prenatally and at ages 3, 6, 9, 12, 15, and 18.

Unfortunately, NIJ and MacArthur reacted to this book not by mounting the project but by suggesting that we have several more years of planning meetings. At this point, Michael, Lloyd and myself decided that we were happy to pass the baton to Tony Earls and Al Reiss, who eventually (in the mid-1990s) mounted the 7-cohort study with over 6,000 participants. I was more concerned to spend time analyzing the data that had been collected in the Cambridge and Pittsburgh studies than to spend more time planning a new study; I had funding in 1984-87 to interview the Cambridge Study males at age 32 (Farrington 2003b).

Not everyone was happy with the enormous investment in longitudinal studies by federal agencies in the 1980s. Travis Hirschi and Mike Gottfredson, in particular, were unhappy and they published several critiques of longitudinal and criminal career research (e.g., Gottfredson and Hirschi 1986), which Al Blumstein, Jackie Cohen, and I replied to (Blumstein et al. 1988). It is not pleasant to be criticized but, as they say, you can't make an omelette without breaking a few eggs. I am very happy for criminologists to read these exchanges and make up their own minds.

While the 1980s were an enormously exciting time for me, because I really felt at the cutting edge of incredible new developments, my effort was also enormous. Between 1987 and 1989, I crossed the Atlantic once a month on average. What with being away for a week and spending another week in preparation, all my British activities were compressed into two weeks every month. In one month (I think it was May 1989) I went back and forth to the United States three times for three successive weekend meetings, and on two of these weekends (in Boston) the hotel had a (false) fire alarm in the middle of the night, which caused us all to stand outside in our night wear. While observing the likes of Al Reiss in pajamas had a certain novelty, I was happy to withdraw from the NIJ-MacArthur initiative in particular in order to have a less frantic life!

Diversifying in the 1990s

Unfortunately, my hopes of a less frantic life were not fulfilled. In the 1990s, my life became frantic in many different ways, as my research became more and more diversified. In 1990, I became President of the British Society of Criminology for a three-year term. I really don't know why I have agreed to be Chair and President of so many committees and organizations; these things seemed noble ventures at the time but usually consumed a lot of time that would have been better spent on research. I agreed to be Chair of the Division of Criminological and Legal Psychology of the British Psychological Society in 1983-85 because of a messianic zeal to advance the cause of psychological criminology, but in many other cases I have been too reluctant to say no to people (as with this chapter!).

Anyhow, I had what still seems a good idea for my Presidential address in 1990, which was to link up national victim surveys, police, court, and prison data to put numbers and probabilities into the flow diagram from crimes committed to persons imprisoned. The first national British crime victimization survey was for the year 1981 and the third was for 1987, so by 1990 it was possible not only to put numbers in the flow diagram but also to track trends over a reasonable (six year) time period.

Filling in the flow diagram for England and Wales was complicated enough, but I then decided to compare England and the United States in collaboration with Pat Langan (see, for example, Langan and Farrington 1998).

This required a huge amount of work to assemble comparable data for the two countries, and I made many trips to Washington. Fortunately, Pat and his colleague Larry Greenfeld have a great sense of humor, although how they could crack jokes all the way from their homes in Columbia, Maryland to Washington at 6.00 a.m. was bewildering to me. I was feeling pretty zonked out at that time in the morning but they started work at 7.00 a.m. every day!

I had also attended a number of meetings organized by Per-Olof Wikström (P-O) in Sweden. P-O is a brilliant researcher and he had great ideas to integrate developmental, ecological, and situational theories and approaches. I am delighted that he is now a colleague of mine in Cambridge. P-O and I had already collaborated to compare criminal careers of males in Stockholm and London, finding many similarities but also intriguing differences (Farrington and Wikström 1994). P-O was much more of a cross-national comparative researcher than I was (he had thought very deeply about all the issues arising), and so he suggested that we should compare the flow diagrams in England, the United States and Sweden over time. After a lot of work, we compared all three countries between 1981 and 1991 (Farrington et al. 1994).

This cross-national comparative study has now been extended to 8 countries between 1981 and 1999: virtually all countries with repeated large-scale national victimization surveys during this time period. However, this effort has become incredibly complex and incredibly time consuming, with increasing difficulty in obtaining

> ### Lessons
>
> *Although we cautioned against drawing causal conclusions from correlations, some politicians apparently used our research to justify their argument that "prison works."*

comparable data and increasing difficulty in herding squirrels; one of our colleagues seemed to be trying to sabotage the venture all the time rather than trying to follow our template for comparable data collection in each country.

A major problem with this venture is our finding that crime rates decreased in the United States between 1981 and 1991 and increased in England and Sweden; and that the risk of legal punishment increased in the United States and decreased in England and Sweden (Farrington et al. 1994). Although we cautioned against drawing causal conclusions from correlations, some politicians apparently used our research to justify their argument that "prison works" (although our findings focused on risk not severity). Because many criminologists feel very strongly that increased imprisonment is undesirable, they had to attack our research (e.g., Doob and Webster 2003). We thought that it was extremely unfair to criticize our research because of the use made of it by others. I can understand the desire to "shoot the messenger," but I would prefer to have critiques of what we wrote, not of other people's faulty and distorted interpretations of what we wrote.

A much happier venture in the 1990s was the OJJDP Study Groups that Rolf Loeber and I chaired, on serious and violent juvenile offenders (Loeber and Farrington 1998) and very young offenders (Loeber and Farrington 2001). In each case, we had meetings every 3 months over a two-year period with very high quality researchers, who buckled down to writing original and excellent chapters rather than trotting out the same old rubbish. Rolf Loeber was always cheerful, optimistic, and enthusiastic, and Buddy Howell, Howard Snyder, and Gail Wasserman (in particular) were wonderful role models who produced brilliant chapters on time and helped to socialize the whole group to produce excellent contributions.

As I said, my research diversified considerably in the 1990s, into shoplifting experiments (e.g., Farrington 1999), citation analysis (e.g., Cohn et al. 1998), bullying (e.g., Baldry and Farrington, 1998), and offender profiling (e.g., Farrington and Lambert, 1997), just to give a few examples. All of these seemed good ideas at the time, and I liked to pursue what seemed interesting. Of course, I also continued the Cambridge Study (with a major follow-up at age 48) and the Pittsburgh Youth Study. One noteworthy cross-national comparative paper was a systematic comparison of childhood risk factors for delinquency in London in the 1960s and Pittsburgh in the 1990s (Farrington and Loeber 1999). Again, while most risk factors showed surprising replicability, there were some interesting differences between the two settings.

I also diversified geographically, for example publishing a paper on victimization in the Caribbean (Painter and Farrington 1998) and on early pre-

dictors of childhood aggression in Mauritius (Raine et al. 1998). Adrian Raine offered to fly me to Mauritius, because I was a consultant on his follow-up project, but I preferred to join him in sampling the nightlife in Santa Monica! I have particularly spent time in the last few years analyzing the Seattle Social Development Project (e.g., Farrington et al. 2003), and Seattle has now supplanted Washington as my second most frequent U.S. destination after Pittsburgh. This is because I am a great admirer of David Hawkins and Rico Catalano and their wonderful array of intervention projects.

I was vice-chair of the National Academy of Sciences panel on violence (Reiss and Roth 1993). This produced very good state-of-the-art reviews—especially in the four supplementary volumes—but was not as exciting as the criminal career panel, when we really thought that we were developing a new paradigm. Partly, this reflected the personalities of the chairs. Al Blumstein was very much a convergent thinker who almost had to be wrestled to the ground to deflect him from moving in a straight line towards a solution. Al Reiss, on the other hand, was very much a divergent thinker who could always think of some new interesting digression at a higher level of complexity. He really wanted to write an encyclopedia, not a report! I collaborated with Al Reiss in writing a paper on the important but surprisingly neglected topic of co-offending (Reiss and Farrington 1991), but if it had not been for me this paper would never have been brought to closure. Al was keen to search criminal records of co-offenders of co-offenders in order to build up a picture of all the co-offending networks in London!

I also enjoyed collaborating with medical and public health researchers like Jon Shepherd of Cardiff and Fred Rivara of Seattle (see e.g., Shepherd and Farrington 1993; Rivara and Farrington 1995). I think criminologists have a lot to learn from medical and public health researchers, and these collaborations seemed to me to involve real science! I have also enjoyed collaborating with psychiatrists such as Jeremy Coid (e.g., Farrington and Coid 2003) because of their commitment to scientific evidence.

Also in the 1990s, I became the first President of the American Society of Criminology based outside North America and simultaneously was President of the European Association of Psychology and Law. I really enjoyed being President of the ASC especially; this was a labor of love, and I have very happy memories of the meeting that I presided over in Toronto (and especially of the fabulous Royal Suite at the Royal York Hotel!). Of course, I felt that the ASC was a bit like an ocean liner that would only be turned slightly and slowly; I was happy to keep a very successful society ticking, with few changes during my year of office.

Intervention Research

Finally, I have been drawn more and more into intervention research in the last 10 years, rather than naturalistic longitudinal follow-ups. I have always been interested in interventions (e.g., my review of randomized experiments: Farrington 1983) and our OJJDP Study Group books focused on both funda-

mental and applied research, trying to be relevant to practitioners and policy-makers as well as scholars. Also, I have completed several reviews of the literature on developmental or risk-focused prevention (e.g., Farrington 1994, 2002), and edited a book on crime prevention (Tonry and Farrington 1995).

In 1998, Larry Sherman persuaded me to join the crime prevention program at the University of Maryland to help update the very influential Maryland report on the effectiveness of crime reduction methods (see Sherman et al. 1997, 2002). This was generously funded by Jerry Lee, who is perhaps the greatest benefactor that criminology has ever seen. Larry Sherman is one of the most incredibly intelligent and incredibly energetic people I have ever met. I feel tired just thinking about him! He also created the Academy of Experimental Criminology to foster randomized experiments in criminology, and I was President of this from 2001-03.

I have been delighted to learn the technology of systematic reviews and meta-analysis in the last few years, and I agreed to chair the Campbell Collaboration Crime and Justice Group in 2000 (Farrington and Petrosino 2001). The aim of this Group is to carry out systematic reviews of the literature on the effectiveness of criminological interventions, and to make these reviews available to everyone (scholars, policy makers, practitioners, the mass media, and the general public) on the Internet. Again, it is a noble cause that has consumed a huge amount of my time so far, and we have not really got it very far off the ground yet! However, I

> ## *Lessons*
>
> *Do not give up...the successful people are those who keep trying*

have very much enjoyed chairing the steering committee meetings (of 16 scholars from 13 countries) because the venture seems exciting and worthwhile and the people are very pleasant and stimulating.

I have also learned that intervention research is pretty controversial compared with the community of longitudinal researchers who are quite gentle and very agreeable in general. For example, excluding studies from systematic reviews on the grounds that they are methodologically inadequate is guaranteed to annoy people, but it has to be done. People were similarly annoyed by our citation research when they found that they were not highly cited. However, I was surprised to receive a bitter and sarcastic critique of what I thought was a straightforward description of how to evaluate a community-based intervention program (see Farrington 1997; Pawson and Tilley 1998).

Inspired by my ex-student Brandon Welsh, I have carried out a number of cost-benefit analyses of the effectiveness of interventions (see, for example, Welsh et al. 2001). The argument that $7 is saved for every $1 expended on a program seems to be very persuasive with politicians and policy makers who do not understand other measures of effect size. In collaboration with my colleague Kate Painter, I have carried

out a number of evaluations of the effects of improved street lighting on crime (e.g., Painter and Farrington 2001). Again, I was amazed to find that these were bitterly criticized by the International Dark-Sky Association and the Campaign for Dark Skies, who are lobbying for less street lighting in order to see the stars. I have had to waste a lot of time answering these criticisms.

Conclusions

Looking back on my career, I have had the great luxury of being able to pursue my interests, which have been very wide-ranging, in Great Britain and North America. I have rather neglected my European activities in this chapter, which for example include five years on the Scientific Advisory Board of the Netherlands Institute for the Study of Crime and Law Enforcement, trying to persuade them to mount a "crime shuttle" longitudinal study that could include various sub-studies after it got off the ground. I am currently exploring collaborative opportunities in Australia, since my daughter and her family have gone to live there!

While I have written many papers, I feel that I should have written more books. In particular, I should have written a research monograph that really flushes out my theory and subjects it to numerous tests. I am moving in that direction (e.g., Farrington 2003a) and so I may yet complete this.

Regarding advice to students; I am torn between advising them to pursue whatever interests them (as I have) and advising them to specialize in one particular area. Perhaps I should have specialized more in longitudinal research. I would not advise them to "chase the bucks," although maybe that is realistic advice in today's demanding climate. Maybe I should also advise them to choose non-controversial topics so they won't get embroiled in answering unreasonable criticism from people who are determined to find every possible fault for ideological reasons. Other good advice is: Do not give up. Everyone has setbacks such as having a journal article or a grant proposal rejected, but the successful people are those who keep trying. Also, the most precious commodity is time, so it is highly desirable to maximize time available for research. This is especially true if you are contemplating cross-national collaborations, which in my view require travel to meetings (e.g., for discussions to achieve comparability).

Perhaps the best advice, certainly for those who are contemplating comparative cross-national studies, is to choose your collaborators carefully. I have collaborated with a very large number of people from many different places, and the vast majority of these collaborations have been absolutely terrific. You can achieve a lot more, and learn a lot more, in collaboration than alone. And by the way: It is a great life as a criminologist!

Selected Bibliography

Baldry, A.C. and D.P. Farrington. 1998. "Parenting Influences on Bullying and Victimization." *Legal and Criminological Psychology* 3:237-254.

Blumstein, A., J. Cohen, and D.P. Farrington. 1988. "Criminal Career Research: Its Value for Criminology." *Criminology* 26:1-35.

Blumstein, A., J. Cohen, J.A. Roth, and C.A. Visher, eds. 1986. *Criminal Careers and "Career Criminals."* Washington, DC: National Academy Press.

Cohn, E.G., D.P. Farrington, and R.A. Wright. 1998. *Evaluating Criminology and Criminal Justice.* Westport, CT: Greenwood Press.

Doob, A.N. and C.M. Webster. 2003. "Sentence Severity and Crime: Accepting the Null Hypothesis." In *Crime and Justice*, vol. 30, edited by M. Tonry. Chicago: University of Chicago Press.

Farrington, D.P. 1979a. "Experiments on Deviance with Special Reference to Dishonesty." In *Advances in Experimental Social Psychology,* vol 12, edited by L. Berkowitz. New York: Academic Press.

———. 1979b. "Longitudinal Research on Crime and Delinquency." In *Crime and Justice*, vol. 1, edited by N. Morris and M. Tonry. Chicago: University of Chicago Press.

———. 1983. "Randomized Experiments on Crime and Justice." In *Crime and Justice*, vol. 4, edited by M. Tonry and N. Morris. Chicago: University of Chicago Press.

———. 1994. "Early Developmental Prevention of Juvenile Delinquency." *Criminal Behaviour and Mental Health* 4:209-227.

———. 1997. "Evaluating a Community Crime Prevention Program." *Evaluation* 3:157-173.

———. 1999. Measuring, Explaining

and Preventing Shoplifting: A Review of British Research." *Security Journal* 12(1):9-27.

———. 2002. "Developmental Criminology and Risk-Focused Prevention." In *The Oxford Handbook of Criminology,* 3d ed., edited by M. Maguire, R. Morgan and R. Reiner. Oxford: Oxford University Press.

———. 2003a. "Developmental and Life-Course Criminology: Key Theoretical and Empirical Issues." *Criminology* 41:221-255.

———. 2003b. "Key Results from the First 40 Years of the Cambridge Study in Delinquent Development." In *Taking Stock of Delinquency,* edited by T.P. Thornberry and M. D. Krohn. New York: Kluwer/ Plenum.

Farrington, D.P., L. Biron, and M. LeBlanc. 1982. "Personality and Delinquency in London and Montreal." In *Abnormal Offenders, Delinquency, and the Criminal Justice System,* edited by J. Gunn and D.P. Farrington. Chichester: Wiley.

Farrington, D.P. and J.W. Coid, eds. 2003. *Early Prevention of Adult Antisocial Behaviour.* Cambridge: Cambridge University Press.

Farrington, D.P., K.O. Hawkins, and S.M. Lloyd-Bostock, eds. 1979. *Psychology, Law and Legal Processes.* London: Macmillan.

Farrington, D.P., D. Jolliffe, J.D. Hawkins, R.E. Catalano, K.G. Hill, and R. Kosterman. 2003. "Comparing Delinquency Careers in Court Records and Self Reports." *Criminology* 41(in press).

Farrington, D.P. and S. Lambert. 1997. "Predicting Offender Profiles from Victim and Witness Descriptions." In *Offender Profiling: Theory, Research and Practice,* edited by J. L. Jackson and D.A. Bekerian. Chichester: Wiley.

Farrington, D.P., P.A. Langan, and P-O. H. Wikström. 1994. "Changes in Crime and Punishment in America, England and Sweden between the 1980s and the 1990s." *Studies in Crime and Crime Prevention* 3: 104-131.

Farrington, D.P. and R. Loeber. 1999. "Transatlantic Replicability of Risk Factors in the Development of Delinquency." In *Historical and Geographical Influences on Psychopathology,* edited by P. Cohen, C. Slomkowski, and L.N. Robins. Mahwah, NJ: Lawrence Erlbaum.

Farrington, D.P., L.E. Ohlin, and J.Q. Wilson. 1986. *Understanding the Controlling Crime: Toward a New Research Strategy.* New York: Springer-Verlag.

Farrington, D.P. and A. Petrosino. 2001. "The Campbell Collaboration Crime and Justice Group." *Annals of the American Academy of Political and Social Science* 578:35-49.

Farrington, D.P. and P-O. H. Wikström. 1994. "Criminal Careers in London and Stockholm: A Cross-National Comparative Study." In *Cross-National Longitudinal Research on Human Development and Criminal Behavior,* edited by E.G.M. Weitekamp and H-J. Kerner. Dordrecht, Netherlands: Kluwer.

Gottfredson, M. and T. Hirschi. 1986. "The True Value of Lambda Would Appear to be Zero: An Essay on Career Criminals, Criminal Careers,

Selective Incapacitation, Cohort Studies, and Related Topics." *Criminology* 24:213-233.

Langan, P.A. and D.P. Farrington. 1983. "Two-Track or One-Track Justice? Some Evidence from an English Longitudinal Survey." *Journal of Criminal Law and Criminology* 74:519-546.

———. 1998. *Crime and Justice in the United States and in England and Wales, 1981-96.* Washington, DC: U.S. Bureau of Justice Statistics.

Loeber, R. and D.P. Farrington, eds. 1998. *Serious and Violent Juvenile Offenders: Risk Factors and Successful Interventions.* Thousand Oaks, CA: Sage.

———. 2001. *Child Delinquents: Development, Intervention and Service Needs.* Thousand Oaks, CA: Sage.

Loeber, R., D.P. Farrington, M. Stouthamer-Loeber, T.E. Moffitt, A. Caspi, H.R. White, E.H. Wei, and J.M. Byers. 2003. "The Development of Male Offending: Key Findings from 14 Years of the Pittsburgh Youth Study." In *Taking Stock of Delinquency,* edited by T.P. Thornberry and M.D. Krohn. New York: Kluwer/Plenum.

Painter, K.A. and D.P. Farrington. 1998. "Criminal Victimization on a Caribbean Island." *International Review of Victimology* 6:1-16.

———. 2001. "The Financial Benefits of Improved Street Lighting, Based on Crime Reduction." *Lighting Research and Technology* 33:3-12.

Pawson, R. and N. Tilley. 1998. "Caring Communities, Paradigm Polemics, Design Debates." *Evaluation* 4:73-90.

Raine, A., C. Reynolds, P.H. Venables, S.A. Mednick, and D.P. Farrington. 1998. "Fearlessness, Stimulation-Seeking, and Large Body Size at age 3 Years as Early Predispositions to Childhood Aggression at age 11." *Archives of General Psychiatry* 55:745-751.

Reiss, A.J. and D.P. Farrington. 1991. "Advancing Knowledge about Co-Offending: Results from a Prospective Longitudinal Survey of London Males." *Journal of Criminal Law and Criminology* 82:360-395.

Reiss, A.J. and J.A. Roth, eds. 1993. *Understanding and Preventing Violence.* Washington, DC: National Academy Press.

Rivara, F.P. and D.P. Farrington. 1995. "Prevention of Violence: Role of the Pediatrician." *Archives of Pediatrics and Adolescent Medicine* 149:421-429.

Sampson, R.J. and J.H. Laub. 1993. *Crime in the Making.* Cambridge, MA: Harvard University Press.

Shepherd, J.P. and D.P. Farrington. 1993. "Assault as a Public Health Problem." *Journal of the Royal Society of Medicine* 86:89-92.

Sherman, L.W. 1992. *Policing Domestic Violence: Experiments and Dilemmas.* New York: Free Press.

Sherman, L.W., D.P. Farrington, B.C. Welsh and D.L. MacKenzie, eds. 2002. *Evidence-Based Crime Prevention.* London: Routledge.

Sherman, L.W., D. Gottfredson, D. MacKenzie, J. Eck, P. Reuter, and S. Bushway. 1997. *Preventing Crime: What Works, What Doesn't. What's Promising?* Washington, DC: U.S. Office of Justice Programs.

Tonry, M. and D.P. Farrington, eds. 1995. "Building a Safer Society:

Strategic Approaches to Crime Prevention." *Crime and Justice*, vol. 19. Chicago: University of Chicago Press.

Tonry, M., L.E. Ohlin, and D.P. Farrington. 1991. *Human Development and Criminal Behavior: New Ways of Advancing Knowledge.* New York: Springer-Verlag.

Welsh, B.C., D.P. Farrington, and L.W. Sherman, eds. 2001. *Costs and Benefits of Preventing Crime.* Boulder, CO: Westview Press.

West, D.J. and D.P. Farrington. 1977. *The Delinquent Way of Life.* London: Heinemann.

Wilson, J.Q. and G.C. Loury, eds. 1987. From Children to Citizens, vol. 3: *Families, Schools, and Delinquency Prevention.* New York: Springer-Verlag.

Chapter 7

From Criminology to Applied Comparative Criminology: Life as a Peripatetic Comparativist

Matti Joutsen

Director, International Affairs,
Ministry of Justice,
Finland

The EU is the archetypal example of how some decisions that were once taken nationally (or even locally) are now taken internationally.

1. Prologue: Cultural Blinkers and Criminology

Studying such value-laden concepts as crime and criminal justice is difficult in any country. Although everyone seems to have their own clear idea about what crime is and what should be done about offenders, the picture gets blurred when you get down to specifics. You may condemn thieves with righteous abandon, but then you remember how you yourself broke into your neighbor's house when you were a kid just for the thrill of getting back at that old grouch. You may say with righteous indignation that economic offenders should go to prison, but then mentally discount otherwise morally upright people such as yourself who do some light fiddling on

their tax returns. And while everyone knows that drunk drivers who run over people in the street are really the scum of the earth, you may then remember how you were really quite lucky driving home from that late party. You had joined your good friend in finishing off a bottle or two, celebrating the fact that she had finally got that raise she so richly deserved. On your way home, you were lucky you were such a good driver and could swerve to avoid that young kid who darted out onto the street from behind a parked car, chasing his ball.

Analyzing the concepts of crime and criminals becomes even more difficult when we try to free ourselves from our cultural blinkers. One of the more invisible straitjackets on the development of hypotheses in criminological (or, in general, sociological) research is the status quo. Living in one society makes us accustomed to certain values and certain ways of doing things. We take it for granted that certain behavior should be criminalized and certain other behavior should be allowed, that the police, the prosecutors and the courts should act in certain ways, and that the attitudes we happen to have towards offenders and victims are "natural."

Imagine a colleague at work in Tokyo, Moscow or Buenos Aires on a criminological research project, for example on the prevention of thefts or vandalism by juveniles. He or she will also be working on the basis of an unconscious set of assumptions and values. Consequently, the research approach and the policy recommendations will probably differ from that of a New York criminologist. The Tokyo researcher might be interested in effective social control, the Muscovite might focus on technical means of prevention, and the resident of Buenos Aires might underline "social defence" and rehabilitation.

Even if the New Yorker were aware of what his or her foreign colleagues were doing, their efforts might be dismissed without a second thought. After all, the reasoning might go, Japan, the Russian Federation, and Argentina are so different socially, culturally, legally, and economically that what goes on there has nothing to do with everyday reality in the United States. Why bother to find out what goes on elsewhere?

The answer is that the researcher who ignores alternative paradigms unnecessarily hampers his or her own

work. The researcher should try to find out how other societies define, experience, and deal with crime because this may provide new insights into what is going on in his or her own country. There are some 200 countries in the world, all with quite different backgrounds and criminal justice systems. Even so, they all have to deal with basically the same crime and crime control problems: how do you prevent theft, rape, or robbery, what do you do with the offender, and how do you help the victim?

Both the similarities and the differences that the researcher comes across may prove beneficial in the formulation of new theories and the development of policy recommendations. For example, similarities between systems may inspire a new recognition of problems in one's own country. The researcher who goes to a foreign country does so with fresh eyes, and may find many things to criticize. After all, it is always easier to find fault with your neighbor than with yourself. If there are other basic similarities between the two countries, it is quite possible that there is the same scope for criticism in both countries.

Differences, in turn, point to the fact that other societies survive and may even flourish with, for example, a less repressive control strategy or with a lesser fear of crime. The researcher is then led to more fundamental questions of structure and approach. How have the Japanese been able to manage with a prison rate that is only a fraction of that of most other industrialized countries? Why is it that crime is not seen to be a problem in Switzerland despite the fact that it appears to have at least as many robberies and drug offences as its neighbors?

2. Growing up on Two Continents

I got into the business of comparative research by living a comparativist life. By the time I graduated from high school (i.e., comprehensive school) in Finland in 1970, my family had jumped back and forth several times between Finland and the United States. Partly because of the confusion of living in two different countries, half of our family preferred to speak in English, the other half in Finnish (and whenever she had the chance, my mother spoke in Swedish). Having lived at a dozen different addresses on two continents during my first sixteen years (according to Wolfgang's research, frequent changes of residence constitute a factor that correlates with delinquency), I had become used to moving from one cultural paradigm to another. It became obvious to me that not only do people speak different languages, but they can think in different ways, value different things, and use different criteria when deciding how society should be organized.

On graduation, and very much on a whim, I entered the political science faculty at the University of Helsinki. This was a period of considerable radicalism in Europe (as well as the United States), with student demonstrations and sit-ins being par for the course. The political science faculty was almost by definition one of the focal points for activism—against the Vietnam War, against apartheid in South Africa, for independence for Biafra, for radical feminism, whatever. Finland is a relatively small country, and student life

had a strong international flavor. Although at that time there were very few foreign students in Finland (perhaps the incomprehensibility of Finnish or those long, cold winter nights helped convince foreigners that there were warmer, more accommodating academic environments in, say, Paris or Bologna), Finnish students closely followed developments elsewhere in the world, whether in Berlin, Berkeley, or Beijing.

Again very much on a whim, I decided to write my undergraduate thesis on corruption. Spiro Agnew was very much in the news, and at the Faculty I had become fascinated with muck-racking journalism from the early part of the nineteenth century. I spent my last summer before graduation doing background research on the subject at the Library of Congress in Washington, D.C. Upon graduation, I was at a loose end. A degree in political science is all very well, but then (as now) it wasn't a meal ticket. I desultorily applied for various jobs through the summer of 1974, but few employers were interested in expertise in corruption, even if the candidate was bilingual in English and Finnish. I had a steady job at a bookstore and was able to pick up nice pocket change as a freelance translator and interpreter, but that didn't seem very attractive as the basis for a career (however, it did give me great respect for the mental gymnastics required of professional interpreters. The ability to convey a message in a different language, when the listeners often have a different mind-set, has quite aptly been described as applied schizophrenia).

Toward the end of the summer, I

saw an advertisement for a job opening as a researcher at the National Research Institute of Legal Policy. This institute, which is part of the Ministry of Justice of Finland, had just been created by Professor Inkeri Anttila, one of the foremost professors of criminal law in Finland, and a pioneer in criminology and victimology. She was an anomaly in Finland: the first woman to enter the law faculty in Helsinki (way back in 1933), the first woman to graduate from the faculty, the first woman to become a professor at the faculty, and the first person in Finland to seriously start thinking about the causes of crime and about the operation of criminal justice.

By coincidence, at that time she had become interested in expanding the horizons of her research institute by becoming more involved in international cooperation. One way to do this was by translating the research reports and other materials produced by the research institute into English. I seemed to meet the implicit job description, and I became, by default, a budding criminologist. Not surprisingly, my first job—in addition to translations—was to write a report on the potential for corruption in Finland (not by any means an easy job. According to consistent data from Transparency International, Finland is one of the least corrupt countries in the world).

For the next eight years, I did studies on a range of topical issues in Finland, such as child offenders, bank robberies, violent crimes, prosecutorial decision-making, and solitary confinement. The studies were often commissioned by the Ministry of Justice, and related to a proposed change of legisla-

tion. Some, such as the studies on prosecutorial decision-making and on solitary confinement, formed the Finnish contribution to wider comparative studies (at the same time, following much prodding by Professor Anttila, I returned to the University, this time to the law faculty to get my law degree).

3. Getting my Feet Wet: Applied Comparative Studies within the United Nations Framework

Soon after joining the research institute, at the end of the summer of 1975, I was asked by Professor Anttila to join her on a trip to Geneva. The United Nations organizes global congresses on crime and criminal justice every five years, and the Government of Finland had already decided on who was to represent it. With my nose buried in books and primary source research data, I had only dimly noted that there was once again a governmental crisis in Finland. A caretaker government had been formed, one that was expected to be in office only a few months, until the political parties were able to decide on the composition of the new Government. The new Prime Minister had decided that Inkeri Anttila would be a suitable Minister of Justice for the duration—which would extend over the time for the UN Congress. Obviously, she would head the delegation going to Geneva. At the last minute, one of the members was unable to come, and I was tapped to fill the empty slot. Since I had no recognized abilities to speak of, my position was that of secretary to the delegation.

There I was, fresh out of the university, wandering the august halls of the

Lessons

While being polite and respecting the importance of the occasion, you had to try to get an edge over other players by emphasizing your own importance.

Palais de Justice in Geneva, a novice among Ministers of Justice, Supreme Court justices, and other senior officials from some 120 countries around the world. The United Nations, of all organizations in the world, is very aware of the symbolism of power. Since 1975 happened to be International Women's Year, it was self-evident that the congress would be presided over by a woman. This, in turn, called for protocol; not just any woman would do. It had to be the head of a delegation, and so the field was narrowed down to two: the Minister of Justice of Bulgaria, and the Minister of Justice of Finland. Whether this was due to the Cold War or to Professor Anttila's prominent international reputation as a scholar, the powers that be wasted little time in putting her name forward, and she was elected President of the Congress by acclamation.

Suddenly, Professor Anttila became the key person at the Congress and was courted by the many delegations that wanted to advance their own agendas in criminal policy. As her secretary, I soon found myself playing apprentice diplomat and criminologist—and loving it. A Norwegian criminologist, Thomas Mathiesen, in a fascinating analysis of United Nations Congresses (based on participatory observation, in the best

tradition of his compatriot, Johann Galtung), has concluded that such international Congresses are steered by five norms of behavior: the politeness norm, the importance norm, the self-importance norm, the consensus norm, and the my-country norm. Perhaps ever since the so-called waltzing congress in Vienna in 1813, international conferences have tended to be a mixture of substance, diplomacy, and one-upmanship. Mathiesen's analysis bolsters this view. While being polite and respecting the importance of the occasion, you had to try to get an edge over other players by emphasizing your own importance. And while trying to reach consensus on all of the issues at hand, you had to be careful to ensure that your own country's interests remained protected (according to Mathiesen, when applied to UN crime congresses, this means that you should never agree to anything that would require your country to change its own criminal policy).

Professor Anttila was therefore faced with the problem of getting some 120 fractious national delegations to agree on a number of resolutions and decisions on matters ranging from capital punishment to imprisonment, and from corruption to the victims of crime. By tradition, all matters had to be decided by consensus, and the trick was to find the proper wording so that everyone could agree, and no one would lose face. As her English-speaking secretary, I found myself in a position of being able to make suggestions as to what synonym or, to use insider parlance, constructive obfuscation would make everyone happy (or, to use a phrase so often used by chairpersons in the United Nations context, to make

<table>
<tr><td>

Lessons

Concepts that I had grown to understand as self-evident in the Finnish system...were not at all self-evident in other systems.

</td></tr>
</table>

everyone equally unhappy).

The end result was that the 1975 UN Crime Congress in Geneva was able to adopt quite a number of resolutions. Among its more important results was the approval of a "Declaration on the Protection of All Persons from Torture," and the development of a code of ethics for law enforcement officials—both of which had been the subjects of extensive, at times rancorous, debate.

At that time, Professor Anttila was also a member of the United Nations Committee on the Prevention of Crime and the Treatment of Offenders, a small committee of 26 members who met every other year to discuss crime prevention and criminal justice on a global basis. Although she was quite fluent in English, she found it useful to bring an English-speaker along to the sessions of the Committee to act as her gofer and colleague, when needed. My initial contact with the United Nations in 1975 was therefore sustained.

Sustained, and then rapidly broadened. At that time, the United Nations had already set up a regional institute in Japan and another one in Costa Rica. Europe was ripe for a regional institute of its own, one that could at the same time bridge the gap between western and eastern Europe. Professor Anttila

had her own research institute and was an internationally recognized and respected criminologist. It was not difficult at all to come up with the idea that a neutral country such as Finland (as opposed to two other candidates, Poland and Spain) would be a suitable venue for the European regional institute.

Using her contacts, Professor Anttila was able to get the Finnish Government to agree to fund such an institute, even if on a rather modest scale. The new institute, established in 1982, became known as the European Institute for Crime Prevention and Control, affiliated with the United Nations. Since that was quite a mouthful to say when answering the phone, it was referred to as HEUNI. To staff the institute, she brought in a small crew from her research institute. She became the Director, and I took on the job of senior researcher. In addition, there were two researchers and an office secretary—not very many people to start work on a subject as deep and wide as European crime prevention and control!

4. Diving in Head First: Working at an Institute for Comparative Criminal Justice

Moving from a Finnish research institute to a regional United Nations institute led to a fast-growing realization that people in different countries simply didn't do things in the same way. Concepts that I had grown to understand as self-evident in the Finnish system—that victims should play a major part in criminal trials, that governmental policy should be determined by experts on the basis of rational arguments and not by sectarian politics, and that the police, prosecutors, and courts should use common sense when dealing with victims and offenders—were not at all self-evident in other systems.

HEUNI was very much an institute for comparative criminology and criminal justice. Back in the 1960s, the first regional institute connected with the United Nations crime prevention and criminal justice program had been established in Japan: the United Nations Asia and Far East Institute for the Prevention of Crime and the Treatment of Offenders, or UNAFEI for short. A few years later, an institute for the Latin American and Caribbean region was established in Costa Rica. Both institutes were established in regions where, with a few rare exceptions, criminology was a relatively poorly developed discipline. The two host countries, Japan and Costa Rica, sought to encourage national and comparative criminological research throughout the region and to promote best practice in criminal justice in order to solve problems that were common to all the countries: juvenile delinquency, corruption, various forms of organized crime, prison overcrowding, and so on.

The situation in Europe at the beginning of the 1980s was quite different. western Europe had been the birthplace of criminology, and towards the end of the 1980s many western European countries—in particular the United Kingdom, Netherlands, Germany and the Nordic countries—were hotbeds of theory and research. The Council of Europe fostered very close co-operation in criminology and criminal justice. For these reasons, it would have been rather presumptive of a small

institute stuck up north in Helsinki to try to promote good research in, say, Cambridge, Copenhagen, or Cologne.

On the other hand, many people realized (but few people said aloud) that there was a lack of good criminological research and open debate in much of Eastern Europe. It is true that at the beginning of the 1980s Poland, Czechoslovakia, and Yugoslavia had good researchers and a relatively supportive research climate. However, the debate in many other countries—in particular Albania, Bulgaria, East Germany, and Romania—was dogmatic and sterile. Almost everywhere, it was difficult for researchers to get even basic data on crime and criminal justice. Even more, the few criminologists at the time had great difficulties in getting access to the international literature, or participating in international criminological meetings.

HEUNI therefore took upon itself the task of promoting contacts between Eastern and Western Europe, and introducing good criminal justice practice in East Europe. At the same time, HEUNI worked at identifying good Eastern European criminological research and best practices, and making them more widely known in Western Europe.

One way in which this was done was by selecting a topic, preparing a background paper for comment by a number of recognized experts throughout Europe, and then bringing all the contributing experts together to work out a report with recommendations. HEUNI did this in respect of a number of topics, ranging from crime prevention, the exercise of prosecutorial discretion, and non-custodial sanctions, to computerization in the criminal justice system.

HEUNI also soon found that it had another, more global role within the United Nations framework. HEUNI effectively functioned as a channel for bringing European (and to a large degree also North American) criminology and criminal justice debate to the attention of the rest of the world. As HEUNI's senior researcher and, on Professor Anttila's retirement in 1987, its director, I took on the job of trying my best to distill the "state of the art" of European and North American criminological research on a number of topics. In several cases, these papers served as the basis for United Nations global reports, or contributed directly to United Nations resolutions.

The first such report emerged from a rather inauspicious beginning. A telegram was delivered to HEUNI which when unfolded extended all the way down to the floor. The gist: the UN Secretariat wanted HEUNI to prepare a review of all research around the world on juvenile delinquency and submit it to the Secretariat within three months. After checking to make sure that the calendar didn't say it was April 1st, I sat down with my closest colleague to list the reasons why we couldn't take on the task: three months was an absurdly short time, juvenile delinquency is a vast subject and perhaps the most heavily researched subject in criminology; going through the literature would require an army of researchers fluent in at least all six working languages of the United Nations (and preferably quite a number more, besides); almost all research is specific to the culture in which it was carried out and cannot, and should not, be generalized; it is practically impossible for outside researchers to assess how well individual research projects had been done, and how valid and reliable their results were; and so on.

I was therefore rather surprised that when I brought the telegram to Inkeri Anttila, garnished with all my reasons for not doing it, she answered that we have to at least try. She argued that not only was this the first time that we had been asked by the Secretariat to provide them with specific assistance, it was also gratifying that the Secretariat wanted to inject criminological expertise into the UN program—something that had been sadly lacking for years.

At least we were allowed a bit more time to complete the project; six months instead of three. Even then, we were able to pull together information on research around the world almost solely because over the years Inkeri Anttila had developed an excellent network of contacts. We were therefore able to send out an SOS on the grapevine throughout the world community of criminologists: "please summarize what the research in your country says about the causes, circumstances, consequences and response to juvenile delinquency, in 500 words or less"(well, we didn't put it quite that bluntly, but I can readily imagine the frustration of any self-respecting researcher in the United States or England, for example, when asked to provide a *Reader's Digest* synopsis of a library's worth of research).

The result, SecretaryGeneral report A/CONF. 121/11, was submitted to the Seventh United Nations Congress on the Prevention of Crime and the Treatment of Offenders, held in Milan,

Italy in 1985. It provided the background documentation for a research workshop at the congress on juvenile delinquency, a first for the United Nations crime congresses. The tradition was continued at the next United Nations congress five years down the line, when together with Dr. Ugljesa Zvekic of the United Nations Interregional Crime and Justice Research Institute, I prepared a world-wide review of experiences with the use of non-custodial sanctions (Secretary-General report A/CONF.144/13) and helped to organize a research workshop on the theme. By the 1995 crime congress, Secretary-General reports on criminological research, and the organization of research workshops had become institutionalized, and several such workshops were organized at that and each subsequent congress.

5. Victimology and Victim Policy

Back at HEUNI, the first topic selected for a European-wide project was victim policy. By the early 1980s victimology had become a popular topic in a few Western European and North American countries, but was almost unheard of throughout most of the rest of Europe. Preparing that first HEUNI research conference sparked my own interest in victimology and victim policy. At that time, work had begun on the drafting of what was to become the United Nations "Basic Principles of Justice for Victims of Crime and Abuse of Power," a declaration that was adopted by the General Assembly in 1985. I became heavily involved in the drafting work, and used the experience in preparing my doctoral dissertation on "The Role of the

Victim of Crime in European Criminal Justice Systems" (Helsinki 1987).

There were several eminent persons already working on the draft, among them Irvin Waller (featured in a separate contribution to this volume), LeRoy Lamborn, Cherif M. Bassiouni, and the indefatigable Irene Melup of the United Nations Secretariat. What Mathiesen had said about a conflict between a consensus norm and a my-country norm was once again borne out in practice. The drafting involved a lengthy struggle between victimologists, victim activists and idealists on one hand, and lawyers on the other. Lawyers as a group appear to have an innate reluctance to change the legal system. Part of this may be due to a deeply entrenched belief that their legal system, if not the best in the world, is at least uniquely suited to their country. If victims did not have a say in court, if there were no special victim-oriented services, if there was no victim-offender mediation, if there were no special arrangements designed to ensure that victims are compensated for their loss, then there must be a reason for this. "Don't tinker with the system" was a phrase we heard all too often, from lawyers from a number of countries around the world.

Perhaps a typical example of this attitude concerns the issue of violence against women. I recall many discussions with senior governmental experts and practitioners from Central and Eastern European countries, people who were utterly convinced that the fact that their legislation included provisions making assault against a pregnant woman a particularly serious offence was sufficient proof that their laws did

Lessons
I realized once again that there is no one single ideal criminal justice system and what works in one country may not necessarily work in another.

not need any more tinkering. And besides, they would add (usually after a few rounds of drinks), everyone knows that we men in (insert name of country here) love our women, and always treat them with respect (an eminent Latin American lawyer had a different reaction to a United Nations proposal that countries pass special legislation protecting women against violence. He angrily argued that the law should not distinguish between the two sexes—and that if such a proposal were to be adopted he would insist on a parallel proposal calling for special legislation protecting men against violence).

A second difficulty we faced was that in many respects and in perhaps all criminal justice systems there remains a large gap between the "law on the books" and the "law in action." Lawyers appeared to assume that any problems that exist can be solved through simple acts of Parliament. Once a law is enacted, the problem should be solved. Regrettably, however, in many cases the resources do not exist that are required to ensure that the new legislation is understood by the practitioners, and that it is implemented in the way in which it had been intended.

In the process of working out the final draft, I realized once again that there is no one single ideal criminal jus-

tice system and what works in one country may not necessarily work in another (especially—but not only—Americans seemed to be convinced that many features that are typical of their criminal justice system, such as plea bargaining, the jury system, local control of the police and so on, are the answer to the prayers of other criminal justice systems). The needs and interests of victims can, in fact, often be met in different ways which could be called functional equivalents. Two examples are the right of allocution and the question of compensation to the victim.

In respect of the right of allocution (the right of the victim to express his or her views and concerns to the court), I had implicitly assumed that the Finnish approach was the ideal (*Mea culpa*). In Finland, the victim has in effect many of the same powers as does the prosecutor to introduce evidence, call witnesses, ask questions, comment on the different aspects of the proceedings, call for a specific punishment and, finally, appeal the decision. It was quickly pointed out to me that the other countries in the world were not willing to give the victim such powers, and indeed I was told that in many cases the victim would not want such powers. It turned out that many other countries had other ways of allowing the victim to be heard—acting as a subsidiary prosecutor, joining the criminal procedure as a civil plaintiff to claim damages, filling out a victim impact statement, and so on. All could be seen, on a general level, as functional equivalents in respect of the right of allocution.

In respect of compensation from the offender, Germanic countries, with their Adhesionsverfahren, and French-based countries, with their action civile, have found different ways to make it possible for the victim to claim damages. The United Kingdom, with its compensation order, has found a completely different approach, one that does not require giving the victim any standing in the procedure itself.

6. Comparing What Shouldn't be Compared: Working on International Statistics on Crime and Justice

Another standing contribution of HEUNI to United Nations deliberations consists of our analysis of the results of surveys of crime trends and criminal justice systems. Every now and then, the United Nations has asked its member states to report on developments in the amount of crime and in the operation of the criminal justice system. The first survey, covering 1970 through 1975, had been a trial run, and the results were never analysed.

HEUNI entered into the picture when the second survey (covering 1975 through 1980) was underway, and we decided to see if we could help with the analysis of the results from the European and North American regions, for which the data appeared to be relatively reliable (here, of course, "relatively" is used very loosely), and could be flushed out with victim surveys and other data. Each successive report was able to improve on the quality of the data and the type and depth of analysis. Gradually, these reports also served as models for the reports from other regions.

In international comparisons, just as in national research, statistics have become a primary source of data. Many countries obligingly publish regular comprehensive statistics on the operations of their police, courts, and prisons. Some statistics (such as the Nordic court statistics) go back to the beginning of the 1800s, thus providing ample material and long time series for researchers. By far the most widely used statistics are the police statistics.

The dangers of using statistics as a reflection of crime and crime control in one's own country are well documented. We all know that reported crime is not the same as actual crime, that the statistics have been developed for administrative purposes and not to satisfy research interests, and that the vagaries of changing laws, statistical practice and the personal idiosyncrasies of the various persons involved in defining criminal incidents make it difficult to draw any conclusions when comparing statistics from different areas or different times. We also know that the crimes punished under the criminal laws of different countries (the crimes that are usually noted in the statistics, and even in popular debate) do not necessarily have the greatest economic consequences for society. Such statistics focus on the thieves and muggers in our society and not on those in a more privileged position, the crimes of whom may easily have a more far-reaching effect.

Working with the United Nations surveys showed that international comparisons can be even more rife with misunderstandings. Not only are there the same problems as with statistical comparisons within one's own country, there are a considerable number of other problems thrown in.

There are the practical problems of availability and language. Although more and more countries are now publishing statistics on a regular basis, it is often difficult to obtain a copy of the most recent statistics. Since these statistics are in the language of the country in question and the tables often refer to the different penal provisions only by number, the researcher will have considerable problems in identifying the data he or she is interested in.

It is also obvious that the legal definitions of offences vary considerably from one country to the next. For example, "assault" may be an independent category in some jurisdictions while others may not consider an incident to be an assault unless it results in bodily injury. Another example is the extent to which negligence affects the determination of criminal responsibility. A third is the extent of criminalizations. Matters that in some country are dealt with by regulatory authorities (such as labor safety) may be police matters in another country. Acts that are criminalized in some countries (e.g., the possession of drugs, certain sexual behavior, gambling, abortion, and euthanasia) may be tolerated elsewhere.

Also procedural differences may affect what is entered into the statistics (and how the data are entered). It is not always the police and the lower courts that deal with crime: certain cases may be dealt with by special investigatory and adjudicatory bodies. Minor offences may be dealt with by a simplified procedure. Traffic offences provide a good example: in many countries, they are dealt with by a special branch of the police or through a special procedure, and are not considered "offences" (and

thus not included in the statistics). In other countries they are considered offences. If solely the figures given in the statistics are compared, the latter countries will have grossly inflated figures; after all, the bulk of offences *are* minor violations.

Another procedural difference relates to the extent to which discretion is permitted, either formally or informally. Some countries require the various criminal justice agencies to proceed with any prima facie case (the principle of legality). Other countries may allow more discretion as to when measures are necessary (the principle of opportunity), which in practice may mean that further measures are waived in a large portion of the cases. Yet another example: in many countries, the police and prosecutor will not proceed with certain types of cases unless the victim has requested that measures be instituted. If no such request is made, the case will generally not be recorded as an offence.

Related to this is the issue concerning at what stage decisions are made that are reflected in the statistics. For example, the police may record a crime at the time it is reported or at the conclusion of the police investigation. If the first option is used the statistics will include a number of cases in which the investigations later show that no offence actually took place, or that the person reporting the offence had erred as to its classification. Also, the police appear to have a built-in tendency to overestimate the seriousness of an offence when it is first reported: what the police first classify as attempted homicide the court may well choose to classify as aggravated assault or an even lesser offence.

The statistical classification of crime also varies widely. To take the example of theft, it may or may not include theft of a motor vehicle, it may or may not include simple and aggravated theft as defined by the law of the jurisdiction in question, and it may or may not include shoplifting.

Next, the rules for counting offences vary. The statistics of some countries include attempts, others do not. Some count offenders, others count offences; some count each separate incident in a series of offences while others record a series as one unit. One particular difference that has led to considerable confusion is the unit used for the successful outcome of police investigations: some countries use "arrests," other countries "reported offences," and still other countries "cleared offences." Any comparison between statistics based on such different units would be quite misleading.

The comprehensiveness of the statistics varies. Some countries include only the major criminal offences. Others include not only the petty offences, but also violations of tax laws, alcohol laws, administrative regulations and similar subsidiary legislation. Consequently, any comparisons should be made between specific categories of offences, and not to the aggregate.

All of this was clearly brought home to me when I attended a conference in Riyadh, in preparation for the United Nations crime congress in 1985. A researcher from a developing country had been asked by the United Nations to prepare a report on the connection

Lessons
The statistics of some countries include attempts, others do not. Some count offenders, others count offences; some count each separate incident in a series of offences while others record a series as one unit.

between development and crime (presumably, what was expected of him was a reflection on whether the modernization thesis developed by Durkheim, Shelley, and Clinard and Abbott held true). The researcher had confidently turned to the Interpol statistics on crime reported to the police. By dividing this total by the size of the population he had calculated what he referred to as the percentage of criminals in the population. I was bemused to note that, on this basis, Finland was by far the most "criminal" in the world: 8 percent of the population were classified as criminals. (For the record, the researcher himself came from the country that he claimed was the least criminal of all, with only .019 percent criminals. Even after I listed several of the statistical difficulties noted above, he remained unshaken in his conviction that I come from a very criminal country and, who knows, maybe I was a closet criminal myself. It wasn't until I started to point out that among the other "top ten criminal countries" were countries such as Fiji, St Kitts-Nevis, New Zealand, and the Antilles, that also other conference participants began to realize that there was something odd about the results.)

7. Changes in the Rules of the Game: Going From National to Intergovernmental Policy

Although the Research Institute and HEUNI were both financed by the Ministry of Justice, and as a staff member I was a Finnish civil servant, I still remained at arm's length from the rest of the Ministry. The Research Institute sought to provide a criminological basis for decisions made by the Ministry, but the Ministry itself did not seek to influence the research. And HEUNI provided a wealth of comparative data on a number of topics, which often came in handy in the day-to-day work at the Ministry. Otherwise, the only contacts I had with the Ministry (asides from the annual Christmas party) were when I was officially representing the Ministry at the annual sessions of the United Nations Commission, or at the United Nations crime congresses held every five years.

That began to change after I had completed my dissertation and spent a year with the United Nations crime program in Vienna. By accident, it seems, the powers that be in the Ministry of Justice realized that they had at their disposal an English-speaking criminologist who had at least a passing knowledge of how different European criminal justice systems worked. From 1996 to 1998, I was tapped to become a member of a small project group established by the Council of Europe together with the European Union, to advise Central and Eastern European countries on the prevention and control of corruption and organized crime. The project group sought to assess the extent of corruption linked with organized crime, review the capacity of the criminal justice system to control it and propose what steps the Governments in question should take. I was assigned the responsibility for recommending various legislative and practical measures to Estonia, Latvia, Lithuania, and the Russian Federation (an assignment I continue to regard as the height of presumption; fortunately, the four Governments in question took my suggestions with good grace).

Some assignments seem to naturally lead to similar challenges elsewhere. In 1997, the United Nations set up a committee to prepare a United Nations Convention on Transnational Organized Crime, and I found that being able to draft in English and keep copious notes on the hard disk of a laptop helped me (and the Committee) to no end. Also in 1997, I was sent by the Finnish Government to become a member of a group established by the European Union to develop a "European Union Action Plan on Organized Crime." Parallel to this, I represented the Ministry of Justice of Finland at meetings of the European Union's Multidisciplinary Group, which had the responsibility for overseeing implementation of the Action Plan. When Finland's turn came to hold the Presidency of the European Union, I took leave of absence from HEUNI to work directly for the Ministry of Justice. After that period, the international aspect of the Ministry's work was reorganized, and I left HEUNI to become Director of International Affairs. In that role, I became responsible, among other duties, for overseeing Finland's mutual legal assistance in civil and criminal matters, and our cooperation with countries near and far, from the Baltic countries and the Russian Federation, to China, Canada, and the United States.

In a short space of time, I therefore found myself working, variously, with the United Nations, the Council of Europe, and the European Union. Each has rather different styles of work, due largely to their different institutional traditions, their constituencies, and their goals. As it turned out, this period was one when their work was being fundamentally transformed.

The United Nations prior to 1991 was a relatively leisurely environment in which to work. It almost seemed as if the United Nations crime prevention and criminal justice program focused largely on producing resolutions. The work seemed to consist of finding the proper wording that would make everyone happy or at least satisfied with the fact that they had once again made the world safer without having to change their own criminal policy. This attitude began to change when many Governments realized that responding for example to international organized crime required more substantive cooperation. I had the happy experience of working together with senior governmental representatives from Germany, the USSR, the United Kingdom and the United States in planning a complete restructuring of the UN program. The new program, especially with its emphasis on drafting multilateral agreements, proved to be more hard-nosed in getting countries to align their policies. When needed, it could even work remarkably quickly. The Convention on

Transnational Organized Crime was drafted from start to finish in less than three years, followed by the Convention on Corruption, which was drafted in only two years (it is not at all uncommon for draft conventions to languish in committees for decades before finally being adopted).

The Council of Europe also produced a great number of resolutions and recommendations, but these were usually very carefully drafted by experts from the countries concerned, experts who more often than not understood that there can, indeed, be different ways to solve the same problem. These same experts were often involved also in the drafting of Council of Europe conventions which continue to have a considerable amount of influence even beyond Europe. When I began working with the Council of Europe, it was undergoing rapid expansion, taking in many new member states from Central and Eastern Europe. More and more of its work was being directed at assisting these new member states in overhauling their legal systems.

Of these three intergovernmental organizations, however, it was the European Union that underwent the greatest transformation over the past ten years. The genesis of the European Union lay in the "Common Market," a historic attempt to bring peace to Europe by strengthening their commercial and industrial interdependence. Decisions were to an increasing extent made on the intergovernmental level, not by the individual member states.

Prior to the 1990s, this intergovernmental decision-making in the European Union had not extended to the

Lessons

In the aftermath of September 11, 2001, the EU decided that, with a three-month deadline, it would draft and adopt decisions on a so-called EU arrest warrant (essentially, rapid surrender of fugitives from one EU country to another), and on the definition of terrorist offences.

work of the police or to criminal and procedural law. These were regarded as inherently national matters. The growth of terrorism and organized crime had resulted in some informal arrangements for cooperation, and to international discussions on policy, but that was basically as far as it went.

Shortly before I began going to European Union meetings, however, something more fundamental was changing, and with it the practical role of comparative criminology and criminal justice. The leisurely pace that I had been used to during the 1970s and the 1980s in the UN and in the Council of Europe no longer held true. One of the tenets of the European Union (EU) is that there should be free movement of persons, goods, services, and capital from one member state to another. Paperwork at national borders is kept to the bare minimum, and usually travellers are simply waved through. It should not have been a surprise that when people can freely cross borders, so can crime. A number of combined factors—the growing economic integration within the EU, the economic

and political changes in Central and Eastern Europe, the social changes throughout and beyond Europe, and the blessings and curses brought by advanced technology—all increased the political imperative to respond to international organized crime (and terrorism). Within the European Union, this meant that mechanisms had to be found to ensure that all the member states took more or less the same measures.

Accordingly, back in 1992, "home and justice matters" (basically, police, border control, immigration, and criminal justice matters) were brought within the mandate of the EU. The focus was on serious cross-border crime, such as drug trafficking, money laundering, and terrorism. During the first few years, there tended to be more "soft law" decisions (such as recommendations) than "hard law" decisions, decisions that theoretically require each member state to review its legislation and practice in line with a certain standard. As time passed, there were fewer recommendations and more "hard law," and the pace of change began to accelerate.

This was shown perhaps most clearly in the aftermath of September 11, 2001, when the EU decided that, with a three-month deadline, it would draft and adopt decisions on a so-called EU arrest warrant (essentially, rapid surrender of fugitives from one EU country to another), and on the definition of terrorist offences. Half of my working hours during those three months was spent either in meetings in Brussels or on an airplane to or from Brussels. It was no longer a question of finding a soft wording that everyone could accept and that no one actually needed to apply. Every word that we drafted would have a direct impact on the legislation and practice of fifteen countries (twenty-five, if you count the then-candidate countries—primarily from Central and Eastern Europe—which joined the EU in May 2004).

8. Applying Comparative Criminology and Criminal Justice in Europe Today

And what do these changes have to do with comparative criminology and criminal justice? Quite a bit—and they bring us back to the cultural blinkers mentioned at the start of this contribution.

The EU is the archetypal example of how some decisions that were once taken nationally (or even locally) are now taken internationally. The EU is dealing on the intergovernmental level with a wider range of offences and aspects of procedure, in greater detail, and at a faster rate. In the debates in which I have participated in the EU (and in the Council of Europe and the UN as well), there have been countless examples of the clash between the "consensus norm" and the "my-country norm" referred to above. Regrettably, given the underlying political motivation—responding to international organized crime and terrorism—the debates in the EU have favored (in what I have come to see as the EU version of the highest common denominator) the more punitive approach. Attempts to suggest lower sentencing levels, or to exempt certain behavior from the scope of EU decisions will almost inevitably be greeted with an indignant "but that sends the wrong political message."

The dynamics, therefore, appear to favor an increasingly uniform—and punitive—concept of criminal justice across much of Europe. This concept rests on EU decisions on the criminalization of a growing range of offences. Police and prosecutorial authorities in the different countries are being provided with fairly broad powers to investigate offences, and to have more effective international cooperation. Future EU decisions will probably be directed also at the sentencing powers of the courts, seeking to ensure that the sentences that are imposed are more or less the same in the different countries—and in practice on a high level (it is symptomatic that the EU decisions on sentences are firmly based on high levels of imprisonment. It seems as if, for many of those participating in the drafting of these decisions, non-custodial sanctions are beyond the pale).

It is here that a comparativist approach is necessary. The scenarios that most of those drafting EU decisions on crime and justice (and comparable decisions in other intergovernmental bodies) seem to have in mind are the serious cross-border crimes. In practice, however, the decisions will also affect the run-of-the-mill offence and suspect/offender within each member state, in which case the practical application may be overly harsh.

These drafters also appear to work under two assumptions: first, that these punitive measures are necessary in their own country, and second, that these measures are ipso facto needed in every other member state as well, so that there is no "weakest link." The often-repeated argument here is that if the level of punishment in country A is less than in country B, all the potential offenders in B will travel to A to commit their offences—an argument that I find difficult to accept, no matter whether the offence is money laundering or terrorism.

The comparativist is needed to identify both the similarities and the differences in the operation of criminal justice systems, and in particular to point out that there are different ways to respond to any given set of problems. Trying to impose a uniform response in different countries, with different cultural, economic, and social circumstances may not lead to the desired outcome. Moreover, requiring that all criminal justice systems apply the same patent medicine to the same symptoms will make innovation more difficult. If drug trafficking must be punished (for example) by a minimum maximum of ten years, this would not seem to allow treatment-oriented measures as an alternative to imprisonment.

Fifty years ago, Finland had one of the highest rates of imprisonment in Europe: more than 200 prisoners per 100,000 in population. When comparativists such as Inkeri Anttila noted that other countries—such as Sweden, Denmark, and Norway—were able to manage their criminal justice system with a prisoner rate that was one-third of Finland's rate, they were able to get Finland to change its policy on imprisonment. The result was one of the greatest success stories in prisons: a sustained decrease in the prison population to today's rate of some 70 prisoners per 100,000.

Europe—as well as the United States and other countries around the world—is grappling with serious crime problems. At the same time, the large number of criminal justice systems in the world provides a laboratory for testing different policies. Comparativists are needed to analyze how the different systems work, and explain to policymakers how their own criminal justice system can be improved. No system is perfect, not even in "my country."

Selected Bibliography

Joutsen, M. 1986. "Research on European Juvenile Delinquency: A Survey of Research and Research Results." In *Papers on Crime Policy*, publication no. 7. Helsinki: HEUNI.

_____. 1987. *The Role of the Victim of Crime in European Criminal Justice Systems*, publication no. 11. Helsinki: HEUNI.

_____. 1987. "Civilizing the Control of Economic Crime: Alternatives to the Criminal Justice System in the Prevention and Control of Economic Crime." In *UNAFEI Resources Material Series,* no. 31, Tokyo: UNAFEI.

_____. 1988. "Listening to the Victim: The Position of the Victim in European Criminal Justice Systems." *Wayne Law Review* 34(1):95-124.

_____. 1988. "The Role of the Prosecutor: The United Nations and the European Perspectives." In *The Role of the Prosecutor*, edited by J.E. Hall Williams. Avebury, England.

_____. 1989. "Research on Victims and Criminal Policy in Europe." In *Crime and Criminal Policy in Europe*, edited by Roger Hood. Proceedings of a European Colloquium, Oxford: Oxford University

Press.

_____. 1990. *Non-Custodial Sanctions in Europe: Regional Overview* (together with Norman Bishop). Research Workshop on Alternatives to Imprisonment. Rome: UNICRI.

_____. 1990. *Research Workshop on Alternatives to Imprisonment* (in collaboration with Ugljesa Zvekic). Rome: UNICRI.

_____. 1990. "Expanding the Use of Non-custodial Measures." In *UNAFEI Resources Material Series*, no. 38, Tokyo: UNAFEI.

_____. 1991. "Changing Victim Policy: International Dimensions." In *Victims and Criminal Justice*, vol. 52/2, edited by Gunther Kaiser, Helmut Kury, and Hans-Jörg Albrecht. Max-Planck Institute for Foreign and International Law, Freiburg-im-Breisgau.

_____. 1994. "Victim Participation in Sentencing in Europe." *International Review of Victimology* 3 (1/2):57-67.

_____. 1994. "Victimology and Victim Policy in Europe." *Criminal Justice Europe* 4(5):9-12.

_____. 1995. "The Potential for the Growth of Organized Crime in Central and Eastern Europe." In *Contemporary Issues in Organized Crime*, edited by Jay Albanese. New York: Monsey.

_____. 1996. "Managing International Technical Assistance Projects in Criminal Justice: Experiences with Assistance in the Reform of Crime Prevention and Criminal Justice in Central and Eastern Europe." Paper no. 8, Helsinki: HEUNI.

_____. 1998. "Surveying Transnational Organised Crime: The HEUNI Report on Organised Crime around the World." In *Surveying Crime: A Global Perspective*, edited by Anna Alvazzi del Frate, Oksanna Hatalak, and Ugljesa Zvekic. Proceedings of the International Conference, Rome, November 19-21, United Nations Interregional Crime and Justice Research Institute.

Kristiina Kangaspunta, Matti Joutsen, and Natalia Ollus, eds. 1998. *Crime and Criminal Justice in Europe and North America, 1990-1994.* Publication no. 32, Helsinki: HEUNI.

Chapter 8

Restorative Justice in Comparison

Lode Walgrave

Faculty of Law,
Catholic University of Leuven,
Belgium

Differences are best observed through commonalities.

An Autobiographic Introduction

Restorative justice (RJ) basically is a bottom-up approach to the settlement of the aftermath of a crime (Zehr 1990; Van Ness and Strong 2002; Braithwaite 2002). It is oriented towards repairing as much as possible all harm, suffering, and social unrest caused by that crime. The most appropriate way of achieving this is an informal deliberative process that includes all parties with a stake in the aftermath of the offence. For many leading scholars, this inclusionary process is the key characteristic of RJ. However, along with others, I prefer an outcome-based approach. I consider RJ primarily through the outcome it pursues, the best possible reparation of the

harm. If deliberative processes appear to be unfeasible, possible coercive judicial sanctions also should, as much as possible, serve reparative goals (Walgrave 2003). My outcome approach may be partly because of my European continental background.

I became aware of the RJ movement in the early 1990s. My academic career began toward the end of the 1960s. I joined the university as an assistant to a professor in criminology who was a psychiatrist. At that time, I also worked as a psychologist in a clinical observation center for juveniles, referred by a youth court judge. Our recommendations would orient the judge's decision. The Belgian juvenile justice system was, indeed, one of the most treatment oriented systems in the world (Walgrave 2002c). In 1972, a translation of an article by B. Alper appeared in the Belgian *Revue de Droit Pénal et de Criminologie* (Journal of Penal Law and Criminology). Based on the U.S. Supreme Court decision in "re Gault," the article criticized the lack of juridical safeguards for juveniles in most rehabilitation oriented juvenile justice systems. It was an eye-opener for me to learn that children and juveniles, in fact, only have "second hand" rights (meaning that their rights only were operational through their parents or judges).

I became one of the juvenile justice critics in Belgium and in Europe. In the slipstream of the then dominant critical and radical criminology, I enthusiastically crossed swords with justice officials, judges, and clinical workers in articles and debates. Whereas Belgian officials sometimes proudly stated that the Belgian juvenile justice was a justice system without punishment, I replied that the system, in fact, imposed punishments without justice, to the detriment of the underclass. Moreover, I believed in Martinson's "nothing works" (in those days things seemed so much simpler).

But there was a problem: rejecting the treatment orientation in juvenile justice risked handing the juveniles over again to the traditional punitive response. And that was not my ideal. At that time, a Belgian youth court judge, Jan Peeters, regularly gave serious juvenile offenders the choice between being placed in a closed facility for juveniles or fulfilling a number of hours of voluntary work in a public agency. He explicitly told them that it was meant as a kind of compensation for what they

---

> ### Lessons
>
> *Restorative justice (RJ) basically is a bottom-up approach to the settlement of the aftermath of a crime...It is oriented towards repairing as much as possible all harm, suffering, and social unrest caused by that crime.*

---

did to the community. His practice served to fuel my ideas about alternative justice for young offenders. In 1981, I wrote an article in the *Tijdschrift voor Familie- en Jeugdrecht* (Journal for Family and Youth Justice) under the title "Justice in front of Youth Crime: Restrain and Reparation, but no Punishment?" Intuitively, I took a "reparative" position, without knowing about developments in other countries.

My *Aha Erlebnis* came in April 1991, at a NATO Advanced Research Workshop on "Conflict, Crime and Reconciliation," in Il Ciocco, Italy (Messmer and Otto 1992). Among the 40 participants were Burt Galaway, Joe Hudson, Rob Mackay, Tony Marshall, Dean Peachy, Christa Pelikan, Mark Umbreit, Elmar Weitekamp, and Martin Wright. We spent a week in the marvelous Tuscan mountains debating from early in the morning until deep into the night. The hotel bar was as inspiring as were the formal meetings. A kind of conspiracy feeling emerged. I heard for the first time the phrase "restorative justice" and saw the contours of a movement based on a fundamentally different view of doing justice. My earlier intuition fitted into the ideas being shared, and the venue served to broaden and deepen my understanding and ideas around the concept of RJ.

While the process-based view on RJ was manifest in Il Ciocco, because of my limited command of the English language, I still did not fully understand the concept of RJ. I understood the word "justice" in restorative justice primarily as institutionalized justice, as defined by the justice system. But for most participants, "justice" had a primarily moral connotation. That is, the feeling of "doing" justice. The Dutch language (my native tongue) has two distinct words for justice. The justice system is *gerecht*, whereas moral justice is *rechtvaardigheid* or *gerechtigheid*. So, I viewed RJ primarily as a way to escape the unfruitful rehabilitation-punishment dilemma in juvenile justice and a possible ground for a constructive judicial response to youth crime, which would better respond to legal requirements (Walgrave 1994, 1995). I launched the idea in Belgium, and I was, to my knowledge, the first to use the word *Herstelrecht*, as a Dutch translation of "Restorative Justice" (Walgrave 1992).

In 1996, the Flemish Fund for Scientific Research granted the funding for the International Network for Research on Restorative Justice for Juveniles. It provided the opportunity to set up a network for meetings and the establishment of a series of international conferences with the most authoritative scholars in RJ from all over the world. It has been a permanent learning process in international and comparative work. Together with my American colleague Gordon Bazemore, I edited *Restorative Justice for Juveniles* (Bazemore and Walgrave 1999). We proposed a "maximalist" version of RJ that would go beyond the voluntary process-

es and would also include coercive judicial sanctions in view of reparation. The long and deep discussions with Bazemore and the meetings and e-mail correspondance with the contributors (John Braithwaite, Ray Corrado, Barry Feld, Susan Guarino, Russ Immarigeon, Mara Schiff, Klaus Sessar, Mark Umbreit, Daniel Van Ness, and Elmar Weitekamp) confronted me with different approaches to social life and to justice, and I began to suspect that my focus on juridical aspects might be too narrow, and typically continental European. There appeared to be more at hand than just a ground for juvenile justice reform.

The second International Conference on Restorative Justice took place in Fort Lauderdale in 1998. The majority of the participants were advanced American practitioners and activist academics. I experienced it as a "high mass" of RJ and communitarianism but missed the critical approach. I was especially puzzled by what was, in my view, a communitarianist "overacting" and the over-simplified opposition to the state institutions. Who will represent the community in RJ meetings? According to which procedures will the initiatives be conducted? How should abuses of power in the name of community be prevented? The general answer to these questions that the "community works" did not sound convincing.

Critical voices also came from the jurists' side. Feld criticized the lack of due process guarantees in restorative processes (1999). Von Hirsch expressed skepticism with regard to proportionality in RJ (1998). Probably more than the mainstream RJ advocate, I was impressed by these criticisms and found it a constructive challenge.

At the third international conference in Leuven (November 1999), Paul McCold attacked the inclusion of coercion in our maximalist view on RJ and presented his "holistic vision." Our heavy but friendly debate touched a key question, whether RJ can remain a "purist," voluntary, process-based option, or must it make its hands dirty and include judicial interventions, oriented though, as much as possible, toward constructive reparation. The debate convinced me that a crucial task for RJ is to find a combination of the needs for informal inclusionary processes in genuinely restorative actions, with the need for formalized checking of power in any democratic state. I began to understand that mainstream Americans really have a different perspective on the relation between the citizen and the state (McCold 2000; Walgrave 2000).

For the first two months of 2000, John Braithwaite arranged a stay for me with his team at Australia's National University in Canberra. The visit enabled me to see the value of the republican theory of criminal justice as presented a few years earlier (Braithwaite and Pettit 1990). I was especially seduced by its central "dominion" concept because it seemed to complete the state bound legal and institutional guarantees with the community-based assurance and trust in fellow citizens. Maybe it could help to bridge the differences in approach between the Anglo-Saxon communitarianists and the European legalists.

I then also made a trip to New Zealand. In ACT, New South Wales (Australia) and in New Zealand, I saw conferencing practices. I was especially intrigued by the original New Zealand Family Group Conference because of the genuine police role and because of its inclusion in the procedure instead of being a kind of diversion. It used the flexibility of a common law regime, which is difficult in the legalistic civil law regimes on the European continent. It helped me to see the benefits of a common law system and to relativize the strict legalism of our civil law approaches.

Despite common philosophical grounds, RJ appears to be developing differently around the world. A major line seemed to divide these divergences: the countries in the Anglo-Saxon tradition advance the deliberative community-based approaches, whereas the countries on the European continent are more sensitive to the legal issues in the development of RJ schemes. Let me explain now, in more detail, how I see these differences. I shall first offer a very short overview of the differences in the developments, and then point to some possible explanations.

Developments in Restorative Justice

The Victim Offender Reconciliation Program in Kitchener (Ontario) in the mid-1970s is often mentioned as the origin of modern RJ practices. It inspired the spread of VOM (Victim Offender Mediation) and VORP (Victim Offender Reconciliation Programs) in Canada and the United States. It was probably Albert Eglash who first launched the phrase "restorative justice" in 1977 (Van Ness and Strong 2002). Besides victim movements, religious and communitarianist groups were among the driving forces, to the extent that RJ is often linked closely to "community justice" (Bazemore and Schiff 2001). Also important were the aboriginal movements, claiming more respect for the way they traditionally dealt with crime and conflict in their midst (Jaccoud 1998; La Prairie 1995). As a consequence, the United States (and to a lesser degree Canada) has a dense, but not very orderly field of projects with different degrees of integration into the judiciary, different reaches, great flexibility, and creativity based on local community initiatives. Legislation, especially for juveniles, provides spaces for implementation of restorative practices, but is not compulsory on the way that should happen (Walgrave forthcoming).

In Europe, developments were partly influenced by what happened across the Atlantic as well as by "critical criminology" in the 1970s, which stigmatized traditional criminal justice as being socially destructive and, even, a tool in the hands of the ruling class to suppress the labor classes. The alternatives proposed by the so-called "abolitionists" were basically restorative (De Haan 1990; Blad 1996). Practice was focused on versions of victim offender mediation. From the beginning, Europeans tried to insert the experiments within the criminal justice system, or at least in close contact with it (European Forum 2000; Weitekamp 2001). Most current projects have a clear relation to the judicial system, and the procedures and processes are more or less determined (Walgrave forthcoming).

In 1989, New Zealand introduced Family Group Conference in its Children, Young Persons, and Their Families Act, largely influenced by Maori tradi-

tions. The FGC practice was increasingly seen in the restorative perspective, under the influence of the international RJ movement (Morris and Maxwell 2003). Braithwaite, his team, and the practices they supported pulled conferencing in Australia into the restorative stream (Braithwaite and Mugford 1994 Braithwaite 1999). Aboriginal traditions, legalization, practice, and academia have together contributed to identifying RJ in Australasia with conferencing, which is increasingly seen, internationally, as the most genuine restorative practice (McCold 2003).

The several models of RJ practices, mediation, sentencing circles, conferencing, community reparative boards, community service, have predominantly been invented and tried out in Canada, the United States or in New Zealand. Some of these practices made their way to the European continent via Australia and the United Kingdom. Broadly speaking, RJ practices first occurred in countries with common law tradition, and appeared later only in European countries based on a civil law regime. The variety of current restorative practices in mainland Europe is comparatively small. In recent years, I have advanced three possible partial explanations.

Analyzing the Differences

The first possible explanation consists of the peculiarities of the two law regimes. The second is the underlying difference in the relation between the community and the state. The third is the contribution of active indigenous population groups.

Common Law vs. Civil law

RJ that promotes the inclusion of the parties with a stake in the response to the offence is a challenge for the traditional state monopoly in the reaction to crime. Changing this is more difficult where this monopoly is strongly centralized and consolidated by legal dispositions, as in the civil law regimes.

I gradually became aware how important the margins of the common law system in the Anglo-Saxon countries are to allow for restorative experiments. For example, I witnessed the police conducting conferences in ACT and saw the use of police discretion in New Zealand as they participated in conferencing, and I was convinced that such police involvement did not lead to a loss of democracy in these societies.

The opportunity principle prevails in common law while the legality principle rules the civil law on the European continent. Each agent in the common law system, police, prosecuting agencies, judges, has been assigned a broad discretionary power to interpret how to act in the public interest and to implement the measure they think most appropriate. This is not the case in the civil law countries where the legality principle prevails. Police, for example, are bound to mention any case to the public prosecutor. Most legalistic countries also reduce public prosecutor's power to choose not to prosecute in court.

I have learned that the flexibility within common law is crucial for RJ. Carrying out mediation or conferencing outside of the judicial system, within the community for example, or their

inclusion, as police "cautionings" for example, in the procedure is easier. It is not as necessary for the outcomes to respond to legal checks as it is under the civil law regimes. Hence, community service could be invented as an alternative sanction by creative judges and magistrates.

Like most of my European colleagues, I was a neophyte in learning about the use of RJ ideology within a criminal justice system context. Most countries on the European continent have (at least more so than in most common law countries) legislated in detail what procedural phase and for which cases restorative schemes can be implemented, and under what conditions (Walgrave forthcoming). For some prominent European scholars, juridical concerns are a reason to be very skeptical against RJ as a whole (Groenhuysen 2000; Albrecht 2001). For others it is a reason to explore the possible legal frame of RJ, as they consider this one of the most crucial themes to broaden its scope (Eliaerts and Dumortier 2002; Walgrave 2002a).

My intense confrontation with colleagues working in a common law environment has convinced me that the flexibility of such an environment brings it closer to the reality of public life and community, but also that it includes risks of more populist influences and a weaker offer of legal safeguards. The civil law system in which I am working includes more strict legal safeguards. It is much more rigid. Comparative work helps to elucidate benefits and risks, and leads to trials to improve the existing systems.

Community vs. "Citoyenneté"

At the 1998 conference in Fort Lauderdale, I was confronted with a deep belief in community and a mistrust of the state. Community was presented as the niche of informal interactions based on spontaneous human understanding, as opposed to the formal institutionalized society with its rules and rigid communication channels (Pranis and Bazemore 2000). Restorative practices were seen as a way to preserve community life, and to prevent it from shifting toward alienation (Bazemore and Schiff 2001).

I had, like most Europeans, great difficulty in coming to terms with the community notion. No doubt that an informal climate of mutual understanding is crucial for restorative practices, but the confidence in community seemed rather naive, even dangerous. Communities are not always available, nor are they good per se (Pavlich 2001; Walgrave 2002b; Crawford 2002). Most Europeans wonder how to ensure that communities develop good practices and how to check their processes and outcomes with legal standards.

After my discussion with Paul McCold (2000) I realized that our differences in our approach to community rest upon differences in concepts on the relation between the state and the citizen (see also van Swaaningen 1997). In the European vision, the power is concentrated in the authorities that are the holders of the *vox communi*. People are supposed to be fully represented by the democratic state institutions. There is no contradiction between the state and community: the state is the formalization of the community, or the community

of communities. Criminal law is a part of the state's control system over its citizens. Strict legalistic civil law offers state protection against the abuse of power by the state and by the most powerful in community.

I have learned that Anglo-Saxons are more skeptical against state power and feel less represented by the state. This appeared most clearly in the United States where the state is often presented as a bureaucratic taxing machine, an opponent to freedom, located at an unbridgeable distance from real life. In America, the state's institutions with regard to education, medical care, social services, and allowances are reduced. Often, the lack of public provisions is partly compensated by communities based on religion, territory, or ethnicity. This may be why Americans foster the idea of community as opposed to "government" or "state," and are less sensitive to the absence and/or exclusionary anomalies of many communities. Criminal justice in Anglo-Saxon countries is not designed to defend the state's interests, but to preserve the individual citizens' need for justice and peace, so that they can live their lives as they want. Common law regimes offer greater flexibility to respond to these individual needs and individualized problem situations.

Lessons

The "citoyenneté," as the French call it, the citizenship, is a crucial good, which includes all rights and protections offered by the state, but obligations as well.

Europeans also are sensitive to the state's bureaucratic and formalist excesses, but they see it as a tool to be improved. The state is seen a safeguard against abuses of power by the most powerful. The "citoyenneté," as the French call it, the citizenship, is a crucial good, which includes all rights and protections offered by the state, but obligations as well. Communitarianism often has a pejorative meaning in the French society because it is suspected that it promotes the selfish interests of the community to the detriment of the general citizens' interest in the state. Not that Europeans love paying taxes, but they basically consider it a contribution to collective life.

All of this explains why most of my Anglo-Saxon and especially American colleagues saw RJ primarily as a way to extend the reach of the "living" community in dealing with the aftermath of an offence and to push back the interference of formal state power. I still feel skepticism toward this seemingly uncritical reliance on informal communities to settle the consequences of the offence and look for models to locate restorative schemes under state guaranteed supervision, while preserving the benefits of informal deliberation. Europeans try to include restorative practices into a judicial frame.

First Nations and Other Indigenous People

During many conferences and my stays in Canada and in New Zealand especially, I realized the importance of the input of Aboriginal people into restorative practices and reflection. These

Lessons
Some of the traditional ways of dealing with conflict and norm transgression appear to be more constructive for social life, more satisfying for the victims, and more reintegrative for the offenders, than are the criminal justice interventions.

indigenous populations have a strong voice in Canada, the United States, Australia, and New Zealand. Recent emancipatory movements have revitalized their traditions and they claim the right to govern their communities according to traditional customs and rules. Some of the traditional ways of dealing with conflict and norm transgression appear to be more constructive for social life, more satisfying for the victims, and more reintegrative for the offenders, than are the criminal justice interventions. The flexibility of common law has left space for such practices, which were also boosted by the Anglo-Saxon confidence in community interventions.

And so, Maori traditions were a major contribution to the introduction of Family Group Conferences in the New Zealand Children, Young Persons and their Families Act, 1989 (Adler and Wundersitz 1994). Native communities in the United States and Canada largely inspired schemes like the so-called Peacemaking Courts and Circles (Yazzie and Zion 1996; Winfree 2002; Stuart 1996; Jaccoud 1998). By and large, Healing Circles are meant especially to restore peace within the affected native community, and Sentencing Circles are a kind of community co-judgment in the criminal justice procedure (McCold 2001). They all are deeply community based and aim to restore peace through reparation and healing (Van Ness and Strong 2002). Several scholars complain that the original native models have sometimes been lost by their reformulation into Western justice approaches (Blagg 2001; Cunneen 2002). Nevertheless, the native practices have energized the debates on criminal justice, and have deeply influenced thinking and practices on RJ. They have contributed a great deal to the creative variety of practices that may be considered under the RJ denominator.

Conclusion

My contact with colleagues and systems in other countries has opened my mind and my view on the world. Besides meeting very pleasant and good colleagues, I have become aware of tendencies and concerns that are common to many practitioners and scholars, and that have strengthened and deepened my own intuitions and theoretical thinking. But I have also learned that the relation between the justice system and its citizens can be quite different from what was evident in my legalistically ruled Belgium. Confrontation with such difference obliges one to correct or, perhaps, endeavor to better explain one's own beliefs.

It became clear to me that local judicial and socio-cultural contexts largely determine the diversity in how a common theoretical and socio-ethical view on RJ is made concrete in practice. It is a challenge for the RJ movement and for comparative research on restorative practices.

The basic lessons for comparative research I have learned can be summarized in the following statements.

Differences are best observed through commonalities. The more commonalities are observed, the more remaining differences are salient. Commonalities serve as necessary anchors to link the compared units to each other. That is why it is easier to compare European institutions and traditions with North American than with Muslim countries for example.

Be skeptical for superficial commonalities and/or differences. Conferencing, for example is implemented in many countries in the world, but its concrete practices are remarkably varied. The police sometimes act as the convener, as the representative of public order, or simply as one of the possible participants. It is mostly used as a kind of diversion for less serious juvenile offending, while it is in the heart of the procedure for all juvenile crime in New Zealand. Community service is considered a punishment in many American States, as a re-educative measure in Belgium, or as a kind of compensatory obligation in many European juvenile justice systems. Belgium has officially a purely rehabilitative juvenile justice system, whereas most other countries also speak of special punishments for juveniles. But in both regimes, juvenile offenders can be locked up for longer periods in closed facilities. It is therefore meaningless to make superficial comparisons between techniques. Techniques and their appellations must always be considered in the frame of local traditions, include the underlying philosophies, and add the study of concrete practices.

Language is crucial. Obviously, English is now the dominant language in international communication, but it may be a pitfall of inaccuracy and misunderstanding. The same words can be understood differently, and not all concepts from non-English countries can be translated adequately. Moreover, not all non-native speakers have the necessary skills to communicate fluidly in English, while what they have to say may be scientifically very important. After all, one should note that the real international language is not English, but "bad" English. It may cause misunderstandings.

But if well done, the lessons to be learned from comparative work are essential for theory development, and for enhancing the quality of local practices. Comparative work is a terrific, extremely rewarding experience. It prevents you from parochialism, and helps to improve your own parish as well.

Selected Bibliography

Adler, C. and J. Wundersitz, eds. 1994. *Family Conferencing and Juvenile Justice: the Way Forward or Misplaced Optimism?* Canberra: Australian Institute of Criminology.

Albrecht, H.J. 2001. "Restorative Justice. Answers to Questions that Nobody has put Forward." In *Victim Policies and Criminal Justice on the Road to Restorative Justice,* edited by E. Fattah and S. Parmentier. Leuven: Leuven University Press.

Bazemore, G. and L. Walgrave, eds. 1999. *Restorative Juvenile Justice. Repairing the Harm by Youth Crime*. Monsey, NY: Criminal Justice Press.

Bazemore, G. and M. Schiff, eds. 2001. *Restorative Community Justice. Repairing Harm and Transforming Communities*. Cincinnati: Anderson.

Blad, J. 1996. *Abolitionisme als strafrechtstheorie* (Abolitionism and penal theory). Arhnem, NL: Gouda Quint.

Blagg, H. 2001. "Aboriginal Youth and Restorative Justice: Critical Notes from the Frontier." In *Restorative Justice for Juveniles. Conferencing, Mediation & Circles*, edited by A. Morris and G. Maxwell. Oxford: Hart.

Braithwaite, J. 1999. "Restorative Justice: Assessing Optimistic and Pessimistic Accounts." In *Crime and Justice. An Annual Review of Research,* vol. 25, edited by M. Tonry. Chicago: University of Chicago Press.

———. 2002. *Restorative Justice and Responsive Regulation*. Oxford: Oxford University Press.

Braithwaite, J. and Ph. Pettit. 1990. *Not Just Deserts. A Republican Theory of Criminal Justice*. Oxford: Oxford University Press.

Braithwaite, J. and S. Mugford. 1994. "Conditions of a Successful Reintegration Ceremony." *British Journal of Criminology* 34(2):139-171.

Christie, N. 1977. "Conflict as Property." *British Journal of Criminology* 17(1):1-14.

Crawford, A. 2002. "The State, Community and Restorative Justice: Heresy, Nostalgia and Butterfly

Collecting." In *Restorative Justice and the Law,* edited by L. Walgrave. Cullompton, UK: Willan Publishing.

Cunneen, C. 2002. "Restorative Justice and the Politics of Decolonization." In *Restorative Justice: Theoretical Foundations,* edited by E. Weitekamp and H.J. Kerner. Cullompton, UK: Willan Publishing.

Cusson, M. 1990. *Croissance et Décroissance du Crime* (Growth and Decline of Crime). Paris: P.U.F.

De Haan, W. 1990. *Politics of Redress. Crime, Punishment and Penal Abolition*. London: Unwin Hyman.

Eliaerts, C. and E. Dumortier. 2002. "Restorative Justice for Children: In Need of Procedural Safeguards and Standards." In *Restorative Justice: Theoretical Foundations,* edited by E. Weitekamp and H.J. Kerner eds. Cullompton, UK: Willan Publishing.

European Forum for Victim-Offender Mediation and Restorative Justice, ed. 2000. *Vicitim-Offender Mediation in Europe. Making Restorative Justice Work*. Leuven: Leuven University Press.

Feld, B. 1999. "Rehabilitation, Retribution and Restorative Justice: Alternative Conceptions of Juvenile Justice." In *Restorative Justice for Juveniles. Restoring the Harm by Youth Crime,* edited by G. Bazemore and L. Walgrave. Monsey, NY: Criminal Justice Press.

Groenhuysen, M. 2000. "Victim-Offender Mediation: Legal and Procedural Safeguards. Experiments and Legislation in some European Jurisdictions." In *Victim-Offender Mediation in Europe. Making Restorative Justice Work,* edited by

the European Forum for Victim-Offender Mediation and Restorative Justice. Leuven: Leuven University Press.

Jaccoud, M. 1998. "Restoring Justice in Native Communities in Canada." In *Restorative Justice for Juveniles. Potentialities, Risks and Problems for Research,* edited by L. Walgrave. Leuven: Leuven University Press.

La Prairie, C. 1995. "Altering Course: New Directions in Criminal Justice. Sentencing Circles and Family Group Conferences." *Australian and New Zealand Journal of Criminology* special issue:78-99.

McCold, P. 1996. "Restorative Justice and the Role of Community." In *Restorative Justice: International Perspectives,* edited by B. Galaway and J. Hudson. Amsterdam/Monsey: Kugler/Criminal Justice Press.

————. 2000. "Toward a Holistic Vision of Restorative Juvenile Justice: A Reply to the Maximalist Model." *Contemporary Justice Review* 3(4):357-414.

————. 2001. "Primary Restorative Justice Practices." In *Restorative Justice for Juveniles. Conferencing, Mediation & Circles,* edited by A. Morris and G. Maxwell. Oxford: Hart.

————. 2003. "A Survey of Assessment Research on Mediation and Conferencing." In *Repositioning Restorative Justice,* edited by L. Walgrave. Cullompton, UK: Willan Publishing.

Messmer, H. and H.U. Otto, eds. 1992. *Restorative Justice on Trials. Pitfalls and Potentials of Vicitim-Offender Mediation. International Research Perspectives*. Dordrecht,

(NL)/Boston: Kluwer Academic Publishers.

Morris, A. and G. Maxwell. 2003. "Restorative Justice in New Zealand." In *Restorative Justice and Criminal Justice. Competing or Reconcilable Paradigms?*, edited by A. von Hirsch, J. Roberts, A. Bottoms, K. Roach, and M. Schiff. Oxford: Hart.

Pavlich, G. 2001. "The Force of Community." In *Restorative Justice and Civil Society,* edited by H. Strang and J. Braithwaite. Cambridge: Cambridge University Press.

Pranis, K. 2001. "Restorative Justice, Social Justice and the Empowerment of Marginalized Populations." In *Restorative Community Justice. Repairing Harm and Transforming Communities,* edited by G. Bazemore, and M. Schiff. Cincinnati: Anderson.

Pranis, K. and G. Bazemore. 2000. *Engaging the Community in the Response to Youth Crime: A Restorative Justice Approach.* Washington, DC: Department of Justice, OJJDP.

Stuart, B. 1996. "Circle Sentencing: Turning Swords into Ploughshares." In *Restorative Justice: International Perspectives,* edited by B. Galaway and J. Hudson. Amsterdam/Monsey: Kugler/Criminal Justice Press.

Van Swaaningen, R. 1997. *Critical Criminology: Visions from Europe.* London: Sage.

Van Ness, D. and K. Strong. 2002. *Restoring Justice.* 2d ed. Cincinnati: Anderson.

Von Hirsch, A. 1998. "Penal Theories." In *The Handbook of Crime and Punishment,* edited by M. Tonry. New York: Oxford University Press.

Walgrave, L. 1992. "Herstelrecht: een Derde weg in het Gerechtelijk Antwoord op Jeugddelinquentie?" (Restorative Justice: A Third Way in the Response to Youth Crime?) *Panopticon* 1:24-42.

———. 1995. "Restorative Justice for Juveniles: Just a Technique or a Fully Fledged Alternative?" *Howard Journal of Criminal Justice* 34:228-249.

———. 2000. "How Pure can a Maximalist Approach to Restorative Justice Remain? Or Can a Purist Model of Restorative Justice become Maximalist?" *Contemporary Justice Review* 3(4):415-432.

———. 2002a. *Restorative Justice and the Law.* Cullompton, UK: Willan Publishing.

———. 2002b. "From Community to Dominion: In Search of Social Values for Restorative Justice." In *Restorative Justice: Theoretical Foundations,* edited by E. Weitekamp and H.J. Kerner. Cullompton, UK: Willan Publishing.

———. 2002c. "Juvenile Justice in Belgium." In *Juvenile Justice Systems: International Perspectives,* edited by J. Winterdyk. Toronto: Canadian Scholars' Press.

———. 2003. "Imposing Restoration Instead of Inflicting Punishment." In *Restorative Justice and Criminal Justice. Competing or Reconcilable Paradigms?*, edited by A. von Hirsch, J. Roberts, A. Bottoms, K. Roach. and M. Schiff. Oxford: Hart.

———. Forthcoming. "Restoration in Juvenile Justice. In *A Comparative Juvenile Justice Volume,* edited by M. Tonry and A. Doob. Chicago:

Chicago University Press.

Weitekamp, E. 2001. "Mediation in Europe: Paradoxes, Problems and Promises." In *Restorative Justice for Juveniles. Conferencing, Mediation & Circles,* edited by A. Morris and G. Maxwell. Oxford: Hart.

Winfree, T. 2002. "Peacemaking and Community Harmony: Lessons (and Admonitions) from the Navajo Peacemaking Courts." In *Restorative Justice: Theoretical Foundations,* edited by E. Weitekamp and H.J. Kerner. Cullompton, UK: Willan Publishing.

Yazzie, R. and J. Zion. 1996. "Navajo Restorative Justice: The Law of Equality and Justice." In *Restorative Justice: International Perspectives,* edited by B. Galaway and J. Hudson. Amsterdam/Monsey: Kugler/Criminal Justice Press.

Zehr, H. 1990. *Changing Lenses: A New Focus for Crime and Justice.* Scottsdale, PA: Herald Press.

Chapter 9

Being There:
An Interview with

David Nelken

*Distinguished Professor of
Sociology at the University of
Macerata, Italy
Distinguished Research Professor
of Law at the University of
Wales, Cardiff Visiting Professor in
Law at the LSE, UK.*

*Becoming an insider is about learning
to start from "here" rather than there.*

The Personal Informs the Professional

*How do you feel about this invitation to
provide a autobiographical account of
your work in comparative criminology?*

I agree of course that a person's
life and work are interconnected
in various ways but it is usually
extremely difficult for the person concerned to see exactly how, or to talk
about it without being either boring or
self-important (or both!). I'll try to
bring out what I can of the personal
side. But, as the title I have given this
interview suggests, I shall also take this
occasion to provide some reflections on
the opportunities for comparative research that offer themselves to anyone
moving to live in another country.

*How did you first come to be interested
in criminology?*

Late in my universities studies, toward
the end of my history degree in
Cambridge, I was preparing to write an
essay about the causes of the American
civil war, but I had become increasingly bewildered by the way each generation rewrote its history. Turning, in despair, from the shelves of books on the
subject in the University library, I saw
and began reading a book lying on an
adjacent desk. The book, titled *The
Courage of his Convictions* (1962),
written by the remarkable journalist
Tony Parker, described the life of an
unsuccessful, but unrepentant, professional bank robber in the man's own
words. I found it fascinating. After

spending the next year studying law, just in case my academic ambitions came to nothing and I needed to become a lawyer, I then signed on to do a Master's degree in Criminology at the Cambridge Institute and followed this with a Doctorate.

Who have been the main influences on your work?

I do not have a mentor as such. But I got a good start at the Institute, where I taught by Roger Hood and Richard Sparks (though they weren't talking to each other by then), as well as by Derrick MacClintock, Donald West, and David Farrington. Nigel Walker, the Director at the time, firmly but kindly helped keep me going on my empirically based doctorate about rogue landlords, but given his limited interests in sociology we mainly spent our supervision time playing chess. I was fortunate to land my first job teaching law in Edinburgh in a department with outstanding colleagues—Neil MacCormick, Kit Carson, Zenon Bankowski, Richard Kinsey, Peter Young, and David Garland. In order to keep up with them I had to try to acquire the skills in theorizing that I lacked. Feeling the need to do something more practically useful, I also served as a member of the Juvenile Court system of Children's Hearings.

After eight years there, I moved to London. I taught for many years on the London University Law LLM with friends and colleagues such as Roger Cotterrell, Simon Roberts, Tim Murphy, and Robert Reiner, and I learned a great deal from all of them. For moral and intellectual support I have relied, in particular, on two friends—the anthropologist Gerry Mars (whose visiting talk at the Cambridge Institute first led me to specialize on the topic of white collar crime), and Malcolm Feeley, a political scientist in the law school at Berkeley. The book that had most influence on my empirical research was Aaron Cicourel's (1968) *The Social Construction of Juvenile Justice*. My approach to comparative inquiry has been much influenced by the work of the anthropologist Clifford Geertz—as well as the travel writer Paul Thoreaux.

What, if any, are the personal factors that have shaped your research interests?

There has been quite a lot of overlap here, even though I have come to realize much of this in retrospect. My father was a child refugee from Nazi Germany. The contrast between the respectful attitude toward law of German Jews like himself, with that which he claimed characterized some of the immigrants from Russia and Eastern Europe, may have helped lead me toward the sociology of law and criminology (the most plausible explanation of this alleged difference being the contrasting cultures and legal regimes to which each of these minorities had previously been exposed). There is probably a personal aspect to some of my other writings. My enquiries into the competing "truths" of law and science served as an indirect way of continuing to grapple with the challenges of lay scholarship for someone with an orthodox religious Jewish upbringing (as another way of addressing the clash between science and religion). My empirical study of contractual agreements, as a way of externalizing understandings between social workers and their clients, coincided with the collapse of the tacit understandings holding my first marriage together.

Moving on to your interest in comparative criminology. Is there a personal side to this too?

My work in comparative criminology is relatively recent, and yes, biography again plays a large part, given that it was a happy byproduct of meeting Matilde Betti, an Italian judge who is now my wife. She suggested the idea of embarking on a comparative study of frauds against the European Union so as to justify my trips back and forth to Italy! I finally moved there to marry her in 1990 after being invited to take a job as Professor of Sociology at the University of Macerata. Since then, comparative research has allowed me to reconcile the need to learn more about my adopted country with trying to continue to contribute to the larger world of academic scholarship.

What are your current research interests?

Not surprisingly, I have written a lot about judges (though I try not to involve my wife). In Italy, this topic is inextricably linked to their recent attempt to deal with political corruption and the consequent counterattack accusing them of political interference. Living abroad has also given me a new handle on Anglo American practices and scholarship, so I have also been writing about the differences in legal

culture and attempts to transplant it (three of these books have been translated into Chinese but not into European languages...I don't know why). Because Italian scholarship is so much stronger on theory than on empirical case studies, I have chosen to devote most of my energy in the University to empirical research and research training. One of my current projects has to do with the remarkably lenient way juvenile delinquency is handled in Italy (and I am running a parallel study in Wales). Another involves interviewing judges and lawyers about the causes of the incredible court delays here. Finally, and here once again the personal element is evident, I have been conducting extensive interviews with second generation young immigrants in Italy in order to understand how they manage what could be called "hyphenated identity."

Comparative Criminology: What's the Point?

Turning now to more theoretical issues, what do you understand by the term "comparative criminology"?

Well, it certainly has to do with a general interest in differences in national patterns of crime, criminal justice, and criminology. Some countries, such as Japan and Switzerland, have been used as exemplars of the enormous differences in crime rates between some nation states and cultures and others. But other countries, for example India or Saudi Arabia, could be just as interesting from this point of view. Beyond that, it is easier to say what the field presupposes rather than what people

Lessons

A comparative perspective can and should also push one to look at social control more widely outside of the legal system. I think it even more important to connect with other comparative writings (e.g., in law, social theory, political science, or anthropology) than to show how comparative criminology relates to mainstream criminology.

have in common. We would all agree, I suppose, not to be put off by the following objections: (1) there is no need for comparative method, as such, because all social science is inherently comparative; an international perspective offers no more, and no less, than a wider data base for studying variation. Conversely, (2) comparison is impossible because you can never really understand another culture or, (3) cross-cultural comparison is unnecessary because the truths of crime and criminal justice are universal and invariant. Of course there may also be some truth in these claims, which comparativists will do well to bear in mind.

What do you see as the point of studying comparative criminology?

There are an almost unlimited variety of possible motives for this as for any other intellectual enquiry. But, for me, it offers an ideal method for showing the interconnections between crime, justice, and culture. It makes it clear, yet again, how much the problem of crime is constructed by the responses of the larger society and the criminal justice agencies. A comparative perspective can and should also push one to look at social control more widely outside of the legal system. I think it even more important to connect with other comparative writings (e.g., in law, social theory, political science, or anthropology) than to show how comparative criminology relates to mainstream criminology. So I tend to go to "law and society" conferences rather than criminology conferences.

What about comparative criminology as a way of learning how to do things better?

Yes, it has always had and will always have that role, and it is neither desirable nor possible to totally separate theory and practice. On the one hand, the gain from a good explanatory or interpretative account of a criminal justice system will often be to show why and how its attempts to solve problems end up reproducing them. On the other hand, looking for practical advantages can yield unexpected theoretical insights. This is sufficiently illustrated by the contributions to the somewhat obsessive debate over whether the European inquisitorial system represents a better way of solving Anglo American dilemmas of controlling police discretion. But whether we can, or should, "borrow" from other systems or be satisfied only with trying in some way to "learn" from them is always an open question.

What about the future?

Well, it is likely that the attention devoted to this topic will expand enormously in the coming years. There are globalizing trends of both crime (especially transnational organized crime) and crime control, including increasing attempts to harmonize criminal law and improve collaboration between states. For better or worse, what can be termed "the global criminological gaze" is spreading a new orthodoxy about "what works" (on the mistaken analogy that organizing an effective criminal justice state is akin to constructing a well-functioning health system). Much work still needs to be done on international criminal law and international legal tribunals courts, as well as the overlap between crime, crime control, and war. Another important focus of comparative criminology continues to be explaining why certain immigrant or ethnic sub-groups of a population have persistently higher, or lower, rates of crime than the majority group. The increasing salience of the field will also create political and moral dilemmas. Comparative Criminologists will not want to be deaf to the cries for justice of victims wherever they live. On the other hand, intervention abroad often has mixed motives and, at a time when the price for political and economic acceptability is to sign on to alleged universal standards, recommending a given model of handling social problems is rarely without wider implications.

It sounds as if you take an open-minded view on the sort of work that is relevant to comparative criminology—Let a thousand flowers bloom?

Not exactly. A lot of what passes for comparative criminology is pretty unimpressive; for example, the sort of comparison by juxtaposition in which experts explain, "this is what we do in Denmark, what do you do in your country?" In general, comparison that is merely descriptive begs the question, "what is to be compared and why?" Caution should be exercised even when reading the type of classificatory approaches commonly employed in textbooks of comparative criminal justice. These too often rely on the rare pieces in English by foreign visitors or on skimpy, insider accounts of the law in books and legal procedure. It is hard to find satisfactory accounts of the law in action or of the wider social and political contexts that give criminal justice its local sense. Anglo-American value choices, such as due process versus crime control, or justice versus welfare, are employed as tools of analysis as if they point to necessarily universal predicaments.

It is more valuable, though perhaps more difficult, to try to highlight differences in the way crime-related social problems are perceived and constructed within different cultures. The idea of functional equivalents (an idea whose roots go back both to sociology and comparative law) can be a good servant but a poor master. As I wrote soon after moving to Italy: living here has given me a jaundiced view of comparative research that sets out to show that all societies face similar problems even if they solve them somewhat differently. What is more striking is the power of culture to produce relatively circular definitions of what is worth fighting for and against, and the way institutions and practices express genuinely different histories and distinct priorities.[1]

Lessons

Unless we can get a grasp on the ways our cultural assumptions shape our comparative project, we are unlikely to make progress in understanding another society in its own terms.

But is it not just as important to look for similarities as for differences?

Yes it can be. This is especially true where we might expect there to be more differences than similarities. What is more, the search for difference itself presupposes some degree of similarity. But interpretative sociological approaches which I favor are best at discovering and explaining differences in the way crime is perceived and handled rather than showing the supposedly universal features of crime and its control. Comparing Italy to the English speaking world throws up such surprising findings: the police here gain more rather than less trust through being militarized; regulatory white collar crimes form a consistent part of the workload of ordinary judges; serious crimes including burglary and rape, until very recently, were usually described as micro crimes (so as to distinguish them from the activities such as organized crime and terrorism, which can threaten the state itself); a large number of young people tried for homicide are dealt with by way of pre-trial probation so that they do not even receive a conviction let alone spend time in prison; and politicians right of center seem

more concerned with blocking the criminal process than seeking to gain votes by increasing its efficiency.

And you think you can make sense of these findings?

Yes! They all have to do with the gulf between the high idea of the state and the reality of government in Italy. They suggest the way historically shaped patterns lie beneath such strange sounding ideas and practices. But, there is one important proviso in talking about such patterns in searching for the interconnection between the puzzling features of criminal justice; we have to be careful not to seek the common denominator of ideas and practices that may be strange *only* because of our own different starting point of experience and expectations (which someone from another society would have equal right to find puzzling!).

Phenomenology and the Comparativist

Is this why you have made so much of the need for the comparativist to be constantly prepared to question her own starting point?

Yes, I do see this as fundamental. Unless we can get a grasp on the ways our cultural assumptions shape our comparative project, we are unlikely to make progress in understanding another society in its own terms. Think of the current enormous attention given to victims of crime. In this (Italian) Catholic culture the victim (or relatives of victims) of horrendous crimes are less likely to be involved in rhetorical justifications of the need for greater severity than they are to be asked by journalists if they are willing to forgive the offender! In fact, my first piece in Italian was written in response to a leading left-wing criminal law philosopher who argues that state punishment can only be justified and its measure fixed in terms of its role in saving criminals from victims' revenge.

Must we question what we take for granted also if we are trying to learn from elsewhere?

Certainly. For example, if we are interested in having Anglo-American societies learn about better ways of handling juvenile delinquency, we will not get far by merely trying to identify what is special about Italian legal procedures. Past efforts in this direction, notably an article on the subject by Edwin Lemert (1986),[2] hardly got beyond labeling the Italian system as formalistically legal and spurious because it did not seem to be crafting the individualized welfare measures assumed to be the quintessence of juvenile justice. What we should be doing is looking at the interconnections between juvenile justice and the way young people are treated within society at large— in families, schools, and elsewhere. Terms like "informal social control" provide poor signposts for what would be involved in studying the emotional intelligence and skill that Italian adults, in all these spheres, use when encouraging youngsters to communicate and collaborate rather than aim at individualistic assertiveness. My offer to provide just such a report was turned down

by the Canadian Law Commission in its recent "What is Crime" initiative.

But what of the criticism that the sort of "reflexive criminology" you recommend could end up producing accounts that tell us more about the writer than what she is writing about?

Yes, we need to guard against that. As with all post-positivist approaches to social science, the effort to put the author into the picture can become self-indulgent (just as the attempt to include the process of creating accounts into the account itself can lead to infinite regress). But, on the other hand, the author is present even when not announced. The work of so many English language criminologists is heavily influenced by their personal circumstances and cultures precisely because of their *un*willingness or inability to question their Anglo-American common law assumptions about the way crime is, or could be, handled. What a leading writer calls "the culture of control" of high modernity fails to recognize the variety of actually existing different *cultures* of control. If the Anglo-American culture of control (leaving aside the large differences between these two cultures) becomes more widespread on the continent, this will not be so much because of the pre-existing homogeneity of underlying conditions and values in contemporary society than because of the self-fulfilling prophecy and the scientific hegemony of the latest fashions in English language criminology.

But surely your focus on "telling difference" does give undue priority to method over substance? In his review of your book "Contrasting Criminal Justice" (2000) Paul Roberts writes: "Nelken certainly invests the discipline he refers to as "comparative criminology" with moral significance, but his primary focus appears to be on the ethical dimensions of the research process itself, as opposed to the substantive issues of crime and justice...The question...ultimately boils down to the neo-Socratic introspection: How should one live a moral life in research?"[3] Would you accept this characterization of your approach?

Well, I agree the book does focus on comparative research methods. Little is written about this, and many see no need for it to be given special attention. My aim was to illustrate the style and implications of the methods I called "virtual comparison," "researching there," and "living there." I have elsewhere asked what comparative criminologists can learn from comparative law scholarship—two worlds of discourse rarely put together. At the same time, what I am not interested in is methodology as an end in itself but, rather, how method affects substance.

Most of my comparative writing has, indeed, been concerned with substance not just method. I have written comparatively about trust; discretion; the rule of law and the role of law; criminological theory and punishment; the construction of social problems; judges, prosecutors and lawyers; corruption; organized crime; European Union fraud; juvenile delinquency; the globalization of crime; immigration and crime; repeat victimization; legal delay; and breaches of legal confiden-

tiality in criminal trials. And I have tackled other substantive topics on the civil side in my work in comparative sociology of law.

Another criticism of the interpretative approach could be that it gives too much importance to local difference at a time of increasing globalization. Is it not a reification to talk about Italian criminal justice at a time when crime is increasingly transnational and criminal justice ideas know no frontiers?

I don't think anyone has the answer to this. Comparison, as such, is no longer an easy panacea for parochialism. As Maureen Cain argues, it can easily be corrupted by the opposing vices of occidentalism or orientalism, whereby we either assume that other cultures are bound to be inherently like us—or else, using them as a foil, we transform them into something intrinsically other.[4] Certainly, when we talk about "Italy" we are speaking of a society that is internally complex, contradictory, and changing, and very much linked to changes in the larger world. Here, too, situational prevention is the new game in town with Italian buildings increasingly festooned by surveillance cameras. And mediation and restorative justice are the latest ideas, even if they are not yet widely implemented. But it is

Lessons
Our goal should be to try to illuminate the relationship between the particular and the universal and the local and the global.

also important not to deny particularity and resistance, the persistence of differences, and the way these affect what appear to be similar trends or practices. Our goal should be to try to illuminate the relationship between the particular and the universal and the local and the global.

The "Insider-Outsider" Problematic

In "Contrasting Criminal Justice" you have tried to generalize from your experience of moving to Italy by writing about the role of the observant participant and the "insider–outsider." Can you say more about this?

Well, I was trying to draw attention to the increasingly common experience of academics emigrating, for shorter or longer periods, to work in other societies. Moving to work or study in another society is not the same as setting out to do ethnography. But it does provide many of the opportunities sought by the anthropologist as compared to comparative research based on more detached investigation or only brief visits. Most obviously, spending an extended period of time in a society gives you a better chance to get things straight (or at least straighter). For example, most outsider accounts I have read have difficulty in explaining the link, if any, between the anti-corruption investigations of the early 1990s and the anti-Mafia investigations of the same period. The experience of "the everyday" enables one to assign the right level of importance to phenomena that are otherwise either exaggerated or minimized in newspaper reports or in the accounts of direct protagonists. And what once seemed liked

hazardous first impressions can be confirmed by repetition.

On the other hand, you also get to witness social change at first hand. When I arrived in Italy the governing parties still seemed in charge of things and the judges had not yet started their anti-corruption investigations. I experienced the public enthusiasm that characterized *Tangentopoli* and, in more recent years, the counter offensive by Berlusconi. As important, I saw how the problem of street crime arrived, for the first time, on the political agenda, coinciding with the first large-scale wave of immigration into Italy. Living in what had been called "Red" Bologna, I experienced the shock when the (ex)communists lost power there after 50 years largely, according to many observers, because of the rising level of conventional crime. And I walked past the spot in Bologna where the revived Red Brigades struck down Professor Marco Biagi only two hours later.

Is it enough just to "be there" to understand another society?

Of course not, otherwise natives would always be the best anthropologists. To make an academic contribution as an "observant" participant one has to be continually looking for pertinent clues and mining their significance in terms of larger questions and wider literatures. But once one grants that crime and criminal justice are not artificially cut off from the rest of life, almost every aspect of everyday experience is potentially relevant, for example, going to the shops (whether and when one is given a tax receipt), bringing up kids (strategies for getting into the school district, how parents do their kids homework etc.), buying a house (encountering the lawyer-approved custom of not declaring the real price), and many other social and practical contexts.

Are there also drawbacks to observant participation?

Undoubtedly. No method is right for all purposes, nor can it be self-sufficient. When you live in a place you can no longer pretend a useful naiveté. And once you have an internal identity those with competing loyalties will be less willing to trust you and everyone is in competition with you for resources. Furthermore, the insider-outsider is not someone without a role but rather occupies exactly that role, which means that her experience corresponds neither to that of the native Italian nor to that of the real outsider. The places where you live and work will not be representative of all other places (Bologna is one of the most "well-off" and law abiding Italian cities). And you lack the long historical memory of the real insider. Because you can experience directly only a small slice of life, you are still largely reliant on others for your ideas and information. To contribute to the larger literature your work necessarily has to refer to, and link with, wider academic debates, whether you are writing about prosecution discretion, political clientilism, corruption, juvenile delinquency, organized crime, or anything else.

Has actually living in the country been of benefit for your work?

Frequently. For example, it has given me the opportunity for numerous encounters with law officials and criminological colleagues who have told me things "off the record" (though these are matters that always need to be interpreted with caution). You get to meet the judge who slips you a case file of organized crime telling you that the government has suppressed the case, or the senior finance policeman who tries to persuade you that there is a tacit accord between government and business—if the former does not check tax returns too closely, the latter will accept inefficient and corrupt government! Many years ago I even found myself at dinner with Romano Prodi (now Head of the European Commission) who, at that time, in his efforts to become Premier was more worried by the electoral chances of Judge Di Pietro than those of the official contender and now Premier Berlusconi. In addition (and the list could go on), it is only through living in a place that you can learn to see where participants in academic debates are coming from, intellectually and politically, which is especially needed in a country like Italy, which is so thoroughly politicized. It makes a difference when you read an article in the *British Journal of Criminology* that criticizes Italian judicial prosecutors if you know the that Italian author has made his career by constantly and extravagantly attacking the judges.

And what about the university world?

Unfortunately, the Italian university itself is not well organized as an environment for producing or discussing research. But some key insights have come from just doing my job. Why do so many of my students not get the point of anomie theory? Because they cannot believe that personal success could be held out as a collective social ideal or value. How can it be that university professors are routinely obliged to carry out actions that carry potentially long prison sentences for maintaining false records? Because the way to get around certain formal requirements of running university oral examinations relies on the covert exchange of favors behind a screen of inflexible rules, rather than actually trying to change the awkward rules. From this experience I was led to hypothesize that the role of rules at any and every level in Italy often seems to have more to do with setting out an ideal of unrealizable order rather than actually creating predictability in social life. As far as learning about more conventional crime, I have also benefited greatly from participating in the regional government crime committees that sprang up in the 1990s.

What other everyday sources of data do you consider useful?

The media: television, radio, and newspapers provide a rich index of commentary (including the strange obsession with why Italy isn't normal). Italian newspapers are extraordinarily factional and provide an endless succession of scandals with appropriate censures of standardized hate figures: on the one hand, corrupt politicians and businessmen, on the other, freedom-hating (ex)communists and judges. Other forms of mass communications, such as those used in commercial and/or political advertising, can also be of interest.

Lessons
Moving to another society in which you have to learn to act as an insider requires you to undergo the sometimes painful experience of secondary socialization as an adult.

A large-scale poster campaign in favor of accountants who belong to their professional association (which is known in Italy as an Order) played on the double meaning of the word "order." It announced, "Where there is Order there is someone taking care of you," before listing the names of local accountants. Remarkably, this slogan manages to mobilize a Statist, top-down, paternalistic idea of imposed order as part of a selling technique to send people to a profession who are used (and not only in Italy) largely to reduce (and here we are being euphemistic) the tax burden that needs to be given to the government. So this advertising copy serves as yet another example of the endemic contrast between the lip service paid to the ideal order of the State (or the state of ideal order) and the practical tactics for getting by in everyday life.

Is there a direct link between the vantage point of an "insider-outsider" and the study of criminology?

Yes, I think there is. Moving to another society in which you have to learn to act as an insider requires you to undergo the sometimes painful experience of secondary socialization as an adult. Everyday mechanisms of social control and social order are inscribed on your own body and soul! More specifically, you need to understand what is going on, know the rules, and make alliances. The insider-outsider's need to (re)discover cognitive order, normative guidance, and affective/affiliative attachment can lead to valuable insights about the culture she finds herself in. Take the question of rules; you can do nothing without knowing which rules must be followed, which rules may be bent, and how this is done.

And are there rules about this?

Of course not! Like so much about everyday life, you can only learn by doing, and the proof of having understood is the practical accomplishment of whatever it is you are trying to achieve.

Do you think that things change over time?

Inevitably your starting point recedes. Becoming an insider is about learning to start from "here" rather than there, accepting the need to work with, rather than in opposition to, native categories even if they are different from those you are used to.[5] The process of beginning to see what it would be like (and why it might make sense) to start from here can also provide new insights into the society of origin, making you realize that you never really understood it.

Do you try to take part in Italian policy debates?

In Italy there has been relatively little space for policy, as opposed to political,

debate. And much of the political battle in Italy consists of telling and re-telling recent (and not so recent) events so as to put your reference group in a good light. So, anyone who writes about Italy can get drawn in to these debates—even against their will. For example, in 1996, well into the *Tangentopoli* anti-corruption campaign, I published a chapter in an authoritative historical series setting out the events up until that date.[6] I thought the account was reasonably balanced (and leading left wing judges later made complimentary reference to it). At the time it appeared, however, a politician (for whom I have little sympathy, aligned with Silvio Berlusconi's right of center opposition party) praised the chapter both in a parliamentary speech and then in his daily television broadcast. Next, I was called up by lawyers for a suspect fighting extradition from New York and asked if I would be willing to use my credibility as a presumably unbiased outsider to act as an expert witness explaining to the American judges that these investigations were politically biased and, thus, that their client should not be extradited.

So, what did you do?

I refused. He lost his fight against extradition and was obliged to return to Italy. A high level Italian court then set him free saying that leaving the country and spiriting away the proceeds of questioned transactions did not constitute sufficient grounds for arrest. This experience taught me a lot about the difficulties of trying to tell both sides of the story in Italy!

Presumably, the more you become part of the society the more your views will be taken seriously?

Yes and no. Certainly the organic intellectual is always fully employed, but paradoxically, the outsider's opinion is more valued the less she is seen as part of things.

Are you saying that as you get to know more about the society your opinion may count for less?

In Italy, yes, because you are assumed to have lost the role of unaligned outsider and to have joined one of the internal and, hence, ideologically predictable competing groups. On the other hand, it is exactly the Italian audience that matters more to me now that I have lived here for so long. While it remains good for my morale to accept invitations abroad, explaining Italy to those who do not live here increasingly seems too facile; it feels more appropriate to measure my interpretations against those of other commentators coming from the culture I am studying. In my case, this means I have to engage principally with the ideas of two friends and colleagues who teach at the University of Bologna: Dario Melossi, a broad ranging sociologist who has also worked for many years in California, and Massimo Pavarini, one of the most cosmopolitan of Italian criminological theorists.

How do you feel about this new challenge?

Well, on the one hand, given their deeper rootedness in the society, it seems pre-

sumptuous of me to question their presentations of Italy. Yet, on the other hand, when they write for outside audiences, I find I want to give my opinion too. Take the following intriguing claims by Massimo Pavarini, as he tries to explain in a recent English language article the implications of the Italian rejection of the State and the absence of Protestant structures of responsibility. "It's raining...damn the government," he says, "very aptly sums up how an abstract, impersonal entity is blamed for everything that is seen as socially evil, unjust, undesirable and frightening. The Italian political lexicon is a complex weave of two historic traditions; the catholic matrix with its providential conception of history in which universal judgment has always outweighed individual judgment, and the Marxist matrix with its belief in the rebirth of society through revolution. Both these cultural traditions have encouraged the process whereby social expectations do not entail individual responsibility for society's ills."[7]

And, you do not agree with this?

It is not so much that I disagree, rather, I wonder how far an already simplified message will be even further misunderstood when read by those with no first hand experience of Italy. What does it mean to say that social expectations do not entail individual responsibility? In my experience of everyday life I see a rich texture of intertwined social and individual demands and expectations. So how far should this account be read more as a critical "intervention" by an engaged participant than an effort at pure description? Is it relevant that this statement is being made by a leading (ex)Marxist criminologist in a book edited by a Marxist scholar? What of the fact that Pavarini himself (once, and perhaps still) Marxist, whatever that means, is also one of the most personally responsible people I have ever met? Does this affect his thesis? Do Pavarini's remarks offer further proof of the extent to which Italians are disposed to speak badly of their society? Even the most well informed Italian criminologist, thus, provides me with an interpretation of his society in the form of a riddle. It seems right to say that whatever else we may learn from them, texts like this also reflect the culture they are portraying.

Including this interview?

Yes, this too.

Notes to Budding Scholars

What advice I have to offer is contained in my remarks about looking for similarities and differences, starting points, thinking carefully about your sources, being an observant participant and so on. Questioning culturally accepted assumptions about how to handle crime is intellectually very interesting and very open ended. In teaching Master's courses as a Visiting professor in Sydney and Melbourne this year, my students (some of them with practical responsibilities for the topics concerned) tackled subjects such as:

- The differences in the role of the victim in the legal cultures of common law and continental criminal justice systems.
- In the war on drugs what we are witnessing is not globalization but Americanization.
- A history of legal transplants in Vietnam through Confucianism, Western (French) law and state communism.
- A comparison of prosecution culture with regard to prosecutorial discretion between Japan and Australia.
- Until there is a cross-national definition of corruption it will not be reduced by international efforts.
- A critique (by a native Australian) of the attempt to introduce the Canadian approach of circle sentencing for cases involving Aboriginal people.
- A comparative study of Indonesian and Australian anti-terrorism law.
- How far transnational terrorism, and responses to the same, strengthens the nation state.
- Amnesty in exchange for truth at the Truth and Reconciliation Commission in South Africa.
- The transplantability of restorative justice into Japan.

On the other hand, in policy contexts, the lesson of interpretive comparative criminology often seems to be the negative one that attempts to resolve crime problems often fail because they come from, or have to work in, the same cultures that produced the problem in the first place. There is more to be said but this lesson is over.

152   David Nelken

Notes

1   Nelken, D. 1992. "Law and Disorder in Italy." *Socio-legal Newsletter* winter:3-5.
2   Lemert, E. 1986. "Juvenile Justice; Italian Style." *Law and Society Review* 20:509-544.
3   Roberts, P. 2002. "The Ascent of Comparative Criminal Justice." *Oxford Journal of Legal Studies* 22(3):539-561.
4   Cain, M. 2000. "Orientalism, Occidentalism and the Sociology of Crime." *British Journal of Criminology* 40: 239-260.
5   See the editor's chapter in M.H. Bond (1997), *Writing at the Interface of Culture.*
6   "Il significato di Tangentopoli: La risposte giudiziaria alla corruzione e i suoi limiti." In *Storia d'Italia 14: Legge, Diritto e Giustizia*, edited by Luciano Violante Einaudi, 1997, pp.597- 627.
7   The quotation comes from *Social Control and Political Order*, edited by R. Bergalli and C. Sumner, 1997, p.95. London: Sage.

Selected Bibliography

Nelken, D. 1984. "Law in Action or Living Law? Back to the Beginning in Sociology of Law." *Legal Studies* 4:152-174.
_____. 1987. "Changing Paradigms in the Sociology of Law." In *Autopoietic Law: A New Approach to Law and Society,* edited by G. Teubner. Berlin: De Gruyter.
_____. 1991. "Lawyers in Society: Comparative Theories." In *International Journal of the Sociology of Law* 19(1):101-107.
_____. 1994. "Whom Can You Trust? The Future of Comparative Criminology." In *The Futures of Criminology,* edited by D. Nelken. London: Sage.
_____. 1995. "Legal Culture, Diversity and Globalization." In Special Issue of *Social and Legal Studies.* UK: Sage.
_____. 1995. "A Legal Revolution? The Judges and Tangentopoly." In *The New Italian Republic: From the Fall of the Berlin Wall to Berlusconi,* edited by S. Gundle and S. Parker. New York: Routledge.
_____. 1997. *Comparing Legal Cultures.* Dartmouth, UK: Dartmouth Publishing.
_____. 1997. "The Globalization of Crime and Criminal Justice: Prospects and Problems." In *Law and Opinion at the end of the 20th Century,* edited by M. Freeman. Oxford: Oxford University Press.
_____. 2000. *Contrasting Criminal Justice* Dartmouth, UK: International Library of Criminology.
_____. 2001. "The Meaning of Success in Transnational Legal Transfers." In *Windsor Yearbook of Access to Justice* 19:349-366.
_____. 2002. "Changing Legal Cultures." In *Transnational Legal Processes,* edited by M.B. Likosky. London: Butterworths.
_____. 2002. "Comparative Sociology of Law." In *Introduction to Law and Social Theory,* edited by M. Travers and R. Benakar. Oxford: Hart publishing.
_____. 2002. "Comparing Criminal Justice." In *The Oxford Handbook of Criminology,* 3d ed. Oxford:

Oxford University Press.

_____. 2003. "Criminology: Crime's Changing Boundaries." In the *Oxford Handbook of Legal Studies,* edited by P. Cane and M. Tushnet. Oxford: Oxford University Press.

_____. 2003. "Corruption in the European Union." In *Corruption and Scandal in Contemporary Politics,* edited by M. Bull and J. Newell. London: Macmillan.

_____. 2003. "Comparativists and Transfers." In *Comparative Legal Studies: Traditions and Transitions,* edited by P. Legrand and R. Munday. Cambridge: Cambridge University Press.

_____. 2003. "Beyond Compare? Criticizing the American Way of Law." *Law and Social Inquiry* 28(3):181-213.

_____. 2003. "Legitimate Suspicion? Berlusconi and the Judges." In *Politics in Italy 2003,* edited by P. Segatti and J. Blondel. Published in English by Bergahn books, and in Italian by Il Mulino.

_____. 2004. "Comparing Legal Cultures." In *Blackwell Handbook to Law and Social Science,* edited by A. Sarat. Oxford: Blackwell.

_____. 2004. "Gobalization and Crime." In *Handbook of Comparative Social Policy,* edited by Patricia Kennett. Bristol: Edward Elgar Publishers.

_____. Forthcoming. "The Concept of Legal Culture." In *Australian Journal of Legal Philosophy.*

_____. Forthcoming. "Waiting for Strasbourg." In *The Role of Lawyers in European Integration,* edited by Schepel and Jettinghoff. Recht der Werkelijkheid: special issue.

_____. Forthcoming. "In search of secu-rity." In *Problems and Opportunities in Multi-Disciplinary Research on Safety and Security in Society,* edited by R. De Mulder. Boom Juridische Uitgevers, Den Haag.

_____. Forthcoming. "Getting it Right or Getting Away with Murder?: Juvenile Justice in Italy." In *The New Punitiveness: Current Trends, Theories, Perspectives,* edited by J. Pratt et al. Willan Books.

Nelken, D. and Piers Beirne, eds. 1997. *Issues in Comparative Criminology.* Dartmouth, UK: International Library of Criminology.

Nelken, D. and J. Feest. 2001. *Adapting Legal Cultures.* Oxford: Hart Publishing.

Nelken, D. and N. Passas 1991. "The Legal Response to Agricultural Fraud in the European Community: A Comparative Study." In *Corruption and Reform* 6:237-266.

Nelken, D. and Mike Levi. 1996. "The Corruption of Politics and the Politics of Corruption." *Journal of Law and Society.*

Nelken, D. and N. Passas. 1993. "The Thin Line Between Legitimate and Criminal Enterprises: Subsidy Frauds in the European Community." *Crime, Law and Social Change* 19:223-243.

Nelken, D. and Jiri Priban. 2001. *Law's New Boundaries: The Consequences of Autopoiesis.* Dartmouth, UK: Dartmouth Publishing.

Chapter 10

Finding New Frontiers to Cross in Criminology

Frances Heidensohn

Goldsmiths College
Dept. of Social Policy and Politics
University of London
London, England

If I were advising someone who wanted to pursue comparative criminology, I would suggest that they first consider what frontiers tempt them to cross...to observe outside influences closely...and to look for key concepts.

Setting Out

In many ways, I had a most auspicious beginning for a career in comparative criminology. While I was studying, at the London School of Economics in the mid-1960s, the influence of the three great European scholars, Max Grunhut, Hermann Mannheim, and Leon Radzinowicz, was still very apparent (see below). The London School of Economics had a notably diverse student body, with many postgraduates from the United States, Europe, and the Commonwealth. New ideas in social science, culture, and politics were energizing the academy and the wider society, with profound consequences for criminology. While Britain produced its own distinctive version of the paradigm-shift we call the "new deviancy" its origins were international, a mix of European and North American theories. Politically, these were turbulent times too with much street-level action over a variety of issues and in a multitude of settings. Massive anti-Vietnam War protests filled streets and campuses in the United States, Australia, and Britain. "Events" in Paris destabilized the French government and the Prague spring flowered briefly in the communist bloc. Civil rights activists marched in the United States in support of disenfranchised African Americans; and they influenced similar actions in Northern Ireland. Key aspects were thus in place to foster international comparative work in criminology: an increasingly global forum for events and debates, major changes, challenges, and new concepts in the subject and the presence of growing numbers of lively young students in the academy. In short:

* the scenario,
* the ideas, and
* the people

were all in place. Yet the synergy did not work at that point to produce an outpouring of comparative work. Instead, those of us who are members of what Paul Rock has called "the fortunate generation" took other paths. Much later, in the 1980s, many of us began to produce comparative studies. This chapter outlines my own part in this development, analyses this contribution and suggests some important lessons I have learned.

Writing about comparing criminal justice, David Nelken (presented in this collection) suggests that:

> [W]ithin the social sciences, some argue that *all* sociological research is inherently comparative. The aim is always the same: the explanation of 'variation.' (Nelken 2002:184)

He goes on, however, to consider whether good comparative work is a practical possibility, given all the known difficulties inherent in the study of crime and criminal justice and the added complexities of understanding definitions, institutions and cultures. Nelken is not the only modern criminologist to stress the importance of international studies; David Bayley (1999) has argued: "There are…substantial benefits from cross-national

study of criminal justice" (p.5).

While it may be possible to claim that "cross-national" means any project which covers more than one country (thus includes almost all the work I have ever undertaken), I intend to follow a more precise definition and confine the description "international" to the later research when I consciously pursued comparisons. Before recounting that history I turn to my first studies of women and crime.

Framing Feminist Perspectives

My earliest studies in criminology, and those with which I am most closely linked (Eaton 2000), focused on women and crime. I was interested in a series of questions about this topic. Why were women and girls so much less likely to contribute their "share" to recorded crime levels than were men and boys? Why had this difference, the most notable, persistent and widespread in all data on crime, not been more fully explored? Why were the few studies available limited and stereotyped yet subject to little critique? Finally, were there not fundamental issues of justice, fairness, and penal policy that should be considered? (See Heidensohn 1968, 1969, 1970.)

Lessons
What we still lacked was the language and the concepts of modern feminism, shortly to arrive in Europe from the United States, which were to provide new ways of framing these problems.

It proved more difficult and took longer to answer these questions than I had, with youthful optimism, anticipated. One problem was the way I formed the questions I was raising. While they dealt with all the major issues which feminist criminologists have addressed since; explaining sex crime differences, considering sexism in the academy, the rationality of female offending, notions of "standpoint," and other theories, none of these are expressed in today's vocabulary. What we still lacked was the language and the concepts of modern feminism, shortly to arrive in Europe from the United States, which were to provide new ways of framing these problems. At this stage I recognized that:

> we barely possess the basic components for an initial analysis of the deviance of women. (Heidensohn 1968:170-1)

Further, the cultural shift which would favor debates about these issues had not yet happened.

In due course, new perspectives were successfully imported into criminology and made a profound impact on the subject. It is especially crucial, in view of the themes of this collection, to record that, it was a new set of ideas from both within mainstream criminology *and also* not from the new sociology of deviance. In presenting another account of these developments elsewhere, I have suggested that they can be described as a series of "awakenings." Four linked awakenings were significant:

Naming:

> A range of concepts, processes and constructs has been named by feminist scholars. This enabled us to see that gender, power and control were relevant to the analysis of both serious assaults and comparatively minor incivilities. (Heidensohn 1998:159)

While this "naming" of sometimes hidden or anonymous topics was stimulated by academic feminists, vital roles were also played by activists and campaigners. Issues such as domestic violence, rape, and trafficking were highlighted by campaigners and notably altered awareness and public policy responses to them (Heidensohn 2000).

Discovering:

Describes the profound awakening achieved through new ways of undertaking research, widely applied to female offenders (Carlen 1984, 1985) and other "deviant" women (Heidensohn 1994a).

Spreading:

Indicates that "a high *recognition* factor...has increasingly been attached to feminist issues, even in criminology" (Heidensohn 1994a:60) so that no criminology course nor serious textbook would be complete without considering them today.

Debating:

The final, feminist-inspired awakening, reflects the series of challenges and debates which have both enlivened the subject and extended its range, for instance, in studies of victims and gendered violence.

By the early 1980s, criminology had altered dramatically, its encounter with feminism counting as one of the major change-agents. Carol Smart's path-breaking book was a landmark and was followed by a series of studies which energized the field (e.g., Rafter and Stanko 1982; Price and Sokoloff 1982). Downes and Rock (1988:273) declared:

> from the late 1970s to date the most notable development in theorizing about deviance has been the emergence of…'feminist criminology.'

At this stage, (having spent five years away from academia as a civil servant) I tried to draw together the debates of the previous years on women and crime, criminology's neglect of women, and also to theorize about female conformity. *Women and Crime* (1985 and 1996a) is the result and has become a "key text in the development of a feminist criminology" (Eaton 2000:20) and has proved to be a lasting success. Following its appearance I have continued to research and publish on related themes (Heidensohn 1986, 1987, 1989, 1994, 1997). However, at this point, I want to turn to the development of my interest in comparative work and to comment on what I had learned from my researches on women and crime and how these influenced my approach to comparative work.

Coming to Comparisons

As I have already suggested, I have never ceased to explore within the framework of feminist perspectives. Rather, the series of projects which I began in the 1980s and am still concerned with, have focussed on making international comparisons using gender-related topics. By this time, I was in my forties and in mid-career. I was able to reflect on what I had achieved so far and on what direction I should take next. Crossing frontiers, in an intellectual sense, appealed to me. Applying feminist perspectives gave me a taste for shifting paradigms, as I believe we did. It was a taxing, but exciting task. Another lesson was the importance of drawing on the widest possible sources to invigorate our subject. Criminology, I had discovered, is not self-renewing, it needs to be regularly refreshed from other sources. In a book about crime and society that I wrote about this time, I described this process:

> The coasts of Britain used to be dotted with tide mills. These mills gained the power to turn their wheels from the water flooded into their mill pools at high tide. Criminology in Britain has functioned rather like a tide mill. The source of its power…came from outside. (Heidensohn 1989a:186)

Outside influences and conditions were critical too: only when there had been key social, cultural, and political shifts had it been possible to engage a wider audience in dialogue about feminist perspectives. Direct proof of this contention comes in an account from a female criminologist writing about her work in Poland before the fall of communism:

> Our main problem was communism and how to get rid of it. Criminology seemed likely to be helpful in unmasking the communist state. Women? Female perspectives? No, there was no place for that....We (women) did not feel unequal and the American women's liberation movement seemed a whim of people with too much free time. (Platek 1995:127)

At a more pragmatic level, it had become clear to me that, in order to establish a really successful academic career, it was necessary to work on the bigger picture, both to pursue cross-national comparisons and to gain wider recognition. (This much was apparent to me when I planned my first-ever study leave from my university in 1987.) It is interesting to observe that the gradings brought in the following year and applied subsequently every four years to all U.K. academic departments in higher education, give the highest scores (and thus the most funding) to work of international repute.

Embarking on my next project, exploring women's experiences as police officers in the United States and Great Britain was thus driven by a number of aims. Most important undoubtedly, was my continued interest in engendering criminology; more specifically, in writing *"Women and Crime: Questions for Criminology"* in 1987. I had found virtually no literature on the significance of women officers enforc-

ing the law with female offenders.

One British-based study of equity in policing had appeared (Jones 1986) and there was a range of U.S. research studies evaluating post-integration developments there. On the U.K. experience there were historical accounts, but very little else. No one had so far attempted to make cross-national comparisons. In sum, what drew me to this topic was, first of all, a spirit of adventure, the realization that there was a new frontier to cross, albeit with more maps and guides than on my first journey. Second, the international dimension had high salience for this issue. Studies of policing, which had grown rapidly as an area of criminology, used various models to analyse the field since police and policing were held to have universal features (Reiner 2000). A widely used model identified "Anglo American Policing" as a distinctive form (Miller 1977) with a common history and shared characteristics (McKenzie and Gallagher 1989). Yet none of the already considerable literature on this topic had considered the entry of women and their subsequent histories within this framework.

Some external factors were propitious: Britain had passed a Sex Discrimination Act in 1975 which applied to the police. The United States had similarly legislated for equality. In both countries, questions about women's role in law enforcement were on the agenda, not least because their full acceptance as police officers had been highly contended by their male colleagues (Halford 1993). One advantage this created for me was that while I failed to gain support from the main funding body for social science research in Britain for my project, I was given an award by The Police Foundation, an independent body which commissions relevant research in this field.

This practical point is not a trivial one. I shall say more below about the costs of doing international research. For the moment, I want to indicate some of the problems which arose in undertaking such a study in the 1980s and how they contrast with today. First, I had to establish all my own contacts in both Britain and the United States: there were no obvious links to use, and some bodies turned down or ignored my requests. Nevertheless, without the benefits of email, with no fax, I managed to set-up a total of fifty interviews with serving or very recently retired female officers in the two countries. Once I had made initial contacts with key informants in the United States, via some informal networks, there was a classic "snowball" response from eager respondents. One of the most interesting aspects of the responses I received, and one on which I have reflected elsewhere, is the degree to which my own earlier work, together with my colleagues, had contributed to the consciousness which these women had of themselves; they were interested in themselves and knew themselves to be interesting. They had become "knowing" about their gender and status, had moved from acceptance to resistance of it and had found their own voices (sometimes using writers like me to express their views) (Heidensohn 1994b).

The comparative study of women in law enforcement proved to be very rewarding. It did prove to be illuminat-

ing to contrast history and experiences in the two nations. There were more similarities than differences and some of the latter were surprising. I was able to construct a framework to analyse women's policing careers in Britain and the United States, finding for instance that in both, women reported harassment and opposition from male colleagues. A key career stage for both groups was what I called "transformation scenes," where female officers gained their male colleagues' respect and were permitted entry into the force, after performing an outstanding act of heroism or recklessness (Heidensohn 1992). Counter intuitively, I observed that Britain, with its more restricted equality laws and less confident feminist culture, had nevertheless achieved a higher proportion of female officers than had the United States, a position which remains unchanged in the twenty-first century (Heidensohn 2003). More vitally, I had found evidence of a distinctive female culture in policing. Despite "the observed differences between women's experiences in the two nations, enough similarity between them (exists) to suggest that they have more in common with each other than with their male colleagues" (Heidensohn 1992: 224).

As it turned out, *Women in Control?* was not to be my first international publication. Although the study on which it is based was carried out in 1987-1988, and I did produce a report on the United States for the Police Foundation (Heidensohn 1989a), it was not published until the end of 1992.

At the same time as carrying out the research for *Women in Control?*, I had become involved in another, very different project which was very much international, this time the focus was on Europe. The U.K. is a European nation and a member of the European Union; yet we have tried to look to North America as both example and comparison for ourselves. Of course, we have a language in common with the United States, as well as a shared history and institutions, such as the law and forms of policing. In the late 1980s, developments in Europe began to alter this bias in criminology. There had, as I noted at the very beginning of this chapter, been seminal contributions from continental scholars to British criminology at a much earlier phase in its history. Max Grunhut at Oxford, Leon Radzinowicz at Cambridge and Hermann Mannheim in London, all émigrées from the Third Reich, had played key founding parts in the subject's growth in Britain (Garland 2002; Radzinowicz 1999). All brought international visions to bear on their work. Mannheim's last major work is even called *Comparative Criminology* (1965); it is an immensely erudite collection of a vast amount of knowledge, drawing on studies from many European countries, as well as Britain and the United States. Yet while these European scholars had lead and encouraged criminology in Britain, they had not inspired it into European orientations. European influences were visible in social theory where great thinkers such as Marx and Durkheim remained inspirational and had been joined by Foucault. Otherwise, interest in *crime as a European issue* had been very limited until the late 1980s.

This period saw several key publications, notably David Downes' seminal case study on Dutch penal policy (1988), as well as conference-based collections which recorded growing interest (see Hood 1989 and Cain 1989). The appearance of these texts paralleled a number of political and policy developments within the EU at this time. Briefly, these included the Single European Act, designed to remove non-trade barriers and due to come into force in 1992; and a series of developments in security at the intergovernmental level, known as the four TREVI groups (Heidensohn 1996b:84-6). These external circumstances formed the environment in which a small British institute lead the way in launching the first major conference on crime in Europe in 1988. This event which I helped to organize with Martin Farrell, required us almost to start from scratch. We had a rapid education in criminology in Europe and held a hugely successful conference, deciding at the outset to publish a book based on our deliberations. We determined that we wanted to promote debate about crime and criminal justice in Europe, both inside and outside the then member states of the EU. We also wished to provide a range of material on issues that we saw as truly "European" because they were transnational: policing, drugs, terrorism and fraud, as well as the possibility of one day having "Eurocops." Finally, we sought to:

> show the scope of systematic study of crime...and of future work in this field. (Heidensohn 1991:4)

Producing *Crime in Europe*, in 1991, involved far more than the usual tasks of editing. We had to search for datasets (before the availability of the internet) and to try to achieve comparability across language barriers. Among many useful findings from this work were that:

> in order to study crime comparatively three conditions need to be met. There must be sources of material and data with which to make comparisons: crime statistics, victim surveys, research studies. Second, translatable concepts have to be available to make possible the collecting, ordering and analysis of such data. Finally, some kind of framework, part universe of discourse, part set of common concerns, must exist. (Heidensohn 1991:10)

I would still stand by these observations and have indeed applied them to my subsequent work.

The next comparative project with which I became involved proved to be a happy marriage of feminist and comparative perspectives and also grew from a conference base. In 1991, three feminist scholars organized the first international congress on women, law, and social control at Mont Gabriel in Canada. At this key event, sixty invited scholars from eighteen countries came together and discussed the chosen topics intensely and comparatively. Explicitly feminist in orientation, the meeting was also aimed at including the most global perspectives and understandings. I found it exhilarating to meet so many names and scholars in the field and to hear their views and histories. For me, this encounter with Kathy Daly, Dorie Klein, Marie André Bertrand, Nicky Rafter, Chris Alder, and many others were amongst the most significant in my career.

Until then, most of my research had been done alone, or at least without a sense of a community who shared my approach to criminology. At home in the U.K., I was firmly placed in a university post and with contacts to local scholars, a few of whom had similar interests. Mont Gabriel was a watershed, however, for me and for many others who attended it.

It lead directly to two other conference contributions and to collaborating with Nicky Rafter on a book based partly on papers given at Mont Gabriel. For *International Feminist Perspectives in Criminology* (Rafter and Heidensohn 1995) we did set out with very clear purposes. We asked all our contributors to catalogue how criminology had evolved in their respective countries and what form its encounter with feminist perspectives had taken. Finally, they were to forecast future directions the subject might take.

Amongst many conclusions we drew from analysing these reports was that:

> Sharing fears of male violence, women around the globe are already bound by strong ties. But recent years have witnessed an *internationalisation of women's concerns* about crime and justice. More than a recognition and acknowledgement of mutual interests, this phenomenon is self-consciously feminist. And it aims explicitly at creating transnational and transcultural alliances that will respect diversity. (Rafter and Heidensohn 1995:9; added emphasis)

We noted that there was now "an international audience for information on gender, crime and social control" (Rafter and Heidensohn 1995:9).

International Feminist Perspectives in Criminology is the book in which two of the main themes of my work in criminology (feminist and international perspectives) are brought together and used to illuminate each other. For the most part, it is gendered questions which are explored using the scope offered by the comparative method. To cite one example, our authors were asked to comment on the sites of criminological production in their countries. We found that where criminology was well-established feminist work was marginalized, whereas it flourished where it was not dominated by a strong criminology. We did not probe the place of international studies in the same way, although, as outlined above, we noted growing globalization of women's concerns.

Nicky Rafter, with whom I edited this volume, has been a great friend and mentor and a major influence on my comparative work. We first met at Mont Gabriel and have continued to meet at congresses. She is, of course, American, but with a very sophisticated appreciation of Europe and European criminology. Her recent work includes translating and editing Lombroso's works (Rafter and Gibson 2004 and 2005). She guided me to much valuable American material and we have also worked together on an international Encyclopaedia of Women and Crime (Rafter 2000).

This book and *Crime in Europe* derived from international conferences,

Lessons
We found that where criminology was well-established feminist work was marginalized, whereas it flourished where it was not dominated by a strong criminology.

both of which had been very consciously planned to stimulate cross-national work. *Crime in Europe* was to promote new comparative angles. In the latter case, we sought to give a European dimension to British comparative studies. Both Martin Farrell and I had strong personal ties to Europe and were convinced that it was both too narrow a view only to look for examples and comparisons in the United States. Moreover, as members of the EU, we had formal links with nations from which we could learn much about criminal justice policies and with whom we were likely to have to cooperate in the future. As events have transpired, British governments have persisted until the present day in seeking solutions to crime problems in the United States (Newburn 2000). At the same time, the Maastricht Treaty and other developments in Europe have meant that the U.K. is now much more closely involved in criminal justice policy in Europe (Heidensohn 1996b).

Having been involved in two comparative studies which were not based on empirical research, I was determined that the next one must be. By this time, in the mid-1990s, I had reached the mature phase in my career: I occupied an established chair in the University of

Lessons
There are still important tasks still to complete and I hope that students in upcoming generations will tackle them with vigour. I see these as:
·   *the theory gap,*   •   *the problem of colonialism, and*   ·   *the question of view point.*

London, was head of my academic department and held a number of professional and public service positions outside the University. My work on a variety of topics was reasonably well known and thus I was approached in 1992, around the time *Women in Control?* was published by Jennifer Brown, then head of research for Hampshire Police, who shared my interest in this topic and had already carried out a survey of her own on women officers.

She has become another significant influence and a research collaborator. She is responsible for the innovative use of conferences as research sites, not in the way I had, with colleagues, previously used them as *sources* of papers and arenas for debate, but as the actual places where subjects might be sought and interviewed. Jenny and I both wished to take further the work on women in law enforcement which we had begun separately. In particular, we were concerned with issues such as sexual harassment and what coping strategies female officers employed to cope and survive their occupations. Using the serendipitous occurrence of two

international conferences on women in policing, and a variety of other links, we were able to contact a large, international sample to whom we administered a questionnaire and a smaller one whom we interviewed face to face. In all, we collected over 800 usable questionnaires from women serving in 35 countries, together with 47 full-length interviews of policewomen from 19 states (Brown and Heidensohn 2000: 109, 172).

Our purposes in seeking this amount of comparative data were similar in part to my own in *Women in Control?*: we wanted to test hypotheses about women's common experiences in police culture transnationally. We also wanted to explore different models and cultures of policing. In addition, we wanted to widen our international scope beyond the anglo-centricism of earlier work and include women from "the South," the non-western world; further, we aimed to reach officers in transitional countries, undergoing rapid political and social change and some from smaller, remoter countries with few female officers.

As I outlined above, we circulated our (pre-piloted) questionnaire through conference mailing lists and research links and at actual international meetings of policewomen. More originally, we decided to use one of these events, in September 1996, as a research site. Initially, the benefit of leading our team of researchers at the conference and interviewing there all day was to give us access "to an international sample, gathered in one place at one time and to a group of criminal justice professionals who can prove elusive" (Heidensohn 2000:68). As it turned out, we gained much more than this: fortuitously, the design of the conference centre ensured that our subjects were "on display" to us for much of the time. We were able to add a good deal of participant observation of their behaviour to our interview records, thus enriching our qualitative and quantitative data enormously (see Heidensohn 2000 for more analysis).

In analyzing and writing up the material from the interviews, I was able to undertake quite a sophisticated comparison which reflected the evolution of my approach to comparative work over a considerable period. First, we constructed *comparative models of policing* derived from our own larger data set as well as from mainstream policing studies. Our framework yielded four discrete models: Cops (i.e., the Anglo-American notion of my earlier study) Colonials, Transitionals, and Gendarmes (Brown and Heidensohn 2000:30-31). Using this taxonomy showed some significant differences between respondents. In addition, when examining the interviewees, I employed the same conceptual framework as I had in *Women and Control?* Thus both a global and a time line dimension was produced. One repeated observation was that of:

the part that transformation scenes played in achieving acceptance into the occupational culture. (Brown and Heidensohn 2000:142)

Gender and Policing is another pioneering text. It is the first international empirical study on this topic and, while there are limitations on the sample we obtained, we were able, by using an innovative method to benefit from having an international conference as our research site. This project was quite costly, and was very tiring, but it yielded great results in a short period. We would have spent far more time, effort, and money to reach a sample anywhere near as rich as this one. This does raise a number of the practical issues for conducting research on a worldwide scale, especially costs, complexity, and compliance. We carefully asked all conference attendees if they wished to be interviewed; one initially refused, then changed her mind as she heard from others how much they had enjoyed the experience.

An irony of taking a long-term interest in international work is that one can become perceived as an expert on the globalization of crime and be invited to take part in congresses and events which focus on that theme. Thus I have now taken part in four international policing conferences as a speaker as well as in the criminological ones described above. This does raise some issues about reflexivity: how far can an observer also be a participant? Indeed this brings in more fundamental questions about comparative method and how researchers obtain their material. Nelken (2002) discusses the advantages of "being there" and "going there." Can we find out much if we do not speak the local language? How long is a long enough stay in a strange place to gain trust/acquire material?

My next international assignment brought home some of these questions as I worked with a group of (mainly Helsinki-based) colleagues to plan and then run a "stream" of the Tenth United Nations Congress on the Prevention of

Crime and the Treatment of Offenders on Women in the Criminal Justice System (see Matti Jousten in this volume). The aims were to share good practice and research findings, and contributors ranged from hands-on workers with the most deprived groups to senior government ministers. Since UN delegates can and do attend, the entire event is continuously translated into all official languages. This resulted (when protocols were being drawn up in another "stream") in lengthy debates about the use of terms such as "gender." Debates were not between groups of feminists but between diplomats over linguistics (Ollus and Nevala 2001).

Comparative criminology is now well-established. Organizationally, the American Society of Criminology has a flourishing International Division, the European Society of Criminology was founded in 2001 and is growing fast. It has a new journal and there are many more. A huge mass of material is now regularly collected by numerous agencies to provide international comparative data on victims (Proband 2003), juvenile delinquents, violence against women (Ollus 2001), and many more subjects. In short, comparative work is now much easier to carry out, not least because electronic communications reduce distances to zero. Almost all the material I gathered on trafficking for my paper at the UN Congress came from Internet sources (Heidensohn 2001). Perhaps it can now be said that most of the frontiers have been crossed.

There are still important tasks still to complete and I hope that students in upcoming generations will tackle them with vigour. I see these as:

- the theory gap,
- the problem of colonialism, and
- the question of view point.

The Theory Gap

While there have been surges of new comparative studies, these have not so far been matched by strong developments of theories which can be used to analyse and explain the material being collected. There are examples of interesting frameworks which have been fruitfully and constructively used as with the various approaches to policing worldwide (see Brown and Heidensohn 2000 for a summary and review). Braithwaite's interpretation of the theories of Elias and his own further application of these to shame and reintegration is another case. But too many studies have sought to compare without allowing sufficiently for contrasts and significant differences. Those writers who focus on governmentality, claiming it to be a global phenomenon, have been particularly challenged over this (see Young 1999): they have been taken to task for assuming that trends which may be marked in the USA and the UK are universal, yet they ignore evidence from Europe and elsewhere which contradicts this view. This is an area where the gap needs to be bridged quickly so that comparative studies can be carried out with more sophistication and the subject as a whole can be enriched.

Another problem is caused by the "colonial" assumptions which underpin some comparative work. Increasingly in criminology, the United States is the "colonial" power, so that other countries and systems are brought into comparisons with the United States in order to demonstrate the salience of an American conceptual approach or a criminal justice policy.

Finally, there is what I have called "the viewpoint problem." Most comparative research is done from the standpoint of the researcher. The assumption tends to be that information is gathered for the purpose of illuminating "home" as against "away."

Before drawing some final conclusions, I want to refer to findings from another study, which is focussed at the international level, indeed at international agencies and networks in which women have taken part in order to promote social control and law enforcement. This is the most fully international project I have so far undertaken and has involved a variety of methods. These have ranged from interviews and observations in various countries, analyses of documents and historical accounts and archive searches at, *inter alia,* the League of Nations in Geneva. What I have so far discovered leads me to revise what I and others have taken for granted about our modern, international projects in our shrunken, globalized world.

Almost strikingly, internationalism is nothing new: more than a century ago, determined groups of women campaigned to get women into policing by systematic use of the media and the political system. Yet they did not have the vote and would not serve in most of the positions they sought to open to their own gender (Heidensohn 2000:45). Contrary to our present views about ease of communication, global networks were established and linked-up without benefit of any of our mod-ern technology. They also regularly collected data, for instance, on trafficking of women and children, and even the League of Nations undertook major, fact-finding voyages around the Far East (Heidensohn 2000). The thrust of all this work was very much affected by external factors, as is so often true in this area. In this case, the externals were the rise of fascism and the outbreak of World War II.

If I were advising someone who wanted to pursue comparative criminology, I would suggest that they first consider what *frontiers tempt them to cross?* That is, what new unexplored land needs discovery and mapping. Secondly, I should encourage them to *observe outside influences closely*, since they can make the difference between times being right or out of joint for any given project. I would look too for *key concepts* and consider with care the existing repertoire and how best to apply them. At a mundane level, I would look to international conferences as a source and focus of activity and consider carefully if your career will be helped by this involvement. In the end, however, it comes down to your own interests and enjoyment.

Selected Bibliography

Bayley, D. 1999. "Policing: the World Stage." In *Policing Across the World*, edited by R. Mawby. London: UCL Press.

Bertrand, M.A. 1992. "Some Concluding Thoughts." In *Proceedings of the International Feminist Conference on Women, Law and Social Control*, edited by M.A. Bertrand, K. Daly, and D. Klein. Quebec: Mont Gabriel.

Brown, J. and F. Heidensohn. 2000. *Gender and Policing.* Basingstoke: Palgrave/Macmillan.

Cain, M., ed. 1989. *Growing up Good.* London: Sage.

Carlen, P. 1984. *Women's Imprisonment.* London: Routledge.

_____. 1985. *Criminal Women.* Cambridge: Polity Press.

Carlen, P. and A. Worrall, eds. 1987. *Gender, Crime and Justice.* Milton Keynes: Open University Press.

Downes, D. 1988. *Contrasts in Tolerance.* Oxford: Clarendon Press.

Downes, D. and P.E. Rock. 1988. *Understanding Deviance,* 2d ed. Oxford: Clarendon Press.

Eaton, M. 2000. "A Woman in Her Own Time: Frances Heidensohn Within and Beyond Criminolgy." *Women and Criminal Justice* 12(2/2):9-28.

Garland, D. 2002. "Of Crimes and Criminals." In *The Oxford Handbook of Criminology.* 3d ed., edited by R. Maguire, R. Morgan, R. Reiner et al. Oxford: Oxford University Press.

Garland, D. and R. Sparks, eds. 2001. "Criminology, Social Theory and the Challenge of Our Times." *British Journal of Criminology* 40(2):189-204.

Halford, A. 1993. *No Way up the Greasy Pole.* London: Constable.

Heidensohn, F.M. 1968. "The Deviance of Women: A Critique and an Enquiry." *British Journal of Sociology* XIX(2):160-175.

_____. 1969. 'Prison For Women'. *Howard Journal* (1969):281-288.

_____. 1970. "Sex, Crime and Society." In *Biosocial Aspects of Sex,* edited by G.A. Harrison. Oxford: Blackwell.

_____. 1985. *Women and Crime.* London: Macmillan.

_____. 1986. "Models of Justice: Portia or Persephone? Some Thoughts on Equality, Fairness and Gender in the Field of Criminal Justice." *International Journal of the Sociology of the Law* 14:33-46.

_____. 1987. "Women and Crime: Questions for Criminology." In *Gender, Crime and Justice,* edited by P. Carlen and A. Worrall. Milton Keynes: Open University Press.

_____. 1989a. *Women in Policing in the USA.* London: Police Foundation.

_____. 1989b. *Crime and Society.* London: Macmillan.

_____. 1991. "Introduction: Convergence, Diversity and Change." In *Crime in Europe,* edited by F. Heidensohn and M. Farrell. London: Routledge.

_____. 1992. *Women in Control? The Role of Women in Law Enforcement.* Oxford: Oxford University Press.

_____. 1994a. "From Being to Knowing: Some Issues in the Study of Gender in Contemporary Society.' *Women and Criminal Justice* 6(1):13-37.

_____. 1994b. "We Can Handle it Out Here: Women Officers in Britain and the USA and the Policing of Public Order." *Policing and Society* IV(4):293-303.

_____. 1996a. *Women and Crime.* 2d ed. London: Macmillan.

_____. 1996b. "Crime and Policing." In *The Future of Europe,* edited by V. Symes, C. Levy and J. Littlewood. London: Macmillan.

_____. 1998. "Comparative Models of Policing and the Role of Women Officers." *International Journal of Police Science and Management* 1(3):215-226.

_____. 1998. "Translations and Refutations: An Analysis of Changing Perspectives in Criminology'. In *Thinking About Criminology*, edited by S. Holdaway and P. Rock. London: UCL Press.

_____. 2000. *Sexual Politics and Social Control*. Buckingham: Open University Press.

_____. 2001. "Research on Women in the Criminal Justice System and Transnational Crime." In *Women in the Criminal Justice System: International Examples and National Responses*, edited by N. Ollus and S. Nevala. Helsinki: European Institute for Crime Prevention and Control.

_____. 2003. "Gender and Policing." In *The Handbook of Policing*, edited by T. Newburn. Cullompton: Willan Publishing.

Heidensohn, F.M. and F. Farrell, eds. 1991. *Crime in Europe*. London: Routledge.

Hood, R., ed. 1989. *Crime and Criminal Policy in Europe*. Oxford: Centre for Criminological Research.

Jones, S. 1986. *Policewomen and Equality: Formal Policy v Informal Practice?* London: Macmillan.

Maguire, R., R. Morgan, R. Reiner et al., eds. 2002. *The Oxford Handbook of Criminology*, 3d ed. Oxford: Oxford University Press.

Mannheim, H. 1965. *Comparative Criminology*. Vols. 1 and 2. London: Routledge and Kegan Paul.

McKenzie, I.K. and G.P. Gallagher. 1989. *Behind The Uniform— Policing in Britain and America*. Harvester Wheatsheaf: St Martins Press.

Miller, W.R. 1977. *Cops and Bobbies*. Chicago: University of Chicago Press.

Nelken, D. 2002. "Comparing Criminal Justice." In *The Oxford Handbook of Criminology*, 3d ed, edited by M. Maguire et al. Oxford: Oxford

University Press.

Newburn, T. 2000. *'Atlantic Crossing.' Inaugural Lecture*. London: Goldsmiths University of London.

Ollus, N. 2001. "International Violence against Women Survey." In *Women in the Criminal JusticeSystem: International Examples and National Responses*, edited by N. Ollus and S. Nevala. Helsinki: European Institute for Crime Prevention and Control.

Ollus, N. and S. Nevala, eds. 2001. *Women in the Criminal Justice System: International Examples and National Responses*. Helsinki: European Institute for Crime Prevention and Control.

Platek, M. 1995. "What it's like for Women: Criminology in Poland and Eastern Europe." In *International Feminist Perspectives in Criminology: Engendering a Discipline*, edited by N. Hahn Rafter and F.M. Heidensohn. Buckingham: Open University Press.

Price, B.R. and N.J. Sokoloff, eds. 1982. *The Criminal Justice System and Women*. New York: Clark Boardman.

Proband, E. 2003. "Surveying Victims of Crime." *European Journal of Criminology* forthcoming.

Radzinowicz, L. 1999. *Adventures in Criminology*. London: Routledge.

Rafter, N., ed. 2000. *The Encyclopedia of Women and Crime*. Phoenix, Arizona: Onyx Press.

Rafter, N. and M. Gibson, eds. 2004. *The Criminal Women*. NC: Duke University Press.

_____, eds. 2005. *Criminal Man*. NC: Duke University Press.

Rafter, N. and F.M. Heidensohn. 1995. "Introduction: The Development of

Feminist Perspectives on Crime." In *International Feminist Perspectives in Criminology: Engendering a Discipline*, edited by N. Hahn Rafter and F.M. Heidensohn. Buckingham: Open University Press.

Rafter, N. and E.A. Stanko, eds. 1982. *Judge, Lawyer, Victim, Thief: Women, Gender Roles and Gender Justice.* Boston: Northeastern University Press.

Reiner, R. 2000. *The Politics of the Police*, 3d ed. Oxford: Oxford University Press.

Rock, P. 1996. *Reconstructing a Women's Prison: The Holloway Redevelopment Project 1968-1988.* Oxford: Clarendon Press.

Young, J. 1999 *The Exclusive Society* London: Polity Press.

Chapter 11

On Being a Comparative Criminologist

Roy King

*Centre for Comparative Criminology
and Criminal Justice at the University of
Wales, Bangor and
Institute of Criminology, University of
Cambridge*

*Here, in action, I had found a situation
in which the power of comparative
research had been harnessed to the possibility of making a difference.*

What is Comparative Criminology?

There is a sense in which every criminologist who came to criminology via the parent discipline of sociology is a comparative criminologist. Those of us who imbibed the work of Durkheim from a tender age were brought up to understand that our very subject matter emerges in a changing environment of moral judgements. When Durkheim (1964) wrote about the normality, nay the inevitability, of crime and invited us to consider what form it might take even in a society of saints, he was declaring that moral judgements were inherent to the human condition. Good versus bad, beautiful versus ugly, criminal versus non-criminal: one part of each dichoto-my has no meaning whatsoever unless we are able to compare it with our sense of its opposite, but it is impossible to imagine a society without them. Placing any person, situation or event in one category or the other—or sometimes on the continuum that connects the extremes—requires us to make the judgement in respect to one or more critical criteria.

Durkheim (1964) famously considered, in his rules of sociological method, that it was possible and necessary, for the scientist to stand outside those moral judgements, to treat what he called social facts as things, to mimic the way in which natural scientists are able to regard their subject matter quite dispassionately because they do not have normative components to

Lessons
Through systematic comparison across societies, or across groups within societies, we may discover the factors which, by their presence or absence, seem to underpin particular patterns of crime or punishment.

get in the way of their observations. Most of us, following Durkheim, make fairly strenuous efforts to stand as far away as we can from our everyday moral positions in our criminological work, if only because it helps to bring the rigour of a positive science to bear on our subject matter. But most of us too have come to recognize, following the alternative Weberian tradition, that it is not possible for us to escape from the fact that we were brought up with those moral judgements long before we became scientists. Moreover, there are benefits to derive from our role as participant citizens which we can use to our advantage as social scientists in understanding the meanings of the events we observe (Weber 1949).

But moral judgements are not the only ones in which comparisons are inevitable. In fact, *every* empirical scientist in *any* discipline, is a comparative scientist in that the first task of any science is description, and the second is classification. Classification requires placing one's data into categories (since none of us can deal with the welter of individual variation) and categorization involves categorizing people, situations or events in ways in which the differences between categories are greater

than the differences within categories. Making those scientific judgements involves comparison albeit against well-defined criteria.

These are the inevitabilities. But there are also desirabilities. The intuitive idea, before modern statistical theory, was simply that through the systematic comparison of "concomitant variations" one could tease out explanations of phenomena in ways analogous to the systematic manipulation of variables deployed by natural scientists in laboratory experiments. It was such a method that Durkheim (1952) deployed in his classic study of suicide—but it was Durkheim's particular genius that he chose to compare groups that would critically test his emerging thesis that suicide varied with levels of social cohesion. In it he developed a seminal model of research design using systematic comparisons and carefully selected critical cases to test his hypotheses. Durkheim never attempted an empirical analysis of crime to match his study of suicide, but his insistence that crime arose out of the very social structure of society and therefore that each society in some sense got the patterns of crime and the criminals it deserved, set out both the scope and the essential dilemma of an imaginative comparative criminology. On the one hand, through systematic comparison across societies, or across groups within societies, we may discover the factors which, by their presence or absence, seem to underpin particular patterns of crime or punishment. On the other hand the functions, or perhaps rather loosely to switch to a Weberian discourse, the meanings of those patterns can only be understood in the local context of the social structure within which they are embedded. I shall return to some of the issues associated with doing comparative criminology in an international context in the latter part of this essay.

On Becoming a Comparative Criminologist

I was fortunate to have been taught by some of the world's finest sociologists, although this was not the product of informed choice on my part, still less a career plan. The first member of my family to go to university, I favored the lowly University of Leicester over the much more prestigious London School of Economics for the simple reason that it would mean I would have to live away from home and stand on my own two feet. Having commuted for seven years from Potters Bar where I was born to Hornsey in London where I went to secondary school, I had had my fill of catching the 08.08 train every morning until I was 18. I have managed to live within walking distance of my work ever since. There were other possible universities which were prepared to have me as a student, but I visited Leicester and liked it, and so truncated my search procedures. I went up on to university to study economics for no better reason than that my brother in law had studied it part time as an external student.

It did not take long, however, to become bored with intersecting supply and demand curves and a world predicated upon assumptions of rational choice. So what to do? Our first year course in sociology was taught by Norbert Elias. Though his great work

had been published in German in 1938 it was not until after the English translation appeared in 1978 that he was finally acclaimed as belonging to the pantheon of the world's greatest sociologists. In the interim his work was virtually unknown outside a small group of colleagues and his students. His course was an unfolding stream of consciousness which we struggled to understand—a struggle made harder for us by his impenetrable European accent. Later, we came to recognize that what we had been privileged to hear, was the essence of his work on the civilizing process. I recall one occasion when towards the end of a lecture I raised what I thought was an intelligent question. I was told "Mr King will you please be quiet. You don't know enough yet to begin to formulate the right questions." It is difficult to imagine saying that to students today—but Elias was right. I didn't know enough to ask questions. For the next two years I shut up and listened and absorbed things like a sponge. In those days, 1959, students were always referred to as Mr. or Miss and our teachers always by their titles.

Sometime in my second year Elias touched on criminological topics—Shaw and McKay (1942) and the Chicago School, and Aichorn's (1936) work on wayward youth. Elias painted such intriguing pictures of both these very different traditions that I was entranced, but if anything I was then more attracted to Aichorn than Shaw and Mackay—and even contemplated throwing everything up to train as a psychoanalyst. In fact I obtained places in two London medical schools—Guy's and St Thomas's—but I had by then used up two years of my scholarship, was not eligible for more public money, and my family had no funds to keep me in higher education for a further seven years.

Somewhat disappointed I reconciled myself to returning to my sociological studies. It did not require much effort. In retrospect I much prefer the perspectives of sociology to the cultural blinkers which circumscribe most psychiatry—but I do regret not having the sheer power to open doors that comes with a medical qualification. Ilya Neustadt, the head of the school, had recruited a veritable hot bed of rising stars to make Leicester the most exciting school of sociology around. John Goldthorpe was just beginning his work with David Lockwood (our external examiner) on the affluent worker (Goldthorpe and Lockwood 1969), in the afterglow of which he moved to a Fellowship at King's College, thus becoming the first established sociologist in the University of Cambridge. Percy Cohen, whose flawless delivery of lectures containing the most complex ideas entirely without notes was only matched subsequently by Anthony Giddens. For me personally, and for a whole generation of students through his writings, Cohen (1968) made modern sociological theorizing sufficiently interesting for us to read the entire corpus of work by Talcott Parsons, as well as many much more accessible authors, to supplement the Marx, Durkheim, and Weberian traditions espoused by Neustadt and Elias. Whilst I was at Leicester, Tony Giddens was a tutorial assistant, whose task it was to pick and further elucidate the points raised in the lectures by senior colleagues. Unfortunately, I can scarcely claim to have

been taught by him, on the basis of what was a rather casual contact. He went on, of course, to follow Goldthorpe to Cambridge and thence to become the Director of the London School of Economics, *en route* becoming the guru of the third way (Giddens 2000). There were others too. One way of measuring the strength of an academic department is by the numbers of staff who go on to full professorships elsewhere and to run Departments of their own—also among those were Sheila Allen and Richard Brown, respectively at Bradford and Durham. Though their specialist subjects were of less immediate interest to me, Richard supervised my undergraduate dissertation on juvenile delinquency in Leicester. Looking back—I still have a copy though I would never show it to anyone—this was a wonderfully naïve attempt to explore the extent to which any of Barbara Wootton's (1959) explanations of juvenile delinquency could be discerned from a perusal of the files of young offenders sentenced to probation in Leicester. At the time it seemed really rather good and I shall always be grateful for Richard Brown's enthusiastic support and his belief (though we never followed this up) that with a bit of editing it was publishable.

By any standards it was a formidable array of talent to which I became exposed, and it would be surprising if some of their enthusiasms had not rubbed off on me. Certainly there is a fair sprinkling of their students who themselves occupy positions of influence in their turn.

By 1962 I had a shiny new First Class Honours Degree in Sociology, but I didn't quite know what to do with it. On the one hand I was fascinated by the pursuit of knowledge, for its own sake and committed to the idea of doing research in furtherance of that pursuit. But, like Aichorn with his wayward youth, I also wanted somehow to make a difference. After three years I realized that my head was full of theoretical notions that I found difficult to apply to the real world. Apart from the possibility of becoming a psycho-analyst, I had not really thought about what possible careers might be open to me once I had given up the idea of being an economist. I sought Neustadt's advice. Under questioning I told him that the parts of the course which I had found particularly interesting were those bits on Shaw and Mackay and Aichorn (the only bits of "modern" criminology that figured in the course) and that I still had some difficulty in linking that to the theorizing of law and order to be found in the works of the founding fathers— Marx, Durkheim, and Weber. In an accent almost as difficult to follow as Elias, he told me: "Well then you must go to Cambridge and talk to my friend Radzinowicz." Much though I was tempted, I asked but where will that lead me? "To a good job. That's where."

I wasn't convinced, but there are times in your life when you should follow the advice you are given—especially if you don't have any better ideas yourself. Cambridge it was: following in the footsteps of John Goldthorpe and soon to be joined by Anthony Giddens, I went to King's College albeit in the much lowlier almost invisible capacity of graduate student, and enrolled on what was then the one-year Postgraduate Diploma in Criminology at the newly established Institute of Criminology. As it happened, Radzinowicz

was on sabbatical leave in the United States during the year I spent at the Institute and so I was never subject to his influence as a teacher—though years later I became the most vociferous critic of the penal policy most closely associated with his name—the so called dispersal system for dealing with high security prisoners (ACPS 1968). Graduating with a distinction a year later, one of my teachers, John Martin, encouraged me to stay on to pursue a Ph.D. on White Collar Crime, but although I drew up the proposal my heart was not in it and a variety of factors, both domestic and academic, led me to the conclusion that I should go out into the big world of work.

I resolved to take the first interesting research post that would pay me £1,000 a year (then the marker salary for people of ambition). I applied for posts as a research assistant and was duly appointed by Professor Jack Tizard, then of the Medical Research Council's Social Psychiatry Research Unit at the Maudsley Hospital in London, as one of three research assistants on the Child Welfare Project, a study of institutional care for what were then described as mentally subnormal children, funded by the American Association for the Aid of Crippled Children. And I registered myself as a Ph.D. student at the London School of Economics. Tizard, a psychologist from New Zealand, had established himself as a world leader in the field of mental subnormality and was soon to win the Eunice-Shriver Kennedy prize for this. It was Tizard's inspiration to ask the question why could the mentally subnormal, then largely cared for in the wards of large hospitals and cared for by a succession of ever changing nursing staff, not enjoy the benefits of small family-style environments of the kind that had been increasingly provided for normal, but deprived, children whose parents were either absent or not up to the task of parenting? At the time the unequivocal answer of the medical profession was that the mentally subnormal had on the one hand, special needs that required specialist nursing support, and on the other had disabilities which meant that they would not benefit from more stimulating environments. Tizard had already shown, through his famous Brooklands experiment, that changes could be effected in the regimes for handicapped children in hospital care, at least for a time and under certain circumstances (see Clarke and Tizard 1983). But the traditional structures of conventional hospitals were sufficiently resilient for such changes to be resisted and eventually overcome by inertia.

It was Tizard's genius in the Child Welfare Project to suggest the imaginative comparative leap first by exploring and measuring the patterns of care in publicly provided homes for normal children and then using those measures to rate the quality of care across a wide range of local authority, voluntary, and health service provision for the mentally subnormal. It was my privilege to be part of the team, with Norma Raynes and Bill Yule, struggling to provide those measures and to interpret them. Using the same test applied to the University of Leicester above, both Bill and Norma also went on to full professorships. Here, in action, I had found a situation in which the power of comparative research had been harnessed to the possibility of making a difference. As

we followed staff around recording for every five minute period of the day their interactions with their colleagues and the children in their care we were able to ask the question: Did handicapped children have difficulties learning to speak because of brain defects or because their carer's hardly ever spoke to them (King, Raynes, and Tizard 1971)? I had had my first real taste of how, through research, one can come up with answers that are both scientifically satisfying and which have practical implications that can be translated into policy. That research formed part of a much larger body of work that led to the widespread adoption of "community care" policies. Regrettably, in retrospect, we sold the policy in part on grounds that it would be cheaper. Politicians took us at our word and never provided the resources to make community alternatives work as effectively as they could. So I also had my first taste, then largely by proxy because I was too minor a figure to be directly involved in the policy making process, of the difficulties and dangers of the relationship between researchers and politicians.

When the Child Welfare Project came to an end I was faced with a dilemma. Should I pursue the precarious career path of a researcher going from one short-term contract to another or seek the security of a tenured teaching position? By now I was married with obligations. And my tutor at Cambridge, John Martin, had just been appointed to the Chair of Social Policy at the University of Southampton. He wanted me to join him there, and by way of enticement he explained that David Gould, an iconoclastic and innovative prison governor (warden) in the best tradition of English eccentrics, had offered the possibility of researching his brand new prison at Albany on the Isle of Wight. I was tempted, but made a token exploration of what else was available in the field. The distinguished South African theoretician and expert on race relations, John Rex in Durham was keen that I should go there. But in the end Southampton won the bidding process. Delighted though I was to have the opportunity to study Albany prison I knew that I wanted to make this a comparative study. Accordingly I put proposals to the Home Office Research Unit (as it then was) for funding a comparative study of prison regimes (rather like those comparative regimes for handicapped children and certainly using some of the same conceptual apparatus) that would test the official thinking about the extent to which treatment or training was provided for prisoners in the prison system of England and Wales. Albany became the pilot for what was to become a comparative study of prison regimes (King and Elliott 1977; King, 1972; King and Morgan 1976). Using the same criteria already applied to Leicester and the Child Welfare Project above, it is a source of great pleasure that a key worker on the Prison Regimes Project (Rod Morgan) has gone on to become not merely a full Professor, but Her Majesty's Chief Inspector of Probation and now the Chair of the Youth Justice Board for England and Wales.

It was my study of Albany that led me to challenge Radzinowicz's policy of "dispersing" high escape risk prisoners among lower risk inmates in several high security prisons which would operate a relaxed regime within a secure perimeter. It was a well-meaning, liberal policy designed to avoid what he thought would become a potentially explosive environment if all high-risk prisoners were "concentrated" in a single "fortress" prison. That alternative had been proposed in an earlier report by Lord Mountbatten (Home Office 1966) following some dramatic, and highly politically embarrassing escapes. Albany had been designed as a low security training prison but almost as soon as it was opened it was selected as one of the first four dispersal prisons. As my research unfolded I watched Albany being transformed from a prison dedicated to an exciting adventure in rehabilitation to into one which had become what the press described as the "jail of fear." My critique of dispersal policy was that it irrationally placed far more prisoners than necessary into expensive high security conditions, and because it misunderstood the conditions which gave rise to escape risks and problems of controlling prisoners whilst in custody, it actually made riots and disturbances more rather than less likely.

Advocating a change to dispersal policy did not make me a popular figure. But nor did the results of my comparative study of prison regimes, which produced results that paymasters did not especially wish to hear. Yes, it was possible to identify and measure clear and important differences between prison regimes. But these differences did not make much sense either to prisoners, who experienced them, or staff who administered them. Nor did the differences bear much relationship to programmes of treatment or training (in so far as such programmes were then available in the early 1970s). Nothing in the findings could support the fundamental ideology on which the prison system was founded, and the basis on which funding was allocated as between the impoverished, and overcrowded local prisons (which in essence served a jail function in American terms) and the uncrowded and better resourced training prisons— because there was so little in the form of training that was taking place. Bringers of bad news should not expect renewed funding, and further research in these rather embarrassing areas was not supported.

The Potentialities and Problems of Comparative International Work

I came to internationally comparative work more or less by default. In 1973, in the absence of serious research opportunities in the UK, I went to the United States as a Ford Foundation Research Fellow to participate in a programme organized by Stanton Wheeler under the auspices of Russell Sage. My research was to be on parole systems. Some years earlier I had been appointed to serve on the Parole Board for England and Wales under a boyhood hero of mine, Colonel Sir John Hunt (by then already Lord Hunt), the leader of the first successful expedition to climb Mount Everest. As a boy in short trousers I had sat cross-legged in the school hall watching the film *The Ascent of Everest.* It was coronation year, and small boys in good schools found their chests swelling with pride at Hunt's achievement. Now, only fifteen years later, I was by far the youngest

member of an august body which included, among many illustrious others, a future Lord Chief Justice. The 1967 Criminal Justice Act which had established the Board stipulated that it must contain persons experienced in the study of crime. In truth, I had by then a single criminological publication to my name (Cooper and King 1965), a small scale study of prison employment conducted with my great economist friend from undergraduate days, Mike Cooper, so I did just qualify—but I did wonder exactly how I had become (along with another of my teachers, Donald West) one of the first two criminologists ever to have been defined by statute. I assumed that the appointment had been made upon the recommendation of Radzinowicz because in those days that was how the British establishment worked (these days such appointments are advertised, attract large numbers of applicants, and are made on merit in a more transparent way). Not long after my appointment, Hunt had asked me to visit Germany and Scandinavia to study their parole systems and report back any lessons from which we might benefit. So when I put up proposals for my Ford Fellowship I opted for a comparative study of parole systems. My year at Yale, partly in the Law School and partly in the Sociology department, was one of the most enjoyable in my life, but I have to confess that my study of prison and parole systems played second fiddle to Watergate. I watched, open mouthed, the live hearings on public television by day and the re-runs on the networks in the evenings, little realizing that I would come across one of the principals (at least by proxy) in Russia, later in my career. In the intervals I did manage to get some serious writing done, but it was not upon my all too meagre parole data. The first lesson of international work is not to become so engrossed in the other culture that one becomes diverted from the main task!

For a brief period after my return to the UK, I turned my research attention to other matters in the field of youth unemployment which first brought me into a productive research relationship with my American colleague Kathleen McDermott. But, although I was able—with Rod Morgan and others—to help lay the groundwork for future changes in penal policy in more or less clandestine meetings with senior officials following the publication of our book on the future of the prison system (King and Morgan 1980), I was told that the time was not yet right for me to conduct further prisons research. By then, and not least because of repeated riots and disturbances in our dispersal prisons, what I most wanted to do was to research maximum-security prisons. If I could not undertake a study of dispersal policy in the UK then I resolved to study the alternative policy of concentration as that was practiced in the United States. Not the cursory exploration of other's policies so beloved by politicians, but a serious and detailed research study using replicable procedures. Through the good offices of David Ward I was able to approach the Department of Corrections in Minnesota and the Federal Bureau of Prisons for permission to conduct research in their maximum-security facilities. Thus was born the first leg of my comparative study of maximum-

> ### Lessons
>
> *I was coming to the conclusion that, divided as we are by a common language, British and American officials often talked at cross purposes when it came to prison issues...I was coming to the view that both systems had developed precisely the wrong solution to their problems.*

security custody in England and Wales and the United States—a detailed evaluation of the Minnesota Correctional Facility at Oak Park Heights (King 1991).

By the time of my return to the UK, the politics had changed and I was no longer *persona non grata*. Those officials with whom Morgan and I had earlier laid some groundwork had now reached positions of considerable influence and two of them, Ian Dunbar and Anthony Langdon, had visited the United States whilst I was there to see what lessons could be learned to help us resolve the control problems in our dispersal prisons. Inevitably we met to share ideas.

My research in Oak Park Heights, as well as extensive discussions with staff and prisoners at the Marion Control Unit and in all the Level 5 Federal penitentiaries, placed me in a unique position. I was coming to the conclusion that, divided as we are by a common language, British and American officials often talked at cross purposes when it came to prison issues. In particular it seemed to me that maximum security in the two countries were driven by different needs. In the United States, both the Federal Bureau of Prisons and most state systems had developed a policy of concentration in their maximum-security facilities more to deal with prisoners who were deemed too difficult to manage in other prisons than to prevent escapes. In England and Wales we had developed a policy of dispersal primarily to deal with escape risks in the hope of not turning them also into control problems.

Moreover, I was coming to the view that both systems had developed precisely the wrong solution to their problems. The supply of prisoners likely to make serious attempts at escape is relatively fixed and a policy of concentrating them into one or two prisons makes economic sense. The supply of prisoners capable of making problems for management is relatively limitless, and removing some troublesome prisoners only means that they will be replaced by others. As far as troublesome prisoners are concerned each prison is best advised to consume its own smoke, although they may need some limited temporary relief and support, perhaps in the form of small specialist but non-punitive units. Concentrating difficult to manage prisoners together is likely to lead to mayhem for staff or complete lockdown for prisoners—neither of which is desirable or indeed necessary. In my experience, only Minnesota had managed to deal successfully with both escape and control problems in its new generation prison at Oak Park Heights —thanks to a happy combination of good prison design and inspired management under its distinguished warden, Frank Wood.

I was able to discuss all this with Dunbar and Langdon, long before my findings were finally published in the comparative context outlined above. When their subsequent report (Home Office 1984) was published recommending two prisons along the lines of Oak Park Heights as a possible alternative to our dispersal system for high security prisoners and a series of small units for difficult and dangerous prisoners quite different from conventional control units, I was broadly in sympathy with what they had said—even though I wished it had gone a little further. But at last the conflation of issues about escape and control risks which had bedeviled discourse in Britain had been addressed. The government did not adopt the recommendations to replace the dispersal system, although the prison service did thereafter adopt greater measures of concentration and resisted pressures to expand it as the prison population increased. As a result the high security estate has, with time, become more appropriately proportionate to the needs of the system. The prison service did accept the recommendations on small units and I was invited to join a small advisory group concerned with monitoring their implementation.

Almost immediately on my return it was possible for me to develop a major comparative study which enabled me to replicate some of the things I had studied fifteen years earlier in Britain (King and McDermott 1989). It also afforded the opportunity to study the second leg of an international comparison of maximum-security custody—a study of Gartree prison in Leicestershire (King 1991). For me this was heady stuff. My first taste of serious internationally comparative research, conducted by the same researcher, using the same research instruments on the one hand, and a "that was then this is now" study of five comparable English prisons fifteen years apart. The results were dramatic and could not have been more stark. English prisons had changed significantly. Their performance in terms of rehabilitative activities had vastly reduced, and was overshadowed by increasing concerns with security and control. Moreover, Gartree, the pride of the liberal dispersal policy compared unfavourably not just with Albany, its British counterpart years earlier, but also with Oak Park Heights, admittedly a unique example of the concentration policy as operated in Minnesota, on just about every criterion.

My next foray into internationally comparative work on prison systems came when I reluctantly visited post-glasnost Russia for a holiday in 1991. At the suggestion of a family friend, who was to become my very excellent interpreter, I wrote to the Ministry of the Interior expressing my interest in talking to their researchers about prisons and asked them to reply via the British Consulate in Moscow. They duly invited me to a meeting. After a rather stiff and formal beginning to my meeting with a number of colonels, including Alexander Mikhlin soon to become a dear friend, the atmosphere began to thaw. They asked me if I would like to visit some prisons, and I said yes. I returned the following year to become the first western social scientist to research Russian prisons and corrective labor colonies. It is one thing to do comparative research in Britain and the United States, divided as they are by their common language. It is something else to attempt research in a country, in respect of which one was brought up to fear the four-minute warning, and where one can scarcely read the signs on the subway. I armed myself for this undertaking by talking to Gerald Brooke, now an academic teacher of Russian at the University of Westminster, but who as a student had been arrested and imprisoned at the height of the cold war for distributing religious pamphlets. He was eventually released as part of the exchange which also produced the release of Gary Powers, the U2 pilot, but only after spending several years in Russian prisons.

Thus began an amazing adventure. It took me to the huge remand prisons, Butyrka, in Moscow where Dostoevesky had researched *Resurrection,* and Kresty in St. Petersburg, both of which suffered such severe overcrowding that prisoners sometimes died for want of oxygen. And it took me to representative examples of virtually all types of corrective labor colonies which had outlived the GULag, and to the new and notorious *Byely Lebed* (a kind of Russian equivalent of Pelican Bay) designed to break the spirits of what the Russians called "Thieves-in-Law" as well as to TB Colonies in a prison system where Multiple Drug Resistant Tuberculosis was rife. To some I had to be flown by helicopter, others were reached only after long and arduous journeys by train and car. Between prison visits I enjoyed the dubious pleasures of going down salt mines, being beaten with birch twigs by Russian generals after a Russian bath, and being mistaken as a guest of honor at a symphony concert.

Lessons
It was also possible to begin to get some sense of the extent to which Russian discourse on crime and punishment had begun to converge on Western philosophies—the promotion of religious freedom, the individualization of treatment through the employment of psychologists, and the idea that prisoners should have a right to work rather than a duty to labor.

Such is the life of the comparative criminologist who ventures into unknown territory if one is not careful.

There are things you can do through an interpreter, and things you cannot do. Among the latter is the pursuit of sociological understanding of staff and prisoner cultures that requires lengthy periods of participant observation and the gradual build up of trust. But it was possible to develop a descriptive picture of the system, some kind of assessment of prison conditions, and to measure them against international standards of human rights. It was also possible to begin to get some sense of the extent to which Russian discourse on crime and punishment had begun to converge on Western philosophies—the promotion of religious freedom, the individualization of treatment through the employment of psychologists, and the idea that prisoners should have a right to work rather than a duty to labor, for example—as Russia edged towards membership of the Council of Europe. There was a profound sense of an aching void left by the collapse of the command economy which had undermined both the original *raison d' être* of the labor colonies and their funding. Some officials were already having second thoughts about the speed with which that void was being filled by movements led by evangelical Christian movements, among them the born-again Watergate conspirator Chuck Colson whose White House office famously boasted a sign proclaiming that "When you've got them by the balls, their hearts and minds will follow."

There were spin offs from the Human Rights elements of this work. Although I knew I had only scratched the surface and was far from having a detailed insight into the Russian system, I soon discovered the truth of the saying that in the land of the blind the one eyed man is king. I was invited to become involved in the work of a number of bodies—the Council of Europe, the European Union and others—to prepare reports on the state of various prison systems in former Soviet societies, and also participated with colleagues in Penal Reform International and the Netherlands Helsinki Committee in various endeavors to bring about reforms in Russia and Romania.

Aware of the things you cannot do through an interpreter I was able to recruit a research student, Laura Piacentini who was prepared to learn Russian before undertaking field research in two colonies in Smolensk and two in Omsk, in Siberia. We have recently revisited these experiences and tried to reflect upon how far the Russian system has changed since joining the Council of Europe, and the consequent transfer of responsibility for prisons from the Ministry of the Interior to the Ministry of Justice. It is well known that Russia and the United States between them account for about one-third of the world's prisoners and that England and Wales is now the heaviest user of imprisonment within the European Union. However, when imprisonment rates per 100,000 population are set against recorded crime rates per 100,000 interesting comparisons begin to emerge. These suggest that, whilst remaining a prodigiously heavy user of imprisonment, Russia has increased its prison population more modestly despite increasing crime rates, than either the United States or England and Wales, where imprisonment rates have continued to increase dramatically despite a downward drift in crime rates (King and Piacentini 2004).

At the end of 1994 and the beginning of 1995 there were once again dramatic escapes from two of our most secure prisons and, in something of a moral panic, yet another official report proposed that the Prison Service once again look to the United States for guidance, this time recommending that we consider building two American-style supermax facilities—one for our worst escape risks and one for our worst control problems (Home Office 1995). I was appointed as the academic advisor to a Prison Service working party tasked with examining the feasibility of such proposals. I had been aware of the growth of these facilities in the United States for some time, and in 1994 I had had the opportunity to visit one of them when Amnesty International asked me to advise them on the conditions for

death row prisoners held at Oklahoma State Penitentiary (Amnesty International 1994), the first of several such invitations. By the time the working party was established I had already secured Research Council funding for a comparative study of American supermax facilities. Between 1996 and 1999 I was able to visit many supermax facilities in several states and to collect detailed research data in three of them. The initial results of that research were published quickly (King 1999). More detailed reports, which will include a comparative study of Oak Park Heights in 1984 and 1999, have taken somewhat longer, in part, because other obligations and invitations have gotten in the way.

The working party tentatively accepted the possible case for a new supermax style prison to prevent escapes—albeit one run more along the lines of Oak Park Heights than the more typical American supermaxes—but only if that replaced one or more existing dispersal prisons. It rejected the proposal to concentrate control problems in a second supermax. However, given that the number of exceptionally high escape risk prisoners was too small to warrant a new facility of their own, and given a design that would permit the separation of several different groups of prisoners, the working party allowed for the possibility of bringing together existing small units for the most difficult to manage prisoners into one half of the proposed new prison. In the event, a general election intervened and there was a substantial hiatus in decision making. Once the new government was in place the moral panic had passed, the prison system had settled down, and the proposal was allowed to drop.

Whither the future? In 1997 and 1998 I was invited by Amnesty International to advise them on problems in the Brazilian prison system, following which I put up proposals for an action research programme designed to bring about reform, which would build on the lessons from earlier, and not conspicuously successful attempts at bringing about change in Romania. That project, jointly administered by the Centre for Comparative Criminology and Criminal Justice in Bangor and the International Centre for Prison Studies in London, finally commenced in 2002 and is still underway. The changes are being introduced with the help of interpreters. But the research evaluation is being conducted in Portuguese by the Centre for the Study of Violence in the University of São Paulo.

References

ACPS. 1968. *The Regime for Long-Term Prisoners in Conditions of Maximum Security*. (The Radzinowicz Report) Advisory Council on the Penal System, London: HMSO.

Amnesty International. 1994. *Conditions for Death Row Prisoners in H-Unit, Oklahoma State Penitentiary*, AMR 51/35/94. London: Amnesty International.

Aichorn, August. 1936. *Wayward Youth*. London: Putnam.

Clarke, A.D.B and Barbara Tizard, eds. 1983. *Child Development and Social Policy: The Life and Work of Jack Tizard*. Leicester: British Psychological Society.

Cohen, Percy S. 1968. *Modern Social Theory*. London: Heinemann Educational.

Cooper, Michael H. and Roy D. King. 1965. "Social and Economic Problems of Prisoners' Work." In *Sociological Studies in the British Penal Services,* Sociological Review Monograph No 9, University of Keele.

Durkheim, Emile. 1964. *The Rules of Sociological Method*. Translated by S.A. Solovay and J.H. Mueller. New York: Free Press.

Durkheim, Emile. 1952. *Suicide: A Study in Sociology*. Translated by John A. Spaulding and Georege Simpson. London: Routledge and Kegan Paul.

Elias, Norbert. 1978. *The Civilising Process*, Vol. 1 *The History of Manners,* Vol. 11 *State Formation and Civilization.* Oxford: Blackwell.

Giddens, Anthony. 2000. *The Third Way and its Critics*. Cambridge: Polity Press.

Goldthorpe, John H. and David Lockwood. 1969. *The Affluent Worker in the Class Structure*. Cambrige: Cambridge University Press.

Home Office. 1966. *Report of the Inquiry into Prison Escapes and Security* (The Mountbatten Report), Cmnd 3175, London: HMSO.

_____. 1984. *Managing the Long-Term Prison System* (The Report of the Control Review Committee), London: HMSO.

_____. 1995. *Review of Prison Service Security in England and Wales and the Escape from Parkhurst Prison on Tuesday 3rd January 1995* (The Learmont Report), Cm. 3020. London: HMSO.

King, Roy D. 1972. "An Analysis of

Prison Regimes." Unpublished report to the Home Office Research Unit, University of Southampton.

_____. 1991. "Maximum Security Custody in Britain and the USA: A Study of Gartree and Oak Park Heights." *British Journal of Criminology* 31(2):126-52.

_____. 1994. "Russian Prisons after Perestroika: End of the GULag?" In *Prisons in Context*, edited by R. King and M. Maguire. Oxford: Oxford University Press.

_____. 1999. "The Rise and Rise of Supermax: An American Solution in Search of a Problem?" *Punishment and Society* 1(2):163-86.

King, Roy D. and Kenneth W. Elliott. 1977. *Albany: Birth of a Prison, End of an Era,* London: Routledge and Kegan Paul.

King, Roy D. and Kathleen McDermott. 1989. "British Prisons 1970-1987: The Ever-Deepening Crisis." *British Journal of Criminology* 29(2):107-28.

_____. 1995. *The State of Our Prisons.* Oxford: Oxford University Press.

King, Roy D. and Rod Morgan. 1976. *A Taste of Prison: Custodial Conditions for Trial and Remand Prisoners.* London: Routledge and Kegan Paul.

_____. 1980. *The Future of the Prison System.* Westmead: Gower.

King, Roy D. and Laura Piacentini. 2004 forthcoming. "The Russian Correctional System in Transition." In *Ruling Russia: Crime, Law and Justice in a Changing Society*, edited by W. Pridemore.

King, Roy D., Norma V. Raynes, and Jack Tizard. 1971. *Patterns of Residential Care, Sociological Studies in Institutions for Handicapped Children.* London: Routledge and Kegan Paul.

Shaw, Clifford R. and Henry McKay. 1942. *Juvenile Delinquency and Urban Areas: A Study of Rates of Delinquency in Relation to Characteristics of Local Communities.* Chicago: University of Chicago Press.

Weber, Max. 1949. *Methodology of the Social Sciences.* Translated and edited by Edward A. Shils and Henry A. Finch. New York: Free Press.

Wootton, Barbara. 1959. *Social Science and Social Pathology.* London: Allen and Unwin.

Chapter 12

From Legal Doctrine to Criminology

Hans-Joerg Albrecht

Director, Max Planck Institute for Foreign and International Criminal Law Freiburg, Germany

This orientation suited me well as I have always been interested with the variability of criminal law and criminal justice and comparative methods.

The First Steps

I was born in 1950 in Esslingen, a city located close to Stuttgart in the southwest of Germany. I attended a so-called humanistic (high) school, which placed an emphasis on foreign languages (I studied English, French, and also Russian for two years) and old languages (in particular Latin). With that, a general decision was made not to go into natural sciences but into humanities. My parents supported the decision and they provided me an opportunity to spend most of my school holidays in England and France on the basis of a student exchange between families so I could strengthen my linguistic skills and learn about other cultures.

After completing high school (or Gymnasium) I studied law at the University of Tuebingen and later at Freiburg University. The decision to enter a career in criminology does not come easily within the German context of legal education and law faculties. My decision to become a criminologist can rather be described as a process that emerged over a couple of years, as a "drifting" into criminology. Thinking back, I had the openness for a multitude of perspectives and thoughts, which was important for studying criminology. The decision to study law was influenced, in particular, by the advice that legal studies would widen my professional opportunities. Legal studies within the German university context are dominated by dogma, doctrine, and normative thinking and—this is certainly well-known—German law faculties take particular pride in having a reputation of having developed outstanding systems of legal doctrine and dogmatism, be it civil, public, or criminal law.

When I started to study law at the University of Tuebingen in 1968, however, the student movement peaked; administrative (power) structures as well as historically patterned rituals were overturned, which changed the face of the campus at large. The student movement in Germany pointed toward two main areas of concern. First, the Vietnam War and liberation movements in other parts of the world, in particular in South-America, fuelled the student movement that lasted from the mid-1960s until the mid-1970s. Second, conflicts emerged out of the massive involvement of individuals in senior university educational, judicial, political, and administrative positions who were formerly attached to the Nazi regime and who could be linked ultimately to the Holocaust. Here, it became clear that law and the justice system had been deeply involved in the fascist regime and it also became evident that the political system implemented after 1945 evidently was not able, or not willing, to prevent former supporters and collaborators of the fascist regime to fill important roles in the administrative, political, educational, and justice systems of the new and democratic Germany. It is, perhaps, also important to note that a (well-founded) impression arose that the judiciary only reluctantly opened criminal trials against judges involved in the fascist justice system (in fact, not one

judge actively participating in the Third Reich system of terror justice has been found guilty and sentenced). With that, debates followed about what causes lawyers to be so easily drawn into any political regime and to be so readily usable for political and ideological purposes.

Aside from the general changes brought by the student movement, law faculties also came under pressure to change at the end of the 1960s. In particular a debate developed that focused on the role of law education in training responsible lawyers.

Why Criminology?

At the University of Tuebingen, I had the opportunity to attend criminology courses taught by the director of the Criminological Institute, the late Professor Hans Goeppinger. Goeppinger was, at that time, a major figure among German criminologists. However, I was not that impressed by the case studies and the ideas that were presented in order to explain why certain individuals enter a life of crime while others become law abiding citizens. Although the course attracted many students, I was not convinced that this could be the whole truth in the face of decent citizens having participated voluntarily in unspeakable crimes against humanity.

In order to understand the relationship between criminology and law, it is important to note that the concept of criminology and criminologist are exclusively used within law faculties in order to describe the scope or the range of topics covered by chairs or institutes (located in law faculties). Up to now, there are 3 criminological institutes within law faculties (Tuebingen, Heidelberg, and Hamburg). There are an additional 15 to 20 chairs or university positions that also cover criminology. Thus, criminological courses are *part of* law education insofar as they belong to a group of topics that can be chosen by law students. There are but a few sociologists and psychologists who specialize in criminological topics. Faculties of sociology involved in criminological research are found in Bremen, Bielefeld, and Frankfurt. Psychological institutes or faculties conducting criminological research are found in Nuernberg-Erlangen, Cologne, Heidelberg, and Freiburg. However, criminology in Germany was and still is dominated by law and law faculties, although psychiatrists and psychologists dominate forensic research.

After leaving Tuebingen and enrolling at Freiburg University (in Germany it is quite normal that students change universities), I studied criminology, juvenile law, and penitentiary law. I attended courses held by Guenther Kaiser who was the director of the Max Planck Institute for Foreign and International Criminal Law (hereafter referred to as the MPI) in Freiburg, and head of the criminological research unit established at the Institute. The lectures and seminars I attended served to guide my interest to a range of questions, in particular to questions of how law is implemented and with what effects.

It was perhaps the student movement and rapid social changes at the campus which led me to start studying sociology as a second major topic after I had completed my legal studies in 1973. This overlapped with my starting to work at the MPI, where I was offered a part-time job in the criminological research unit. I accepted the offer, although I was not certain about where I was heading.

The Max Planck Institute for Foreign and International Criminal Law

Criminological research at the MPI has a tradition of over 30 years—having been established in 1970. However, the origins of the Institute go back further. The MPI has its roots in a small division of the University of Freiburg. It was set-up by the criminal law scholar, Professor Adolf Schoenke in 1938. With Hans-Heinrich Jescheck succeeding Adolf Schoenke in 1954, the Institute was made into a public foundation of the Federal Republic of Germany, the State of Baden-Wuerttemberg, and the University of Freiburg. In 1966, the Institute was incorporated into the Max Planck Society. The Max Planck Society is a large private research organization in Germany established to advance fundamental scientific research and to supplement the efforts of university-based research. The relationship of MPI to the universities is not characterized by competition; rather, it is one of close cooperation. The MPI is established close to many universities, and most of the Institute's directors and other Max Planck research fellows teach at nearby universities. Legally, the Society is a registered, nonprofit organization; a vast share of its funding, however, comes from public money. The Society is focused on fundamental research and it is not bound by any political directives. It only occasionally accepts commissions from industry or government to carry out specific research projects. Within the Max Planck Society, the Institutes have considerable independence in the choice and implementation of research projects. Additionally, the Institutes are subject to the oversight of independent committees comprised of international experts. An advisory board visits each Institute every two years to review and evaluate their research and to discuss future plans.

A great accomplishment of the first director of the Institute, Hans-Heinrich Jescheck, was to recognize that criminal law and criminology, by their very nature, are interrelated and that cooperation between these two branches could lead to deeper, reliable, and valid insights regarding national and foreign criminal law and criminal justice. Consequently, in 1970 he initiated the establishment of a criminological research unit with the aim of implementing concepts of coordinated criminological and legal research. Its first director was Guenther Kaiser, who retired February 1997. On the basis of this innovative integration of normative and empirical approaches to the study of crime and criminal law, a special kind of comparative criminal law and criminology developed at the MPI. Both divisions contribute their own questions, methods, and results towards joint projects.

Drifting into Criminology

Studying at the institute of sociology and working at the MPI exposed me to sociological perspectives of deviance

> ## *Lessons*
>
> *Criminal law and criminology, by their very nature, are interrelated. Cooperation between these two branches could lead to deeper, reliable, and valid insights regarding national and foreign criminal law and criminal justice.*

and deviance control. Among them was of Guenther Kaiser, the director of the institute. He was an influential source of information on crime and criminal justice as well as theoretical perspectives. In particular, his texts on social control remind us that control based on criminal law is always part of a general social system of control and that there are significant interactions between penal law and social control. His work also shows how social science research can be combined with normative and legal thinking. It is evident that normative ideals and the statutory basis are decisive on whether a criminal act or an offender will be processed fully through the system. But, it is discretion, the economy of law and justice, political interests, poverty and power, which may help explain variance in the outcomes of the criminal process. It was on his advice that I carefully studied a sociological reader oriented on crime and deviance edited by Fritz Sack and Rene Koenig. Here, I learned about the North American sociological perspective of crime and deviance. Then, it was Erhard Blankenburg, Johannes Feest, and Klaus Sessar and, moreover, Trutz v. Trotha who brought to my attention interesting and promising areas of research as well as the value of theoretical approaches. Trutz v. Trotha introduced me to research and theories of gang delinquency and later into a general theory of (criminal) law while Blankenburg, Feest, and Sessar, carrying out research at the MPI on the "dark figure" of crime, police, the creation of suspicion, and the role of public prosecutors in the criminal justice system, that turned my attention to labeling theory as well as quantitative and qualitative research methods.

The type of research carried out in the 1970s at the MPI marked also a basic shift in German criminology as alternative theoretical concepts on crime and deviance began to be considered seriously, and control institutions such as police, the public prosecutors office, and the courts became targets of research. The basic reason for the shift toward social control lies in the reception of the *labeling approach*, which stimulated the idea that crime and deviance are not self evident and quasi-natural social or behavioral phenomena but socially created concepts or ascriptions, varying over time and space, carrying meanings that differ, in particular, among cultures. By introducing interactionist dimensions of crime and deviance into criminology, sociology claimed priority in defining the core problems in the study of crime and deviance, which should be found in the question of how criminal labels or definitions of crime can be explained.

This development coincided with the societal and political unrest experienced in the late 1960s and the early 1970s, in particular in the student movement—as I mentioned earlier—and was followed by new concerns for

social and legal discrimination. Policy was reshaped to correct the distorted distributional patterns as far as highly rated values such as economic wealth and power or political participation were concerned. On the other hand, the distribution of negatively rated values such as criminal labels, social marginalization, or social disintegration also attracted attention. In general, minorities and marginalized groups, in theory and policy, were perceived to be major forces in promoting social change and challenging conservative social institutions. Criminology and sociology took up corresponding questions of causes and consequences with respect to the distorted distributions of negative values in society.

Going Further

After having passed the second state examination in law in 1976 I decided to start with a Ph.D. in criminology and to study a question I was particularly interested in; that is, the decision-making process on sentencing. This fit into the research program at the MPI which was geared towards studying the major players in the filtering process ranging from the victim's reporting of an offence, police decisions to launch criminal investigations, the prosecutors' decision on bringing a case to court, and finally the judge's decision on what type and amount of punishment to impose. My interest concerned, first of all, the relevance of various legal and extra-legal factors in sentencing decisions. However, I was then fascinated by the observation that judges do not at all produce that much variance in sentencing (as they in principle could on the basis of wide statutory sentencing ranges) but evidently manage to establish a regime characterized by consistency and the reduction of variation, sometimes amounting to tariffs. This finding led me to go deeper into the field of judicial decision-making and study in particular the question of how prosecutors and judges learn about what kind of punishment they should apply for or impose. Having finalized my Ph.D. in 1979, I had to decide on what to do next and I slowly developed a taste for a university career. Within the German academic context this means to do what is called "habilitation," which is carrying out and publishing a major piece of research. I chose again sentencing as the topic and I developed a study that tried to combine normative and empirical analysis of sentencing decisions in order to outline a consistent theory of sentencing. The major conclusion was that a theory of proportionality does best in both explaining current variation in sentencing outcomes as well as providing for a normative framework which allows for consistent sentencing on the one hand and necessary room for changes and adjustments on the other hand.

After having received the habilitation (and with that a degree that allows for a full professorship in law faculties) in 1990, I was offered a position as a law professor at the university of Konstanz, which I accepted. This meant, of course, that I had to go back to criminal law and doctrine and, from 1991 on, I taught criminal law courses. In 1993, I accepted a chair of criminal law and criminology at the University of Technology in Dresden, located in Saxonia in the eastern part of Germany.

There I spent 4 years teaching criminal law, criminology, penitentiary law, as well as juvenile law. It was an interesting time as the faculty of law was established a year after the fall of the Iron Wall and I experienced the building up of a faculty and the problems inherent in merging two completely different systems as a consequence of separate and distinct developments in economy, politics, and the justice system.

In 1996, the Max Planck Society started the process of finding a successor for the director of the MPI for Foreign and Criminal Law, Guenther Kaiser, the head of the criminological research unit. I was offered this position in the spring of 1996 and I accepted it shortly after. However, I decided to stay until the end of the winter term 1996/1997 at the University of Technology in Dresden and I returned to Freiburg in the spring of 1997. The decision to go back to MPI was also a decision to change from a mix of teaching and research to exclusively fundamental research, developing a research program, and administrative tasks.

Studying Crime and Criminal Justice

The most important challenge was to initiate and implement a research program that was likely to broaden and deepen available theoretical and empirical knowledge in the fields of crime and crime control. During the 1970s and 1980s, the focus of criminological research at the MPI had been on the main actors of penal social control (as e.g., police, public prosecutor, criminal courts, the correctional system, and enforcement of criminal sanctions), implementation and evaluation of crim-

---

Lessons

In thinking about cross-national research, three basic questions have to be considered: What is international comparative research? Why do we want to do international comparative research? How does this type of research differ, if at all, from other research?

---

inal sanctions, as well as prison based rehabilitation and victimization surveys.

In regard to the general approach to criminological research, it was clear that the program should be based on an international comparative (in particular European) perspective, that it should be interdisciplinary in terms of integrating normative and empirical elements, as well as combining a range of disciplines like law, sociology, and psychology. This orientation suited me well as I have always been interested with the variability of criminal law and criminal justice and comparative methods. In fact, methodology is a crucial point in comparative social science (and other) research. Although the concept of scientific research basically is comparative in nature, as the French sociologist Durkheim has pointed out in his work on the process of research, intercultural, international, or cross-national; research methodology has not received the attention it should have received (see King in this collection for further discussion). This is especially true if taking into account the paramount interest which cross-cultural comparative research actually receives today in the social sciences, particularly in crimi-

nology and especially in policy research. On the other hand, it has been deplored that comparative social science research has produced little if any meaningful scientific knowledge in the last decade. In thinking about cross-national research, and this is part of the method, three basic questions have to be considered: What is international comparative research? Why do we want to do international comparative research? How does this type of research differ, if at all, from other research? The first question does not present many problems as international comparative research is characterized by using information or data that stem from more than one nation-state, or, if the term cross-cultural research is used, from more than one distinct culture. The question of why international comparative research is needed then requires first an answer to the question why primary or national research is carried through. Here, we find several answers. The most obvious goal of comparative research points toward theory development. This goal is linked to the endeavor of explaining social phenomena, which requires, in turn, a thorough description of the social phenomena in question. Then, identification of the variables that can be manipulated is sought. Finally, comparative research is looking toward policy evaluation. From these primary goals of research we may delineate the answers to the question of why international comparative research obviously is needed and what differences can be observed between international comparisons and national research. The need for comparative research points to the aim of generalizations of empirical observations and theoretical considerations; the study of how and why a social or cultural phenomenon that is relatively constant within a specific society has a broader range of variation when a number of different societies are compared; and the collection of information concerning the extent to which cross-national variation may be explained by variation in other variables (which may be subject to manipulation).

Immigration and Ethnicity

Immigration and minorities are major issues that have to be addressed in criminological analysis and research. European societies have changed into ethnically and culturally heterogeneous societies with ethnicity replacing, to a certain extent, class as a decisive variable in structuring society. The consequences are visible in the justice and correctional system.

In fact, immigration has become a high ranked European concern over the last two decades. This can be attributed, in particular, to the opening of borders between the east and west of Europe as well as to a debate on safety in Europe, the onset of which is marked by the creation and implementation of the Schengen Treaties and the abolition of inner border controls in most of western Europe. Strengthening control of the external Schengen borders certainly has been at the center of the attempt to reduce unwanted and illegal immigration. However, the need for a common European immigration policy—as expressed from the end of the 1980s on—is also caused by displacement phenomenon (which became visible at the beginning of the 1990s when drastic

changes in German asylum law led immediately to increases in the numbers of asylum seekers in neighboring European countries and of course subsequent changes in immigration laws of the respective neighboring countries).

But, it is not only immigration per se that is dealt with in current debates. The topic of immigration is mingled (and actually confounded) with other sensitive, and sometimes emotional, but always ideologically and politically exploitable issues such as ethnicity and ethnic differences, nationality, identity, national identities, and finally order, safety, and stability. Immigration, then, is linked with organized crime, in particular organized drug trafficking, trafficking in humans, the smuggling of illegal immigrants, and the emerging shadow economies (red light districts, prostitution, sweatshop labor), which today absorb substantial parts of the (non-EU) immigrant population. The dominant perspective on immigration and ethnic minorities currently is characterized through crime, deviance, and conflict. Assumptions on causal links between immigration (or the minority status) on the one hand, and crime and deviance on the other hand, point to powerful belief patterns concerning the potential of conflicts and instability associated with immigration and the "alien."

The topics of immigration, ethnicity, and crime are most sensitive as they facilitate polarization and are susceptible to political exploitation. Indeed, the issue of ethnic minorities and especially asylum seekers as well as their perceived potential for threatening public safety has become a rallying point for authoritarian sentiments in European societies as well as for new right-wing political parties and extremist groups. Accounts of pogrom-like (i.e., massacre) events as well as individual acts of hate-motivated violence and bias crime are on display in virtually all European societies. However, statistical accounts vary considerably and, in particular, statements on the trends in hate crime incidents seem almost impossible because they are not common definitions and approaches as to what should be regarded to establish hate-violence or racist violence and related acts (over time and across countries). But, it is the emergence of group violence directed against (visible) minorities that attract attention and evidently have—though they can be regarded also as rare events—the power of creating considerable fear and a feeling of lack of safety not only in minority groups but also in societies at large.

Europe-wide surveys, measured through attitudes and perceptions, confirm that quite substantial parts of autochtone populations (i.e., earliest known inhabitants) see themselves as being (very or quite) racist.

Issues such as immigration and crime are exploited in criminology and social science at large. Critical approaches on the one hand, and "realist" views on the other hand, present their opposing cases, either stressing that absence of research on immigration and crime will make the topic totally exploitable for right wing politicians, or assuming that fear of immigration and ethnic minorities as well as hate crimes committed against members of ethnic minorities are provoked by reporting and publishing on crimes committed by immigrants or members of ethnic minorities. The possible sources of such hostilities and, ultimately, violence certainly are located somewhere in the process of development into modern and then into late-modern societies. However, it should be acknowledged that preying upon minorities, marginalization, and moves toward total extinction are not phenomena that all of sudden have emerged with modern societies and they are certainly not restricted to the last decades of the twentieth century.

European history, from the Middle Ages through to the Enlightenment period and beyond, demonstrates the successful search for folk devils, scapegoats, the demonization of the "other," and permanent exclusion of the "stranger." What actually has changed in modern societies is the wide availability of minority groups that can be scapegoated, the easy exchangeability of ideological prey with mobility and large scale migration and immigration, with a state that evidently has lost substantial power to regulate and to govern with an aim to solve social and economic crises by way of traditional forms of governance. In addition, the issue is compounded by the emergence of mass media (and markets) that in a certain sense are dependent on finding and creating demons and folk devils and constructing pictures that convey messages of threat, tensions, and distraction as well as entertainment at the same time. The mass media have developed the power to create images that are much more influential as they are spread more rapidly. They are more consumer-adjusted and, in fact, they are reaching more consumers than before. What has also changed since the

Enlightenment period concerns the basic concepts of folk devils and demons. Demons and devils have been transformed into dangers and risks. So, demonization has to be replaced by the concept and the strategy of "dangerization." Finally, political governance has become partially dependent on the deviant other and the mobilization of feelings of safety. Political power, its establishment, as well as its preservation, is today dependent on a selection of campaign issues among which safety (and feeling unsafe) are top priority; safety is one of those political topics that forces all political parties and discussants to respond with "more of the same" (that is, more safety and more instruments that promise immediate safety). This can be expected, as safety, more than any other political issue, is exploitable and may serve as an instrument to mobilize feelings and ultimately votes.

Organized Crime and Informal Economies

Organized Crime

Organized crime also has to be placed at the center of criminological research efforts, as it is important from both the theoretical perspective of crime and deviance and from the perspective of crime control. The concept of organized crime should be based on two theoretical approaches. The first approach regards organized crime as linked with the traditional subcultures of the modern metropolis. These subcultures are also dependent on shadow economies that, on the one hand, provide for the economic basis for what was once

called the "professional criminal" (in particular the professional thief) and, on the other hand, provide for an environment for a network of professional criminals on the basis of deviant norms and values. In fact, much of the contemporary literature on these subcultures of organized crime sometimes describes the underworld as a competitor to conventional society. However, as we observe in many societies, there exists a multitude of arrangements between these underworlds and the conventional society, which are functional insofar as the underworld and the shadow economies operating within provide for the supply that is demanded for in the conventional society. The demand for drugs, prostitution or gambling emerges outside shadow economies and keeps these economies alive. The arrangements vary and include also various types of corruptive relationships.

The second theoretical approach that is necessary to understand organized crime refers to crime as a rational and a well-organized enterprise. It is obvious that the enterprise-related characteristics of organized crime prevail today and that the subculture-based characteristics are on the retreat. Organized crime thus comes in the forms, and with the structures, of ordinary and conventional economic behavior. The differences that were once visible now have faded away and organized crime becomes indistinguishable from other types of economic behavior. This can be demonstrated with money laundering where nothing in the offender or in the act itself lends itself to a clear identification of the act as criminal or deviant. The offender and the acts do not carry any of the signs of crime or deviance we are accustomed to rely upon with respect to conventional crime or conventional criminals. The significant difference between organized and conventional crime, therefore, essentially concerns the emergence of new problems in investigation that are the consequence of adjustments and changes in rational, organized enterprises like crime; adjustments that bring this activity closer to conventional society, abolish the so-called related "subculture" and, therefore, the visible differences. Organized crime creates problems for law enforcement because forms and procedures of conventional society are used (which make the identification of criminal acts and suspects a difficult task). Contributing to these law enforcement problems, certainly, are new types of criminal legislation, like money laundering statutes, which take, as a point of departure, perfectly legitimate behavior (handling assets or money) and invoke illegality only by the criminal origins of assets. Organized crime serves also as a powerful argument for demanding new investigative powers for police and law enforcement at large.

Informal Economies

The topics of economy and crime (or the economic causes of crime) are closely related to the topic of organized crime and have always received attention in criminology and in the field of sociology of deviance. This is evident when looking at the various attempts to account for theoretical and empirical links between economy, labor markets, and crime. However, not covered in this type of research, and what should be a point of focus, is the informal economy and their links with crime, crime control, and societies features that relate to both crime and crime control. The traditional approach in criminology with regard to economy and crime was to try to identify economic variables reflecting crisis and exclusion and relating these to crime and deviance. Unemployment, increasing prices, poverty, income inequality, and economic crises in general, thus, have been subject to research. But, the whole field of illicit economies and illicit markets, as well as the participants in these markets and the structure of social interactions have only very rarely made the subject of research. This is true for both microeconomic approaches and macroeconomic approaches. Since the 1970s, and the first economic crises in this respect, the only question that has thoroughly been studied concerns the assumption that unemployment is correlated with criminal behavior. The reason the informal economy and the social contexts established through such informal economies did not receive much research attention might be explained from the perspective of the most important informal market in the last decade, namely, the drug market. It was not the economic

---

Lessons
Organized crime serves also as a powerful argument for demanding new investigative powers for police and law enforcement at large.

aspects that were of interest for research, but the treatment and addiction approach, including the penal law aspects, that have characterized research interests and that have guided empirical research in this area.

Another reason concerns a certain bias towards such illicit markets. The perspective of illicit markets should not necessarily be viewed within a negative context. Yet, the dominant perspective on drugs, red light districts, and undocumented labor has always been one of moralizing. Decriminalizing such offences as consensual sexual behavior as well as related behavior in the 1960s and 1970s and a policy of cleansing criminal law from moralizing elements, criminology lost interest in the study of prostitution, pimps, and other subcultural phenomena.

Modern and industrialized societies have undergone significant changes during the last few decades. These changes have had an enormous impact on those sectors of society where traditional explanations for crime and criminal behavior have been sought. Among these changes are the gradual shifts in labor markets and in the economy, including the "disappearance of work," in particular the disappearance of a labor market demanding unskilled labor, and the development of a service and information economy that puts forward strict demands with regard to education, skills, flexibility, and mobility. Such changes are evidently associated with high unemployment rates among those who are at a disadvantage with respect to those changes; and among these people we find, in particular, newly arriving immigrants from marginalized segments of society.

Safety and Safety Legislation

Anti-organized crime legislation (and after 9/11 anti-terrorist legislation) is part of a general security legislation that, from the view of industrial countries, in particular Europe and North America, represents the response to configuration of problems made-up of immigration, transnational and cross border crime, transaction crime, money laundering, and shadow economies. Such legislation represents cross-sectional legal areas that are made-up of immigration law, police laws, laws on secret services, telecommunication laws, general criminal and procedural laws, economic laws, general order laws, as well as legislation establishing particular powers in controlling professions in sensitive areas. Out of this cross-sectional nature follows a basic problem. This type of legislation interferes in civil society in a way that understands freedom and uncontrolled space as potential risks that are then put under general suspicion. Immigration and asylum, religious organizations and political movements, ethnic minorities, foreign citizens, transnational communities, and a workforce that is associated with security risks are made targets of supervision and partial exclusion.

Anti-organized crime legislation draws attention to the so-called "money trail" and with that to the control of financial and money markets by way of introducing elaborate money laundering control systems. The money trail has been highlighted as an important issue since the end of the 1980s; then the focus was on the control of drug markets. However, the approach has since been generalized and made available for the control of organized and transaction crime at large. The expansion of new investigative (proactive) methods then can be observed in particular in the area of electronic surveillance and control of telecommunication as well as search and seizure strategies based upon systematic collection and use of information based on certain individuals. Such investigative methods play a prominent role in the UN Convention on Control of Transnational Organized Crime 2000. These developments have affected traditional principles of criminal procedure drastically but did not result in empirical research on how such investigative methods are used and to what effect.

The changes in setting-up new security producing mechanisms display also a loss of significance of the nation-state and the monopoly of power. The monopoly of power and the nation-state step back behind international and transnational forms of police and military cooperation, which are expressed in the development of international and transnational forms of police and military cooperation that is expressed in cross-border systems of collecting and exchanging information as well as in the emergence of supranational intervention and task forces. Transnational police are visible in Europol, in systems of liaison officers, and joint investigation teams. This ultimately leads to a precarious reduction in the role of the judiciary, which is nonexistent on the international level and, thus, also demonstrates a strategic defeat for the protection of civil rights.

Current developments in criminal law and criminal procedure point to a strong demand for basic research on what changes in the crime control systems can be observed, what such changes mean in the face of normative principles, and what alternative options are available in forming the future of crime and crime control. I will try seriously to contribute to such knowledge, which will make decisions in this field easier.

Summary

The lessons that I have learned over the years with regard to criminology—I have to admit—are restricted to learning, teaching, and research.

The first lesson is clear and rather simple. It came from the founder of the Max Planck Institute, Hans-Heinrich Jescheck who always insisted that criminal law and criminal justice should be based upon empirical evidence; it should be based upon criminology and criminological research. A pure legal doctrine is neither able to address substantial problems in criminal justice nor able to provide for substantial legitimacy beyond formal aspects of procedure.

Then, it is also clear that criminal law and criminal justice are power drenched as criminal law defines relationships among individuals and between individuals and the state in a way that ultimately allows for coercion and the use of force. Insofar, a criminological approach should always include a critical dimension.

However, despite the need for a critical perspective on criminal law and criminal justice, it should be acknowledged that the successful institutionalization of criminal law in modern societies has brought advantages and added value for society and citizens. It has served to ensure that victims and offenders are alleviated from the burden to pursue justice as well as from the risk of escalation and polarization that lies in the non-availability of a monopoly of power.

Criminology is of an interdisciplinary nature. Explaining deviance, crime, and crime control, as well as their consequences, requires more than one scientific discipline. Criminology, therefore, has the task of constructing a meta-level of theory and analysis where understanding is the by-product of scientific inquiry, which transcends a single disciplinary perspective. Unfortunately, there have not been many attempts to do this. This may be tentatively explained by researchers following the line "separate is better."

Finally, international comparative research, in particular, demonstrates that there is a lot of flexibility and variability in criminal law and criminal justice and that compliance with norms and rules can be achieved through various means. In fact, there are many (functional) promising alternatives to criminal law (provided that the monopoly of power remains unaffected). This, again, means that there are real choices to be made and this message has to be conveyed to politicians and to the political system.

Selected Bibliography

Albrecht, H.-J. 1989. "European Perspectives on Drug Policies." In *Drug Policies in Western Europe,* edited by H.-J. Albrecht and A. van Kalmthout. Freiburg: Eigenverlag Max Planck Institut fèur Auslèandisches und Internationales Strafrecht.

———. 1997a. "Ethnic Minorities, Crime and Criminal Justice in Germany." In *Crime and Justice. A Review of Research,* Vol. 21, edited by M. Tonry. Chicago: Chicago University Press.

———. 1997b. "Dangerous Criminal Offenders in the German Criminal Justice System." *Federal Sentencing Reporter* 10(3):69-73.

———. 1998. "Money Laundering and the Confiscation of the Proceeds of Crime—A Comparative View on Different Models of the Control of Money Laundering and Confiscation." In *The Europeanisation of Law,* edited by T. Watkin. United Kingdom Comparative Law Series, vol. 18. Oxford: Alden Press.

———. 1994. "Sentencing and Disparity— A Comparative Study." *European Journal on Criminal Policy and Research* 2:98-104.

———. 2001a. "Postadjudication Dispositions in Comparative Perspective." In *Sentencing and Sanctions in Western Countries,* edited by M. Tonry and R. Frase. Oxford: Oxford University Press.

———. 2001b. "Restorative Justice– Answers to Questions that Nobody has Put Forward." In *Victim Policies and Criminal Justice on the Road to Restorative Justice. Essays in honour of Tony Peters,* edited by E. Fattah and S. Parmentier. Leuven: Leuven University Press.

———. 2002a. "Juvenile Crime and Juvenile Law in the Federal Republic of Germany." In *Juvenile Justice Systems: International Perspectives,* 2nd ed., edited by J.A. Winterdyk. Toronto: Canadian Scholars' Press Inc.

————. 2002b. "Fortress Europe?– Controlling Illegal Immigration." *European Journal of Crime, Criminal Law and Criminal Justice* 10(1):1-22.

————. 2002c. "Immigration, Crime and Unsafety." In *Crime and Insecurity. The Governance of Safety in Europe,* edited by A. Crawford. Portland: Willan Publishing.

Albrecht, H.-J. and A. van Kalmthout, eds. 1989. *Drug Policies in Western Europe.* Freiburg: Eigenverlag Max Planck Institut fèur Auslèandisches und Internationales Strafrecht.

Albrecht, H.-J. and G. Kaiser, eds. 1990. *Crime and Criminal Policy in Europe. Proceedings of the II. European Colloquium on Crime and Public Policy.* Freiburg: Eigenverlag Max Planck Institut fèur Auslèandisches und Internationales Strafrecht.

Albrecht, H.-J., J. Derks, and A. van Kalmthout, eds. 1999. *Current and Future Drug Policy Studies in Europe.* Freiburg: Edition Iuscrim.

Albrecht, H.-J. and T. Leppä-S. 1992. *Criminal Law and the Environment.* Helsinki: Helsinki Institute for Crime Prevention and Control.

Albrecht, H.-J. and W. Schädler, eds. 1986. *Community Service, Gemeinnützige Arbeit, Dienstverlening, Travail d'intérêt général—A New Option in Punishing Offenders in Europe.* Freiburg: Eigenverlag Max Planck Institut fèur Auslèandisches und Internationales Strafrecht.

Chapter 13

Searching for Answers

Shlomo G. Shoham

Tel Aviv University
Israel

Passion is a prerequisite for success—without it one lacks the attachment to task and the stamina that are key to persevering against all odds.

An Auspicious Start

I was born in Lithuania in 1929 and immigrated to Petach Tikva in pre-state Palestine with my parents in 1930. I spent my formative years in an orange-growing village in the Sharon area. At 14, I joined the Haganah, one of the underground movements fighting for independence from Great Britain. Several years later, because my parents' economic situation was rather poor, I was forced to matriculate externally at the University of London. Later in 1947, I studied philosophy and law at the University of Jerusalem on Mount Scopus and attended lectures at the Hebrew University. When the War of Independence began in 1947, I joined a convoy fighting in Gush Etzion where I fought against the Jordanian army and was captured and spent two years in a P.O.W. camp in Jordan. Although generally uneventful, this experience was still cruel and violent, and confirmed the maxim that what doesn't kill you toughens you. After my release, I resumed my law studies and upon graduation in 1953 was appointed assistant to the Attorney General and my mentor, the late Haim Cohen. As a state prosecutor, I was struck by the inequality of sentences handed out by judges in apparently similar cases. Little did I know at the time that this experience and impression would influence the path I was to follow as an academic. This induced me to carry out a study on the sentencing policy of criminal courts in Israel (Shoham 1966a).

Working as a prosecutor, I quickly learned that variation in sentencing cannot be attributed altogether to the factors involving the offender and the offense, but must be mainly due to a third factor, namely, the sentencing attitude and disposition of the individual judge himself. The inevitable result must be that the public at large may lose faith in the judiciary and, worse, habitual and professional offenders may count on that hazardous element while planning their "jobs." It is from this experience that I concluded that this hazardous element is definitely to the detriment of the presumable deterrent effect of punishment. These observations and experiences also helped to forge my theoretical orientation and passion for social reform along the lines of social defense.

Capitalizing on One's Situation–Opportunity

After having sent hundreds of defendants to prison in the course of my service as prosecutor, I decided to visit several incarceration sites around the country to assess living conditions. I quickly realized I no longer wished to send people to prison. I went to Haim Cohen and announced my decision to him. He looked at me askance, but with a smile leering on the corners of his mouth said that I was being groomed to be Attorney General or a Supreme Court judge and that my decision left him no choice but either to commit me to an insane asylum or send me to Cambridge University to study criminology. Being pragmatic, I chose the lesser evil.

While at Cambridge I was inspired by the works/teaching of Glanville Williams. When I returned from Cambridge in 1959, I established the Department of Criminology at Bar Ilan University in Tel Aviv where I taught for 10 years. There I conducted extensive research in the area of delinquency, deviation, and punishment treatment. It is here I became interested in the most natural area of crime and deviance in a country of mass immigration like Israel, with 90 different ethnic groups scattered across a relatively concentrated area. The most obvious frame of reference for the study of crime and deviance in a country of social change like Israel was *culture conflict*. This frame of reference was especially apt in that context since migration should also be studied on a comparative basis with other countries of mass immigration such as the United States, Canada, and Australia.

In 1968-69, I was a visiting professor at the University of Pennsylvania. Upon my return, I established the criminology department at Tel Aviv University's law faculty where I teach and conduct research to this day.

As will hopefully be evident throughout this contribution, I have spent the greater part of my academic career immersed in two main areas of criminology that have strong national and international routes. I have been keenly interested in applying and developing theory to criminological issues. For example, throughout my career I have developed three different theories and maintained a keen interest in the application of sentencing policy.

While I have spent a significant portion of my life in academia, one of the key events that influenced my interests in the multidisciplinary study of humankind was the tragic death of my oldest son, Giora. He was killed during the Yom Kippur War (October 1973). His falling led to a major shift in my worldview as well as my views about how we attempt to treat and assist criminals, prisoners, and drug addicts. For example, in the 1970s, together with my colleague and friend the late Professor Yehuda Fried, we devised an innovative, existential rehabilitative method by which to treat drug addicts.

The Value of Theory

Academically, my main interests have always been criminology, in particular social deviance, and the application of theory to practice. As I consider myself a pragmatic person, I consequently developed my versions of the culture conflict thesis as a possible means of providing the missing etiological link between these predisposing factors and the dynamic process of association with the criminal or deviant patterns of behavior (other variations were put forth by George Vold and Austin Turk). I developed my interest while applying locally the teachings of my Pennsylvania mentor, Thorsten Sellin who developed the theory in the late 1930s. Without this link, I believe any causal schema of criminal or deviant behavior is bound to remain incomplete. I have successfully tested the theory in relation to violent prisoners, suicides, prostitutes and their pimps, reckless drivers, and drug addicts. Given the significance of the theory in my work, I would like to share some of my observations within the Israeli context.

Recognizing the complexity of human behavior within a heterogeneous society, I argue that there are two types of conflict, which I have attempted to link. They are norm conflict and mental conflict, which may have value deviation that is not necessarily accompanied by overt deviant behavior. The generic syndrome of social deviation, taken as the dependent variable, would have social stigma, deviant behavior, and value deviation as the independent variables. Indeed, norm conflicts as mental conflict are almost *ex definitione* a condition precedent to value deviation.

This dynamic conception of value deviation as a process differs from the exposition of anomie, deviation, and alienation by Robert Merton (1910-2003), Talcott Parsons (1902-1979), and Melvin Seeman. Theirs is more of a static description, a taxonomized typology. In a sense, our conception of an individual's final failure to resolve his/her internal normative conflicts is of the ultimate in despair, value-wise, whereas many instances of anomie as described by Merton and Parsons, are faulty coordination of goals and means with the former and a disjuncture between the congruity motive and the activity-passivity continuum with the latter. This, to be sure, is *the initial normative gap* only prior to ego's involve-

---

Lessons

Recognizing the complexity of human behavior within a heterogeneous society, I argue that there are two types of conflict: norm conflict and mental conflict.

ment to bridge it. Ritualism, for instance, is one of the most coveted "adaptations" or "adjustments" by employers the world over. The ritualist employee at the assembly line or near a desk in the Kafkaesque halls of the mammoth, bureaucratic, impersonal structures is an asset. His ability to raise means to the level of ends in themselves make him an "ideal worker," a "perfectly adjusted individual," and "an integrated teamworker" in the jargon of the industrial psychologist.

Linking Theory to Practice

In my writings, I have two norms and value continua, one for the criminal group and the other for the individuals who are associated with it. These continua would have at one extreme the ideal-type conformist individual (or the group as measured by its total score on appropriate attitude scales) whose discordant values and conflicting norms with the prevailing normative system would be minimal. On the other extreme would be the individuals or groups in total war with the "legitimate" normative system. These complete normative negations would occur with a subculture that is in antithetical normative opposition to the prevailing culture. An individual or group may be placed at a given time on a point on the continua or move along it depending on the amount and severity of their normative conflicts with the predominant normative system. Researchers are currently engaged in constructing some interval scales to measure norm conflict among delinquent youth in Israel as auxiliary tools to action research on "street-corner" youth in some slum areas in Tel Aviv.

The project was planned for boys and girls between 14 and 18 and organized into some thirty informal "street-corner" groups. Coming from slum areas, these boys and girls, by definition, are from families of lower socioeconomic status. They are mostly of oriental origin (Middle Eastern basin and North Africa) and have a significantly high proportion of first generation children of immigrant parents. The groups range *prima facie* from slight deviancy to overt delinquency with heavy police records. We assume also a significant homogeneity of the groups as far as ethnicity, socioeconomic status, and length of stay in the country is concerned.

We have utilized some American inventories to differentiate between criminal or deviant and noncriminal or conformist individuals. We have hypothesized that these inventories would be suitable for our purposes because of the considerable similarity in some relevant aspects between the United States and Israeli processes of social change. Both societies have been the site of mass immigration and accelerated urbanization. Moreover, the discord and ethnic conflict experienced by blacks and more recently by Puerto Ricans in the United States are not dissimilar in content, although infinitely smaller in magnitude and narrower in scope, to the pains of integration of the Oriental Jews in Israel.

After the two extremes of the value and norm discord-concord continuum are determined and the items that discriminate significantly between the delinquent or deviant and the nondelinquent or conforming youth are chosen, the various groups through their individuals would be placed on this interval scale. The latter would be re-administered to the groups every two months to measure their movement along the scale toward or away from conformity. In order to have any effect at all, the field workers have to penetrate the groups and seek the voluntary collaboration of their individuals on *the latter's own terms.* The preventive efforts would evidently not be directed toward the predisposing crimogenic factors. These are inherent in the social structure and cultures of societies.

Fluctuations in crime rates and special types of delinquency and deviation in a given society and their significant links to some sociocultural factors have been a prime area for culture conflict research. Most of the frequently quoted research findings in the field, which have been associated with the culture conflict frame of reference, have dealt with the rates and volume of crime in a specific culture as a unit of analysis. Israel is a natural laboratory for studying the hypotheses related to the culture conflict frame of reference on the social level. This is mainly for the following reasons:

- Israel has more than 70 ethnic groups, which display a wide cultural divergence among its nearly 2.5 million Jews.
- The flow of Jewish immigration into the country was almost continuous from the end of the last century to the present. The most conspicuous fact about this immigration is that it quadrupled the Jewish population of the country. The population census from the beginning of 1948 (toward the end of the British Mandate) showed 649,700 Jews whereas, at the end of 1964, there were 2,155,600 Jews in Israel.
- A quarter of a million Arabs have lived for the last 20 years in Israel and were exposed to Jewish value systems. After the war in June 1967, another million Arabs are being exposed to a sudden culture conflict that, no doubt, engulfs its whole normative system.
- The rural-urban distribution is varied, ranging from the communal Kibbutzim to highly urbanized centers. This affords an adequate application of the culture conflict thesis to the ecological dimension.
- Marked fluctuations from social anomie to extreme eunomie have been observed through the periodic wars, that is, from 1949 to 1956 to 1967.
- The country is relatively small (7992 sq. miles) and all the discordant cultural heterogeneities inherent in the demographic structure of its population are contained within a rather compact arena.

Indeed, some meaningful findings have been gleaned from recent research on culture conflict, crime, and delinquency in Israel. These deal, *inter alia*, with the following: the crime rates of immigrants compared with the rates of native-born and those who immigrated to Israel before the establishment of the State (May 1948); the divergence of types and severity of crimes committed by immigrants from different countries of origin and different ethnic groups; the delinquency of native youth (or those who immigrated very young) of foreign-born parents; the rates of crime and delinquency as related to the cultural gap between the immigrants and the absorbing community; the rural-urban variable, homogeneity of ethnicity or the lack of it in a settlement or a community, and high or low normative cohesion as related to juvenile delinquency; horizontal and vertical mobility of immigrants and the barriers against the latter related to the delinquency and crime rates in some ethnic groups.

In my studies on culture conflict I studied the application of the theory to Arab villagers within the boundaries of the Green Line, as well as in the West Bank. During the 1990s, I organized an international conference in Jerusalem on migration, culture conflict, and crime, after which the International Forum on Migration and Crime was established. This forum resulted in two subsequent international conferences: Trier, Germany, in 2002, and Istanbul, Turkey, in 2003.

Searching for Answers

As stated earlier, I have always been interested in criminology and in particular in applying theory to practice. In the early 1970s I wrote a book entitled *The Mark of Cain* in which I present my

version of stigma theory. The premise of the theory is based, to varying extents, on the works of Erving Goffman (1922-1982) and on Edwin Lemert's (1912-1996) labeling theory of the 1950s. My theory is based on the notion that certain attributes can be deeply discrediting. I have used the theory to explain recidivism in crime and social deviance primarily as related to prostitution, drugs, and group delinquency. Although applied within an Israeli context, the book has been translated into many languages and was reprinted in 1982. Although the theory may no longer be seen as mainstream, I believe it still helps to explain some types of crime and deviance.

Responding to the Evolution of Theory

Most recently, I have developed a new theory on micro and macro criminology. The ideas are expressed in my book *Valhalla, Calvary and Auschwitz* (2001). In the book, I assert that human behavior is both dualistic and associational. This is the focal concern of criminologists. The inspiration for this new theory came through the influence of two of my former teachers, namely, Walter C. Reckless (1961) (i.e., containment theory–1899-1988) and Claude Levi Strauss (1963) (i.e., a structural anthropologist) who attempted to explain different myths from different cultures from around the world seem so similar. I have applied these concepts to the understanding of the recruitment to crime on the individual level and to some processes on the group level. Our hypothesis is that when norms are promulgated in the family and internalized to a deep level by the children, a normative barrier is former against delinquency and the pressures to overcome it.

Juvenile Sentencing

Since the 1980s, the office of juvenile court judge, under the auspices of the Children's Judges' Covenant, has evolved into a major source of indirect criminal prophylaxis. The international meetings decreed that the juvenile court judges should become members of youth protection boards and other organizations concerned with the betterment and coordination of social conditions. The recommendations are strongly based on a social welfare model of juvenile justice that I adhered to strongly. However, I am of the opinion that there is no clear-cut empirical proof that social welfare programs and the amelioration of general socioeconomic conditions have a definite and marked correlation with the decrease in volume and severity of delinquency and crime (see my eight-volume work *Israel Studies in Criminology*). Nevertheless, they have spawned a host of services. These services have different names and different functions in various countries—child guidance clinics, child welfare boards, welfare agencies, family service agencies, etc.—and more often than not crime prevention is but one of their many activities. The international meetings outlined the desirable framework of criminal prophylaxis services, according to which the detection of potential delinquents is initiated by the agencies that, apart from the family, have the closest contact with children—

> ### Lessons
>
> *I am of the opinion that we might even describe the everyday administration of criminal justice in many countries as a curious melange of different and sometimes diametrically opposed aims of punishment.*

schools, clinics, social agencies, police, courts, and religious institutions. In my former capacity as Advisor to the Government on Criminal Policy, I was heavily involved in applying theories of criminology and criminal justice to the prevention of crime and the treatment of offenders. These agencies should help to discover children with adjustment problems, who will be referred by special coordinating councils or referral committees to agencies professionally qualified to diagnose and treat potential delinquents.

It has been interesting for me to see that finally, after 20 years, the international deliberations have shown that a sentencing policy is determined by its ultimate objectives. A sentence will obviously vary according to the court's ideas about the purposes of punishment. A retributive sentence or one destined to appease the wrath of the gods aroused by the offense will be different in nature from a sentence that purports to re-educate the offender and reform him. Fortunately, there is a marked unanimity in opposing retributive punishment in its classic or expiatory aspects, which are quite obviously outdated in the second half of the twentieth century. The realization that a purely or a mainly retributive punishment has no place in a rational and utilitarian criminal policy is not confined to the sentencing of juvenile delinquents but to the sentencing policy as a whole.

Purposes of Punishment

Since my days as deputy attorney general, it has been practically impossible to distinguish the purposes of punishment in any given sentencing policy. I am of the opinion that we might even describe the everyday administration of criminal justice in many countries as a curious melange of different and sometimes diametrically opposed aims of punishment. Yet, the criminal systems of today, which are mainly neoclassic, are slowly catching-up with prevailing ideas in modern penology (see ISC). With respect to young offenders, for example, the prevailing trend is to require that the juvenile sentencing organ, whatever its structure or name, function with appropriate legal guarantees of procedure and appeals.

Another trend is to entrust the disposition of postdelictual cases to juvenile courts and antedelictual ones to administrative bodies. The idea of adult "disposition tribunals" or "treatment boards" composed of behavior specialists with or without the supervision of the trial judge has been widely discussed and adhered to in professional literature, but the separation of the sentencing function from the guilt-finding function and the execution of the former by a quasi-administrative body composed of experts does not seem to have gained much support. This apparently stems from a reluctance to ease

the legal safeguards that prevent the abuse of personal rights and freedoms presumably involved in the operation of administrative disposition bodies.

International Interests

Although I have been engaged in comparative work since the 1960s, my recent work with professors Graeme Newman and Ronald Clarke from Rutgers University in New York represents what I would consider a unique comparative piece of work. In the book we study crime and violence on a situational level.

Fruits of a Labor of Love

Throughout the years I have published literally dozens of books and authored hundreds of articles in the area of criminology and social deviance. I was the recipient of the Sellin-Glueck Award, the most prestigious award given by the American Society of Criminology in 1977 as well as the Israel Prize for criminology in 2003. But perhaps the most rewarding aspect of my work has been treating drug addicts and teaching young students eager to understand how the human psyche goes wrong.

Lessons Learned and Shared

As I reflect back on my efforts and labors of love, I am left with a few lasting impressions that (young) aspiring scholars might find noteworthy:

- Mentorship is extremely important, and for me has always been enlightening. Without Martin Buber, Thorsten

Sellin, and Haim Cohen, I would not have accomplished much.
- Passion is a prerequisite for success—without it one lacks the attachment to task and the stamina that are key to persevering against all odds.
- There is no theory like applicable theory. Kurt Levin's (i.e., field theory) statement that "there is nothing so practical as a good theory," aptly explains why theory is good when it is applicable and bad when it is not.
- Crime and deviance must be studied on a comparative level, otherwise one loses sight of the basic fact that all human beings are essentially equal.

In conclusion, among the many lessons I have learned, the most important is that criminal policy must go hand in hand with the ever-developing fields of the study human behavior on both the individual and group levels.

Selected Bibliography

Levi-Strauss, Claude. 1963. *Structural Anthropology*. Translated from the French by Claire Jacobson and Brooke Grundfest Schoepf. New York: Basic Books.

Reckless, Walter C. 1961. "A New Theory of Delinquency and Crime." *Federal Probation* 25:42-46.

Shoham. S.G. 1964. *Crime and Punishment in Israel*. Tel Aviv: Am Oved Publishing House.

———. 1966a. "Criminology in Israel." *The Juridical Review Part* 1:29-41.

———. 1966b. *Crime and Social Deviation*. Chicago: Regnery & Co.

———. 1975a. *Interaction in Violence: Human Relations*. Megamot: Hebrew.

———. 1975b. "Stigma and Stereotype." *New Perspectives in Criminology*. Zurich Hidden Delinquency. Report to the Council of Europe.

———. 1979a. "Differential Patterns of Drug Involvement Among Israeli Youth." *UN Bulletin on Narcotics*. Geneva.

———. 1979b. *A Text in Criminology*, 2d ed. (Hebrew with G. Rahav). Tel-Aviv: Schocken.

———. 1980. *The Mark of Cain: The Stigma Theory of Social Deviance and Crime*, 2d ed. Queensland, Australia: University of Queensland Press.

———. 1981. "New Paths in Criminology." In *Crime, Deviance & Social Control: New Edition of Social Deviance*, edited by Abeldo Perror. Tel Aviv: Tel Aviv Students Organization.

———. 1986. *Israel Studies in Criminology*.Vol. VII. Northwood, Middx. England: Science Reviews Ltd.

———. 1994a. *Primer in the Psychology of Crime*. Albany, New York: Harrow and Heston Publishers.

———. 1994b. *Violence: An Inter-Disciplinary Study*. Dartmouth Publications.

———. 2001. *Valhalla, Calvary and Auswitcz*. L'Age d'Homme Publications in French.

———. 2004. "The Twenty-First Century

Kulturkampf: Fundamentalist Islam Against Occidental Culture." *Israel Studies in Criminology*, Vol 8. Toronto: de Sitter Publications.

Shoham, S. G. and Sarnoff A Mednick, eds. 1979. *New Paths in Criminology.* Lanham, MD: Lexington Books.

Shoham, S.G. et al. 1989. *The Violent Prisoner: An Interdisciplinary Study.* Cambridge, Mass: Brookline Publishing Co.

Chapter 14

Adaptations

Charles Hou

National Taipei University,
Taiwan[1]

Crime is mostly a phenomenon of poor adaptation.

Culture Shock: An Awakening

My sociology training started in 1972 at Fu-Jen University, a Catholic university in Taiwan. An American born priest, Father Daniel Ross, was chairing the department. It was my first contact with people from the Western world and it was also my first experience with reading sociological textbooks in English. As far as I can remember, we used the textbook *Sociology: Man in Society,* co-authored by Melvin L. DeFleur, William V. D'Antonio, and Lois B. DeFleur. This was my introduction to the discipline of sociological education.

Upon graduating from Fu-Jen University, I received a scholarship from Texas Christian University (TCU) to pursue a Master's degree in sociology in the United States. It was a time when going abroad was unusual and difficult for most Taiwanese graduates. Not only did I have to apply for permission to study abroad from my own country, but I also had to show the host country my financial capability. The economic development in Taiwan during the late 1970s lagged behind most Western countries. Only a very few people could afford to study abroad. In addition, political controls were very strict. I remember that I was required to sit in a class for an entire morning to learn all the techniques of combating Chinese communism. Anyway, after all of these troubles, I finally had the opportunity to eyewitness one of the most advanced and admired Western

Lessons

I quickly learned more about the conflict perspective and developed an understanding of the outcry of the American criminologists against the perceived injustices in society.

nations.

My motive of getting an advanced degree in the United States was also encouraged by the popular ideology of modernization during the 1960s and 1970s in Taiwan. Taiwan was a developing society in those days. There was a strong sentiment that our under-development was linked to the traditional Chinese values or ways of doing things, such as lack of legal attitude, undemocratic political structure, and structure of personal relationships. Nevertheless, it was believed that we could become another modern society if we followed the footpath of the Western world. In particular, we needed to learn all of the psychological traits of being a modern man, such as having an open-mind, a material-oriented attitude, and so on. It was with this belief that I, along with many other Taiwanese university graduates, found our way to study abroad.

I arrived in Fort Worth, Texas on August 22, 1978 with a student F-1 visa. At Texas Christian University (TCU hereafter), I met with Dr. Robert Regoli who introduced me to the field of criminology. It was Dr. Regoli who taught me about criminology and what criminologists were doing (at least, at the time). His influence and enthusiasm helped redirect me towards criminology, a path to which I have dedicated most of my academic life.

The United States in the late 1970s was progressive and prosperous. At least that was how I saw it. The urban buildings were gorgeous and splendid. The streets were clean and had order. Campus buildings and life were much more auspicious than I was used to. I recall my surprise when I saw that my roommate had a car and a color TV. My family, in Taiwan, only had a black and white TV. Many people in Taiwan would have envied the life that I had in the United States.

In spite of my impressions, this lifestyle was not appreciated by most of my instructors at TCU. I was hard pressed to find any faculty members who shared my feelings. They seemed to be unhappy with their social and political environment. In fact, they were extremely critical and even resentful toward the government. Obviously, the years of the 1970s were dominated by a critical sentiment towards higher educational institutions. Scholars were cynical of the government. Not surprisingly, most of my readings at the time could be described as coming from the "conflict perspective." I read the works by Vold, Chambliss, Quinney, Turk, Krisberg, and Taylor, Walton, and Young. The critical perspective was the most dominant viewpoint in my criminological studies while at TCU. Hence, I quickly learned more about the conflict perspective and developed an understanding of the outcry of the American criminologists against the perceived injustices in society.

In spite of my initial indoctrination into the conflict perspective, the imposed baptism did not last long. After receiving my Master's degree in 1980, I moved to Bowling Green University, Ohio, to pursue a Ph.D. degree. There I was able to see the incredible working ethos shared by sociology faculties. Faculty members spend long hours in their offices. Moreover, in some social gatherings, I was surprised to see their concerns for social values and their sentiments on good social order. I would say that the social environment that I encountered in Ohio was more conservative than that of TCU. At Bowling Green I quickly put all conflict textbooks behind me and embraced the more mainstream criminological research and readings.

Back to My "Roots"

I grew up in the southern part of Taiwan. Most of my neighbors were farmers. They were content with their life. Psychologically, I was with them. Besides, Taiwan was under the marshal law for a long period of time and political dissents were treated harshly. For me, I did not have the courage to challenge the existing social or political systems. I did not want to place myself at such a high risk of jeopardizing my future. In fact, some of my friends holding a radical view of the society ended up in jail. Being somewhat more conservative and pragmatic, I was more concerned with finding a good job. I could not rely on my father who had to raise his four children along with my mother. I needed to finish my education, find a teaching job, and get out of poverty.

Fortunately, I finished my doctorial training relatively quickly.[2] Upon my graduation in 1984, I was fortunate to have the opportunity to achieve my "American dream"—a good job. I returned to my home country and found a position at a university at the age of 30.

When I joined the sociology department, I was only the second faculty member who had earned a doctoral degree. The other one before me got her Ph.D. from Texas A&M University. The others had received only their undergraduate or graduate degrees in Taiwan or in Mainland China. Universities, at that time, were certainly not administered or managed in the same manner as those of the Western world. People did not need a doctoral degree to teach. The intention of universities then was to produce graduates so that they could functionally participate in the society. Research and publication did not have a significant role on campus.

When I started my teaching career, I became a major figure in the department. The research methodology and the sociological theory that I taught attracted many students. Students loved the methods of conducting empirical research. They valued the techniques of sampling, measurement, and statistical analysis. American sociological perspectives were also well received. It seems to me that American sociology is the scientific paradigm. With this, the department began to recruit more faculty members with doctoral degrees from the United States. Currently, the sociology department at my university has 12 full-time faculties and all of them now hold a doctoral degree from the United States.

Lessons

Taiwanese criminology was not a reaction to the emerging urban problems. Criminology was established simply because social order had to be maintained. It was a reaction to the needs of administrative purposes.

Finding My Way

Currently, I am a professor of sociology and criminology at National Taipei University. I offer regular courses of introductory criminology and graduate seminars on crime and deviance. I also hold an administrative position as the Dean of Academic Affairs. Within that capacity, I am responsible for all undergraduate and graduate programs at the university. In addition to my academic commitments, I serve as a member of the organized crime committee in Taipei City Police Bureau. We review cases of violent crime and organized crime on a monthly basis and decide which cases should go to the court. On average, we process about 20 to 30 cases a month. Moreover, I am also a member on the Council of Crime Prevention Committee at the Ministry of Interior Affairs. We recommend policies to the Minister of Interior Affairs concerning strategies on crime prevention.

I have been teaching criminology and doing criminological research for almost twenty years now. At present, I am working on the problem of juvenile delinquency. I am particularly interested in studying the various factors that lead to delinquency in Taiwan. I don't intend to defend a specific theory. That is, I don't think criminologists should compete for theoretical paradigms. Criminal behavior is complex. No single theory can provide a complete fit to the truth of the complicated criminal world.

First "Wave" of Criminology in Taiwan

The academic study of crime in Taiwan is a relatively new area of study when compared to how long it has existed in North America and Europe. Taiwanese criminology began in the 1960s when the Department of Crime Prevention was established in 1966 at Central Police University. This is a university where high-ranking police officers as well as high-ranking correctional officials are trained. With the establishment of the academic unit, faculties became involved in the systematic study of crime.

In the beginning, engaging in criminological research was rather limited. Not only were there a limited number of professionals, but also they were constrained by the kind of research they could do. For example, research targets were essentially limited to those who had been incarcerated.

The Chiang Kai-Shek's (1887-1975) regime moved to Taiwan in 1945. Within less than two years, the Incident of 2-28 occurred when many Taiwanese elites were killed. Immediately after the Incident, an order of martial law was declared.[3] Constitutional rights of freedom of speech, press, and the right of the people to assemble were all abolished. However, during the early 1960s, rebellious movements on the island as well as overseas became pretty active and had resulted in many arrests. Naturally, the control of social order was a primacy for the ruling regime and an agency that could train correctional officials to manage the prisoners was then necessary. It was against this background that a criminology program was established. Without question, criminology was conceived as a part of the mechanism of governmental control. It provided an administrative function and served the interests of the ruling party.

Taiwanese criminology was not a reaction to the emerging urban problems. Criminology was established simply because social order had to be maintained. It was a reaction to the needs of administrative purposes. Because of this particular nature, the president of Central Police University had to be, first of all, a police officer, rather than a scholar or a criminologist. Moreover, the Minister of Interior has the authority to appoint the president.[4]

The tight control that characterized the early existence of criminology in Taiwan greatly limited the development of this field. The theoretical ideas were only shared among members of a small community, particularly within members of the administrative community. Criminology was an isolated discipline unto itself. Criminological theories were not used to direct crime prevention strategies or in matters relating to police investigation and patrolling. In fact, criminology was not classified as an independent field by the National Science Council, an agency that sponsored scientific research in Taiwan.

The Growth of Criminology in Taiwan

As Taiwan experienced rapid economic growth, however, the problems of crime increased. For example, the number of offenders arrested for criminal offenses was 30,200 in 1972; 38,285 in 1982; 172,551 in 1992, and 185,751 in 2002. Since the 1980s, official crime rates grew by more than 500 percent. In response to the emerging problems of crime, a second "wave" of criminological study emerged since 1996. At National Chung Cheng University, located near Chia-I, a southern Taiwanese city, a second department of criminology was established. It was named Crime Prevention. The graduate program is dedicated to the study of the nature of crime and the strategies of crime prevention.

In 2001, a third criminology program was established at my university, National Taipei University. It is officially called the Graduate School of Criminology. The proposal was prepared by this author and then was forwarded to the government for approval.

The Graduate School of Criminology at National Taipei University intends to promote an understanding on crime and deviance in Taiwan. It also attempts to develop criminological theories that could better describe the specific nature of crime in Taiwan. Moreover, the training of Taiwanese criminal justice staff is part of the program's focus.

In 2001, Professor Jim Sheu, a Ph.D. from the State University of New York at Albany, and Professor Susyan Jou, a Ph.D. from the State University of New York at Buffalo, joined in the graduate program at National Taipei University. They have become the program founders and symbolized a significant expansion of criminology in Taiwan.

Currently, both the graduate programs at National Chung Cheng University and National Taipei University continue to operate successfully. The programs are able to attract some 200 students from various professions, such as police officers, prosecutors, probation officers, judges, correctional officers, and teachers and the future looks bright. For example, in July of 1995, the *Journal of Criminology* was published through the graduate program at National Chung Cheng University. In July of 2003, another criminological journal, *Crime and Criminal Justice International*, was published through the Graduate School of Criminology at National Taipei University.

Research projects concerning crime and deviance are now increasing in Taiwan. However, most of the theoretical efforts are perspectives borrowed from the United States. That is, Taiwanese criminologists in the past only tried to duplicate American research with minor modifications. Expectedly, the explanations of crime and deviance are pretty much in line with that of American scholars. Theories, such as social bonding, strain, subculture, technique of neutralization, and differential association, are often tested within the Taiwanese context. Even contemporary theories, such as life course and development theory, reintegrative shaming theory, rational choice theory, and the control balance theory, have had their popularity. Not

much has been done comparatively. Taiwanese criminologists today still follow in the footsteps of the American criminologists. More effort is needed to develop its own unique perspective and to conducting comparative research. With few exceptions (see Cao and Hou 2001), little has been done on comparative and criminology.

My View on Crime and Deviance

Each person has his or her own way of growing up and entering society. And this particular experience often becomes crucial for one to perceive the world around them. The following are my observations on crime and deviance and to some extent they are related to my association with the world.

(1) *Crime is Related to One's Structural Adaptation:*

I was born into a life of comparative poverty where resources were quite limited. Private means of transportation was not readily available so I had to get up at 5:00 am every morning so that I could catch the first train at 5:46 for school. Out of family necessity many of my elementary school classmates entered the labor market right after graduating. Coming from a middle-class family that emphasized education, I did not have much choice. Explicitly and inexplicitly, it was impressed upon me that I needed an education in order to "get ahead" in life. When I was a child, I had already made up my mind not to rely too much on my family.[5] With this determination in mind, I worked as an assistant to the department while I was an undergraduate student at Fu-Jen University. Later on, I was a research assistant to many faculties during my six years as a graduate student at the two universities in the United States. All of these experiences helped me in developing my original view of crime and deviance.

Like Herbert Spencer's (1820-1904) ideas on organisms, I saw social life as an extension of the life of an individual natural body. Every individual wishes to have a happy life. Should one fail, one's fate is often unfortunate. On the contrary, if one is successful, he or she would mostly remain a conformist. I would say that personal adaptation provides a basis for all human beings to promote their life and to pursue their happiness and the way that one adapts has much to do with the chance of crime and deviance.

Crime is mostly a phenomenon of poor adaptation. When we look at the criminal statistics in Taiwan, we would find that criminals are most often from a particular group of people, the lower classes. For the past 10 years, the lower classes comprise about 130,000 or 140,000 criminals a year in Taiwan. And the majority of them are from the service sector, the manual labor market, or are farmers or unemployed. Professionals or technicians as well as managers account for less than 1 percent of the criminal population.

The relationship between personal adaptation and crime and deviance also extend to the youth population in Taiwan. In Taiwan, we have found that many of the delinquents are school "drop-outs."[6] Although the true proportion of delinquents among drop-outs

is unknown, criminologists as well as government officials understand that there is a significant relationship between these two phenomena. In response, the government has set up various programs to minimize the problem. They include: mandatory reporting systems, special educational guidance, and mid-way schools.[7] These policies are designed to bring back the drop-outs.

My position is: a stressful life, and/or events in school are potential triggers for juvenile delinquency (Hou 1996). Moreover, I have also observed that many of the stresses at school are structurally constrained. For example, the aboriginals, who mostly reside in mountainous areas, have the largest percentage of drop-outs. Aboriginals have the lowest average income level among four of the major ethnic groups in Taiwan. Many of the aboriginals are characterized as alcoholics and coming from broken families. Under these circumstances, children from aboriginal families have to face many pressures, including troubled families and unfavorable living conditions. These conditions are not conducive to educational achievement.

Second, the statistics also show that more than a quarter of the drop-outs come from broken families. Many of the drop-outs experience a stressful childhood and frustration, which according to strain theory prompts many of them to turn to a life of crime and deviance.

In essence, I believe that adaptation is an important criminological concept. It is an issue that everybody has to deal with. And the way that one adapts to society has much to do with the possibility of having trouble with the law.

(2) *Any Structural Adaptation Needs to Consider the Characteristics of Society, such as: Culture, Norms, Religion, and Various Social Institutions:*

My view of adaptation is not biological, like that of Lombroso or Darwin. Mine is rather sociological. I see society as a gathering of human social minds, not simply a gathering of human animals. There are norms, culture, laws, and regulations, as well as all kinds of social institutions which help society to operate. Therefore, any attempt to understand the adaptation, we need to understand the content of these human designs.

As a sociology-trained criminologist, I believe that social characteristics represent human solutions to the problems that face every society (Hou 1995). These are symbols that the majority of a society's members share. Without knowing the meanings of these symbols, we cannot know the expectations of other people. And most importantly, we wouldn't know how to act or behave. Therefore, social characteristics, which make human interactions possible, are necessary for individual survival and also for societal survival.

Here, I would mention two of the most important social contents in Taiwan—family and educational institutions. I will summarize these two distinguishing Taiwanese characteristics because they have much to do with the problems of crime and deviance and may well provide "food for thought" for other cultures.

Family in Taiwan: Family is perceived to be the fundamental social institution in Chinese society. While Beccaria (1738-1794) believed in a contractual individual in the state of nature, the Chinese believe human beings are necessarily born in a family-society. Most Chinese people are convinced that a harmonious family will assist one in having a brighter future. They also think that a broken family can destroy a person. If a member of a family is destitute and refuses to work, the Chinese say that it is a misfortune for the entire family. However, if a member of a family becomes an official, Chinese people would then say that it is a great honor for the entire family.

Contemporary empirical research in Taiwan shows that the family is an important social value shared by the majority of people. For example, husband and wife share similar responsibilities in taking care of a family. Mothers often come to a quick decision concerning a choice between family and their professional careers (in any case, women do most of the housework so that men can concentrate on their jobs). Children are considered as the future their families. Children assure the continuity of one generation to the next. Because of this particular status, children are often under careful protection. Children share very little of the household cores.

When family value is extolled, it is significantly integrated into many of the social functions such as: education, religion, politics, and economy. Therefore, the Taiwanese see the importance of making a family successful. The failure

Charles Hou

of the family as a social entity would cause many troubles for the children, including poor peer relationships and school performance, discrimination, and crime and deviance.

Criminological researchers in Taiwan continue to show a significant relationship between family and delinquency (Sheu 1997; Hou 2001). Major conclusions are: family structure is related to delinquency, with children from intact families experiencing less delinquency and children from broken families experiencing more delinquency. Moreover, family relationships such as family atmosphere, kinship conflict, communication and mutual trust, and mutual understanding are important predictors of delinquency. Good family relationships promote good behavior and poor relationships cause deviant behavior.

Yes, family in an oriental society like Taiwan has its dark side. Sometimes, overemphasis of family solidarity can also lead to deviance. Professor McCaghy and I interviewed 89 prostitutes in Taipei. We were surprised to see that the majority of the prostitutes claimed to be maintaining good or very good relationships with their parents. However, about one-third of the sample entered the occupation from a sense of filial responsibility toward their debt-burdened or impoverished families (McCaghy and Hou 1994). We found girls from poor families take up their life of vice in order to survive. Our conclusion demonstrates the importance of family influences, although in a different way.

Education in Taiwan: Education, particularly formal education, is impor-

> ## Lessons
>
> *We found girls from poor families take up their life of vice in order to survive. Our conclusion demonstrates the importance of family influences, although in a different way.*

tant in the United States. It serves one to achieve a social status and the opportunity of upwardly mobility. Education in Taiwan is also perceived to be important. However, it has a different meaning to Taiwanese. The meaning that Taiwanese give to education becomes significant concerning crime and deviance.

When we refer to the role of education in Taiwan we are really referring to the elite school system. Most people are more concerned with entering an elite school, rather than seeking personal development through education. Because of this, a "good" school often means attaining high academic standards. It is seen as a symbol of success and pride. In addition, teachers and principles from "good" schools receive higher social prestige.

I consider it a good thing that education is emphasized as it plays a major role in one's social development. However, a culture that places too much on education, particularly, on school elitism, does create problems. For example, I was able to witness students who did not do well in school were purposely ignored by their teachers. When these underachievers were absent from school, most of the time, the teachers did not call or make a family visit. As a result, these underachievers became alienated and they started to dislike the school. Their behavioral problems would then be accelerated, from being absent to skipping class, from skipping class to dropping out, and from dropping out to running away from home.

Often times, if one adapts well, his behavior is good. However, if one has trouble learning, he or she is likely to experience behavioral problems. Therefore, in Taiwan, you would easily find "good" schools to have fewer delinquents, and "bad" schools to have more delinquents.

As a result of the sociocultural situation, I have engaged in research that explores the relationship between the role of the family and education and how they interact to account for crime and deviance (Hou 1996). Criminologists in Taiwan confirmed the relationship to be significant. Taiwanese delinquency has much to do with the problems that a juvenile faces within the family and at school.

(3) *The Study of Social Control and Social Process Could Help Criminologists to Achieve a Better Understanding of Crime and Deviance:*

Hirschi's (1969) theoretical tradition, including *social bonding theory* and Gottfredson and Hirschi's (1990) a *general theory of crime*, has greatly impacted the development of criminology in Taiwan. Many Taiwanese empirical studies concluded that the social control explanation of crime and deviance has explanatory power (Wang 1988; Hou 1998, 2000). The research shows: (1) low self-control is associated

to delinquency; (2) social bonding factors, such as commitment and attachment, were related to delinquency; and (3) a considerable proportion of young people who visited KTVs, pubs, and dance halls exhibited greater tendency toward deviant behaviors. Moreover, the researchers here also find Hirschi's argument to be applicable to a variety of deviances, such as cigarette smoking, alcohol drinking, and illicit drug use (Sheu 1997).

In fact, the mechanisms of social control are explicitly perceived to be important in Chinese society. Confucianism emphasizes the importance of *Li*, translated as ceremony and courtesy. *Li* is a good virtue and it serves as the basis of social order. Confucianism also emphasizes the virtue of *Ren*. *Ren* represents the characteristics of kindness, and benevolence for a person.

I tend to see many similarities between Hirschi's social control tradition and the Chinese cultural value. The value of good self appears to be significant both in Taiwan and in the United States. It serves as a defense against committing criminal and/or deviant acts. Obviously, it is this individual's social psychological complex that makes a boy or a girl obey or defy the law.

However, the theme of social control alone is not sufficient to explain crime alone. Hence, I add another component to criminology—that is, the social process factor. Social process determines how one defines a situation, and it is also related to how one develops his or her own self. Sociologists under the tradition of W. I. Thomas in the 1920s saw the relationships between one's behavior patterns and the total personality and the individual's definition of situation to be relevant. That is, when one defines a situation as real, its consequence would become real too. Likely, when one defines the violation of law to be acceptable, the chance of one becoming a delinquent is higher.

For me, social process has much to do with one's life experience, particularly, the personal encounters with family, school, religion, job setting, and others. Here, I would mention two aspects of the social processes. First, we need to examine the creative and the initiative aspects of interactions that one enters. A person would engage in all kinds of activities by his or her own will. He or she would decide what friends to be associated with, or which schools to attend. Under this circumstance, he or she would have the chance to learn and to develop his or her own social constructions. For me, the context of the ongoing process of social interactions and communications provide a basis for one to develop the social self. If the interactions are comfortable and satisfactory, a good self then can be developed. On the contrary, if a person finds his or her own initiative in reaching out to the world to be frustrated or full of endless conflicts, the development of social self could become miserable.

Second, we need to study how one experiences and reacts to the social responses of others. The social responses help one to learn the meanings regarding this social world. For the most part, I subscribe to the functional side of positive reactions. Taiwanese criminologists are able to confirm the positive impact that social reactions such as support, caring, concerns, and understanding, have upon young offenders (Hou 2003). Positive reactions would enhance the progress of social self and lead one to stay away from trouble. However, if the reaction is negative, harsh, or discriminatory in nature, often times, it causes roadblocks to developing a strong self.

Unfortunately, the social response to youth crime is often harsh in Taiwan. When one is labeled as a deviant, or when one has a criminal record, he or she will be closely supervised, not only by the police officers, but also by the general public. The police refer to them as "dangerous" and their neighbors see them as criminals and a threat to the security of their community. Because of these harsh reactions, the opportunity for a criminal to be reintegrated back into their community is not good. This is why the rate of recidivism is growing higher here, about 30 or 40 percent.

I agree with the position taken by Christopher Uggen (2003), a professor at the University of Minnesota. Professor Uggen suggests we pay closer attention to the effects of labeling. He argues that labeling should be one of the crucial themes in criminology. Unfortunately, labeling seems to have lost its luster among most criminologists. For me, however, Uggen's emphasis on labeling should be taken seriously. Stigma and deviant labels have played a decisive role on an individual's life chances as well as on our political and economic institutions.

With the above remarks, I intend to address the importance of social

---

Lessons

Crime is transcending international boundaries and globalization is facilitating the process. It is clear that a greater number of crimes will require global solutions and international cooperation.

control and social process factors concerning our understanding of crime and deviance. The meanings that one attaches to this world and the social self that one develops through social process are paramount in our daily life. It is important because it can be used to explain how one becomes a law-abiding citizen, or contrarily, it explains how one might turn to a life of criminal activity.

Summary and Perspective

My childhood, my graduate education, and my professional career as a professor in Taiwan have all enlightened me on crime and deviance. I reviewed the importance of unavoidable human adaptations. How well one adapts to society impacts one's chance of having trouble with the law. However, I argue that a full understanding of crime and deviance needs to be seen as the process of human interactions, particularly concerning one's integration into a functional society.

Family and education are two major institutions in Taiwan. They are related to many aspects of the Taiwanese social entity. Again, these two social institutions play a significant role in one's

functional integration in society.

The sociological traditions of Durkheim, Weber, and Merton, as well as scholars of *symbolic interaction* have all served to enrich my life and academic career. For a better understanding of crime, we need to consider the "social ladder" *and* focus on social control and the process of human interaction. There is a mutual interaction between the individual and social group. Individuals make choices, but the choices they make and outcomes are constrained by society.

The Future of Criminology

First, I have observed that Laub and Sampson's (1993) *life course* approach is helpful to the study of crime and deviance. Human beings often face different types of "social capital" embodied in the relations among persons and the turning points in our life course. We all will grow and change with the passing of time. Most likely we will get a job or change our job. We will likely get married or enter into a romantic relationship with someone. Or we might decide to become a Christian and begin to believe in God. All of these create different contingencies and encounters for us. That is, we turn to a variety of social control mechanisms as we go through our life course. It is these events that become the turning points for us to make our life different.

Second, I have also observed that more and more people choose their careers as criminals, that is, they intentionally follow criminal careers rather than traditional jobs. I am a member of the Gang Committee in the Taipei City

Police Bureau. As a member, I was able to witness the extensive criminal records among gangsters. Many of them built their own reputations as hardcore criminals. Future research is needed to examine these career offenders, especially the factors that contribute to the stabilization of their careers throughout their lives (keeping in mind Laub and Sampson's life course approach).

Third, for the past twenty years, an economy based on knowledge has dominated social development and its' impact on the nature of crime and deviance are tremendous. An economy based on knowledge has created a new division of labor and class structure as well. More and more people are moving away from the traditional job markets and many of them are unemployed. Additionally, social inequality has widened. For example, in Taiwan the rate of unemployment and the gap between the rich and the poor are the largest this year. New patterns or changes in social systems effectively influence crime. At least, the number of property crimes in Taiwan will continue to mount significantly in the near future.[8] I suggest that criminologists watch over the interactions between crime and the changing social situations emerging today.

Fourth, we need to recognize that globalization is affecting our daily lives. Crime is transcending international boundaries and globalization is facilitating the process. Taiwan, for instance, recently uncovered a high profile, tax return fraud, however, the police were challenged by the international nature of the operation. It is clear that a greater number of crimes will require global solutions and international cooperation.

Lastly, although my training has been in sociology, I now embrace criminological inquiry. My interest and enthusiasm for studying criminology will surely continue, and I know that my criminological imagination will remain rooted within a sociological frame of mind.

Notes

1. Taiwan has a population of about 23 million. Its official name remains as The Republic of China (ROC), which lost its control of China to the Chinese communists in 1949. Since then, the ROC moved to Taiwan and has been governed as an independent political entity. That is, Taiwan sets its own policies, conducts its own national defense, and engages in formal and substantive relations with other countries of the world. However, it does not have a place in the United Nations and it is not recognized by the United States as an independent state.

2. I had Professor Steve Cernkovich, a Ph. D. from Southern Illinois University, as my dissertation advisor. He carefully guided me to study the social control perspective of delinquency and the relationships between the social content and various criminal behaviors.

3. The martial law ended in 1987. This tightly-controlled political situation lasted for more than 40 years in Taiwan.

4   This tradition remains even today. The current President, Dr. Te-hui Tsai, was also once a police officer and he was appointed by the Minister of Interior.

5   My father received high school education and worked as a government clerk. His salary was low, less than $100 a month during the 1950s and about $250 during the 1970s.

6   There are about 8,000 to 10,000 "drop-outs" for the past few years, which account for about 0.3 percent of the student population.

7   The mid-way school runs like a school within a school. It is located within the school. However, the mid-way school has its own teaching materials, which are often easier than that for normal students. Moreover, the program focuses more on treatments and psychological counseling.

8   Professor Cao (1999) made an observation on the increasing crime rates in Taiwan during the 1980s and 1990s. His analysis is in line with me. According to Professor Cao, the transition from an authoritarian regime to a democratic government, the difficulties that many people have experienced in adapting well with the newly-gained freedom from the government, and the increased stratification all breed more criminal activities and social disorder.

Selected Bibliography

Cao, Liqun. 1999. "Security in Taiwan." In *Taiwan in the 21st Century: Mainland Chinese Scholars Looking Ahead* (in Chinese), edited by Zhang Jie and Yu Yanmin. River Edge NJ: Global Publishing Co. Inc.

Cao, Liqun and Charles Hou. 2001. "A Comparison of Confidence in the Police in China and in the United States." *Journal of Criminal Justice* 29:87-99.

Hou, Charles. 1995. "Social Disorder, Self-Protection, and Fear of Crime in Taiwan." *Journal of Criminology* (in Chinese) 1:51-75.

_____. 1996. "Macro-Sociological, Micro-Sociological Social Control and their Impacts on Delinquency." *Journal of Criminology* (in Chinese) 2:15-48.

_____. 1998. "A Study on Juveniles Involved in Disfavored Activities." *Fu-Jen Studies* (in Chinese) 28:1-22.

_____. 2000. "On Juvenile Delinquency—An Integration of Social Control and Social Learning Theories," *Journal of Criminology* (in Chinese) 6: 35-62.

_____. 2001. "Family Structure, Family Relationships, and Delinquency." *Research in Applied Psychology* (in Chinese) 11:25-43.

_____. 2003. "Rational Choice and Criminal Decisions: A Case of Juvenile Burglars." *Crime and Criminal Justice International* (in Chinese) 1:36.

Laub, John and Robert Sampson. 1993. "Turning Points in the Life Course: Why Change Matters to the Study of Crime." *Criminology* 31:301-325.

McCaghy, Charles and Charles Hou. 1994. "Family Support and other Contingencies of Career Onset

among Taiwanese Prostitutes."
Archives of Sexual Behavior 23:
251-265.

Sheu, Jim. 1997. *Studies on the Earlier
Indicators of Juvenile Delinquency*
(in Chinese). Taipei: National Youth
Commission, Executive Yuan.

Uggen, Christopher. 2003. "Criminology
and the Sociology of Deviance." *The
Criminologist* 28(3):1-5.

Wang, Shu-Neu. 1988. *Testing Criminological
Theories in an Oriental Society* (in
Chinese). Taipei: Bou-WinTang
Company.